Cultural Diversity and the Curriculum

Volume 1

The Foundation Subjects and Religious Education in Secondary Schools

Edited by

P.D. Pumfrey and G.K. Verma

 The Falmer Press

(A member of the Taylor & Francis Group)
London • Washington, D.C.

UK   The Falmer Press, 4 John Street, London WC1N 2ET
USA   The Falmer Press, Taylor & Francis Inc., 1900 Frost Road, Suite 101, Bristol, PA 19007

© P.D. Pumfrey and G.K. Verma 1993

First published 1993

Library of Congress Cataloging-in-Publication data are available on request

A catalogue record for this book is available from the British Library

ISBN 075070 1390
ISBN 075070 1404 (Paperback)

Jacket design by Caroline Archer

Typeset in 10/12pt Bembo by
Graphicraft Typesetters Ltd., Hong Kong

Printed in Great Britain by Burgess Science Press, Basingstoke on paper which has a specified pH value on final paper manufacture of not less than 7.5 and is therefore 'acid free'.

Cultural Diversity
and the Curriculum

Volume 1

Other Titles in the Series

Cultural Diversity and the Curriculum
Volume 2
Cross curricular Contexts, Themes and Dimensions in Secondary Schools.
Edited by Gajendra K. Verma and Peter D. Pumfrey

Cultural Diversity and the Curriculum
Volume 3
The Foundation Subjects and Religious Education in Primary Schools.
Edited by Peter D. Pumfrey and Gajendra K. Verma

Cultural Diversity and the Curriculum
Volume 4
Cross Curricular Contexts, Themes and Dimensions in Primary Schools.
Edited by Gajendra K. Verma and Peter D. Pumfrey

Contents

Contents

Preface

In May 1992, once again, the sociological tinder box of Los Angeles exploded literally and metaphorically. The idealistic concept of the USA as a 'melting pot', in which differing groups establish mutually acceptable *modus vivendi*, was once more challenged. The feelings aroused amongst black communities, following the verdict in the trial of four police officers charged with assaulting Rodney King, at which an amateur video-recording of his arrest was presented, can well be understood. Was the subsequent rioting, looting, arson and murder justified? Was nothing learned from the Watts riots of twenty-seven years before? There are crucial lessons for individuals and institutions to be learned from this latest manifestation of minority-group alienation by all members of society. No country, no ethnic, religious or social group can afford to adopt a 'holier than thou' attitude. The riots in Manchester, London, Bristol, Liverpool and Leeds during the 1980s and the ethnic, religious and social tensions that exist in the 1990s show the fragilities inherent in our own social cohesion. They underline the importance of multicultural education if the concept of 'one nation' is to be approached.

This series of four books has two major purposes. The first is to describe and discuss cultural diversity and the curriculum from various curricular perspectives. The second is to consider how the legitimate educational concerns of minority ethnic groups, and the aspirations of larger groups, can be constructively addressed within the framework of the National Curriculum and those equally important aspects of the curriculum subsumed under the broader headings of the 'basic' and 'whole' curriculum respectively. To this end, specialists in the key components of the curriculum have considered some of the challenges and describe promising practices in a number of specific subject and cross-curricular fields.

In education, theory and practice are equally important to the teacher. Being an effective teacher, but not being able to reflect upon and communicate the reasons for such success, is professionally insufficient. The bases of effectiveness must be made explicit in order that expertise can be developed and disseminated. The central objectives of any profession considering any phenomenon are fivefold: conceptualizing its nature, describing aetiologies, specifying presenting symptoms, making prognoses and evaluating responses to various interventions. The causes and effects of particular patterns of behaviour are of crucial importance in education. All five are set within a range of culturally linked value systems.

Should the contributors to an edited book such as this be required to write from a common theoretical position? It would be one means of ensuring coherence, but this apparent gain could easily be offset in the present state of knowledge. 'Political correctness' is an ever present danger in the social sciences.

J.D. Saxe wrote a poem entitled 'The Blind Men and the Elephant'. It began with the following lines:

There were six men of Hindustan
To learning much inclined,
Who went to see an elephant
Though each of them was blind . . .

Their comments, consequent on their respective encounters with different parts of an elephant's anatomy, demonstrated six conflicting interpretations concerning the nature of the phenomenon under scrutiny.

Disputes between individuals trained in the many differing disciplines interested in theoretical and applied aspects of education are well known. To conceptualize and describe 'Contexts', identify 'Challenges' and advocate 'Responses' in relation to cultural diversity and the National Curriculum are important objectives. Each discipline and profession has something to contribute towards these ends, as has each subject specialist in relation to the National Curriculum. In the quest to do this in a field as complex and controversial as that covered in this series, it is almost inevitable that individual contributors will hold differing theoretical positions. In this respect, no one has a freehold on 'truth'. The same applies to the variety of policies and practices that are advocated.

Consideration of hypotheses and their antitheses, of their related policies and practices in the dialectic, can be a constructive activity. Presenting and evaluating theories and evidence matters. The absolute certainty of the fundamentalist, whether secular or otherwise, is typically less than helpful in any search for the disinterested resolution of conflicting views.

When social scientists consider a phenomenon, we all too frequently and easily suffer from a conceptual 'tunnel vision' imposed by whichever disciplines and sets of beliefs have influenced our modes of thinking. Recognizing this is mutually beneficial to improved communication. By reading the book colleagues will be able to make judgments concerning the contributors' present insights and/or illusions. The analyses, evidence, suggestions and reflections of highly experienced educators on key curricular aspects of cultural diversity and the effective delivery of the National Curriculum, cannot lightly be dismissed. The contributors provide many practical suggestions for improving education in a multicultural society and for improving delivery of the National Curriculum to all pupils. As such, the varied contributions merit the attention of all citizens in our multiethnic community.

Fortunately, for pupils, parents, professionals, schools and communities within our country, the messages contained in the series *are* increasingly being received, considered, modified to fit specific circumstances, and implemented.

The last line of Saxe's poem puts the central point concerning both theory and practice that we ignore at our peril: 'Though *each* was *partly* in the right, they *all* were in the wrong.'

The series begins with two volumes devoted to the secondary school. The editors deliberately chose to start with the secondary stage of education. Much remains undecided concerning the structure, content, pedagogy and assessment of many components of the secondary-school curriculum. Despite these considerations, and virtually irrespective of the decisions reached concerning them, the multicultural nature of the population and of schools will develop. Demographic data presented in Chapter 3 confirm this point and provide indications of the demographic changes that are likely to take place in the future. These changes, and their educational implications, must be considered if the educational system is to respond adequately. The issue of cultural diversity and the curriculum cannot wait until the full implementation of the ERA 1988 is in place. We have deliberately ventured into this controversial field whilst the 'rules of the curricular game' in state secondary schools are still being negotiated in relation to certain aspects of the curriculum. We do so because of the importance with which we view the increasing ethnic diversity of the school population and of the country. Janus-faced, that ethnic diversity represents both problems and opportunities. To deny either would be a disservice to the pupils and the communities that the educational system exists to serve. It would also limit the chances that an education meeting the requirements of the Education Reform Act 1988 would ever be provided.

Finally, the views expressed in this series represent the considered opinions of the individual contributors and are not necessarily those of the editors.

Acknowledgments

We thank the Office of Population Censuses and Surveys for permission to reproduce tables in Chapter 3 based on their research.

List of Tables and Figures

Tables

Figures

List of Abbreviations

AIMER	Access to Information on Multicultural Education Resources
AIMS	Art and Design in a Multicultural Society
AMA	Association of Metropolitan Authorities
APU	Assessment of Performance Unit
ARE	Anti-Racist Education
AREAI	Association of Religious Education Advisers and Inspectors
ARTEN	Anti-Racist Teacher Education Network
ASE	Association for Science Education
AT	Attainment Targets
BCPE	British Council for Physical Education
BTEC	Business and Technical Education Council
CARF	Campaign Against Racism and Facism
CARM	Campaign Against Racism in the Media
CATE	Council for the Accreditation of Teacher Education
CDT	Craft, Design, and Technology
CPD	Continuing Professional Development
CPVE	Certificate of Pre-Vocational Education
CRC	Community Relations Commission
CRE	Commission for Racial Equality
CSE	Certificate of Secondary Education
DART	Directed Activity Related to Texts
DES	Department of Education and Science
DFE	Department For Education
EC	European Community
EFL	English as a Foreign Language
EMAG	Ethnic Minority Advisory Groups
ERA	Education Reform Act 1988
ESRC	Economic and Social Science Research Council
ESL/E2L	English as a Second Language
GCSE	General Certificate of Secondary Education
GEST	Grants for Educational Support and Training

GRIST	Grant Related In-Service Training
HMI	Her Majesty's Inspectorate
HMSO	Her Majesty's Stationery Office
INSET	In-Service Education for Teachers
IT	Information Technology
ITT	Initial Teacher Training
KS	Key Stages (of the National Curriculum)
LEA	Local Education Authority
LINC	Language in the National Curriculum
LMS	Local Management of Schools
MCE	Multi-Cultural Education
MFLWG	Modern Foreign Languages Working Group
NAHT	National Association of Head Teachers
NAME	National Anti-Racist Movement in Education
NAT	National Attainment Target
NC	National Curriculum
NCC	National Curriculum Council
NCDP	National Curriculum Development Plan
NCMT	National Council for the Mother Tongue
NERIS	National Educational Resources Information Service
NFER	National Foundation for Educational Research
NSC	National Science Curriculum
NUT	National Union of Teachers
OAT	Original Attainment Target
PC	Profile Components
PoS	Programme of Study
RE	Religious Education
RI	Religious Instruction
RoA	Records of Achievement
RT	Runnymede Trust
SACRE	Standing Advisory Council on Religious Education
SAIL	Staged Assessments In Literacy
SAT	Standard Assessment Task
SEAC	School Examinations and Assessment Council
SCDC	School Curriculum Development Committee
SNC	Science National Curriculum
SoA	Statements of Attainment
SSD	Social Services Department
TGAT	Task Group on Assessment and Testing
TVE	Technical and Vocational Education
TVEI	Technical and Vocational Education Initiative

Part 1

Towards Cultural Pluralism through the Curriculum in Secondary Education

Chapter 1

Introduction

Peter D. Pumfrey and Gajendra K. Verma

'I think the school is a very good school but I don't think it's right when she comes home singing in Pakistani' (Mrs J. Carney on why she wished her daughter to change schools in Cleveland LEA, 1991). Mrs Carney asked for her daughter to be transferred from a school comprised largely of British children of parents of Asian origins to a school with mainly white pupils. The Commission for Racial Equality challenged the LEA's approval of the move. The High Court has decided that parental choice was the prime consideration in deciding the above issue. In law, Mrs Carney has the right to have her daughter educated in what she sees as mainstream British culture. The judgment raises many highly controversial issues. For example, what is the position of members of any minority linguistic community which asks for equivalent moves where these are possible? The Commission for Racial Equality may yet appeal (see Chapter 2 and Appendix 1 for a further consideration of this issue).

Earlier, on 17 September 1986, Ahmed Iqbal Ullah, a 13-year-old pupil attending a secondary school in Manchester was stabbed by another 13-year-old pupil, Darren Coulburn. Ahmed Iqbal Ullah died as a consequence. In February 1987 Coulburn was found guilty of murder and was ordered to be detained indefinitely. The LEA had a well-developed antiracist policy. What had gone so tragically wrong? Manchester City Council appointed an independent inquiry led by a barrister, Ian Macdonald, an expert on immigration and race-relations law. He was assisted by three assessors: Lily Khan, a commissioner in the Commission for Racial Equality and director of Asian studies at Tower Hamlets Adult Education Centre in London; Gus John, then assistant education officer (community education) for the ILEA; and Reena Bhavnani, tutor in sociology at Ruskin College, Oxford. On 21 May 1987, the Macdonald inquiry opened at Longsight Library. It took evidence and visited schools until the autumn. Relationships between the 'inquiry' and the LEA became extremely strained (Hill, 1990).

Reading about such events, rather than being even marginally involved, inevitably tends to minimize them. Involvements sensitize. A group of post-graduate students from the University of Manchester School of Education was on a visit to the Lake District. All the members of the group were mature, qualified, experienced and highly responsible members of the teaching profession in their various countries. Hawkshead was visited one evening. The group decided where and when it was to reconvene later, and then dispersed to look around this attractive small town. One of the female students from an African country was openly and publicly verbally abused with racist name-calling by a group of young adults sitting outside a public house. The effect on her, and on the other members of the group, was devastating. Her subsequent reflections on her visit to the UK were profoundly coloured by this incident. Whether or not the young persons involved in the racist verbal abuse were also visitors to Hawkshead, or not, was irrelevant to her reactions. In her eyes, they were British. They were abusive. They were racist. What did this say about both our society and our educational system?

Early in 1992, one of the authors was returning home from work during the evening. In the centre of a suburb of Manchester known as Withington, on an arterial road leading out of the city, a serious assault had taken place on a 60-year-old Asian shopkeeper, Siddik Dada. The assault took place in the 'Popular Delicatessen', a business that he had built up and run for many years. Teenage gangs were reported to have 'stormed his shop late at night' on previous occasions. After a period of thirteen days on a life-support machine in intensive care, he died. The community's abhorrence of this senseless attack on a respected member of the community was reflected in both the tributes that were publicly paid and in the presence of members of the community's many ethnic groups at his funeral. 'Withington stood in silent respect for a loved member of the community' was the headline in the local paper *The South Manchester Reporter*. At the time of writing, four young persons are in custody awaiting trial on charges related to the assault which led to the death. Irrespective of cultural and/or ethnic background, such a crime is reprehensible. The implication that this was a racist attack must be addressed if anything is to be gained from this tragedy.

Incidents such as the four described above provide illustrations of matters that concern individuals, families, schools, communities and society. They are selected for that purpose. The aim is not sensationalism. The same points are unfortunately reinforced by more substantial findings.

A study of racial attacks in eight areas of Britain demonstrated clearly that many minority ethnic groups continue to experience a range of serious racist harassments (Commission for Racial Equality, 1987). Moving into the field of education, a survey of racial harassment in schools and colleges revealed clearly that a serious situation exists there also (Commission for Racial Equality, 1988). A useful and extremely worrying survey by a member of staff of the University of Sheffield summarizes research findings on ethnicity and education. It also includes findings from a two-year field study of an inner-city comprehensive school. He found that the methods of control and sanctions used with white pupils differed from those used with pupils of Afro-Caribbean origins. The latter were amongst the most criticized and controlled students in the group. 'Report cards' represented one means whereby teachers identified and formally recorded offences. Variants of such a system have a widespread currency in secondary education. In the particular school, whereas 37 per cent of pupils of Afro-Caribbean origins had received at least one 'report card', only 6 per cent of pupils of all other ethnic groups received such a card. The author considers that the giving of these punishments was likely to be based on 'offences whose identification rested primarily on the teacher's interpretation of pupil attitude and intent' (Gillborn, 1990).

As the proverb suggests, coming events do, at times, cast clearly their shadows before. According to the Swann Committee report racist name-calling is insidious, damaging and dangerous to all because it 'can convey to a child the accepted value judgment which the majority community has passed on to his or her community' (DES, 1985). The importance of this issue has been subsequently highlighted by both the Macdonald inquiry (op. cit.,) and the Elton report. What has been learned during the primary-school stage of education inevitably subsists into secondary education.

One ethnographic study, sponsored by the Economic and Social Research Council (ESRC) into the use of racist name-calling, involved research workers in discussions with 160 pupils aged 9, 10 and 11 attending three, mainly white, primary schools. Its aims included the identification of pupils' perceptions of 'race' and their interpretations in everyday life. Typically, visitors to the school would see all the pupils playing together and would observe no evidence of interethnic antagonisms. Hearing racist remarks would be exceedingly unlikely. The conclusion could be reached that, in such circumstances, racism is not an issue demanding the serious attention of the school (Troyna and Hatcher, 1991). According to the research workers, such an assumption is totally unjustified in the light of the evidence that they obtained. The comment, by one white 10-year-old boy when asked his perception of 'coloured' people, 'we don't really want any more here do we, because they take over, don't they?', is illustrative. On the positive side, some pupils showed evidence of antiracist good sense as when a white pupil stated that she had stopped using racist name-calling because she now realized how much it hurt. The researchers distinguished between 'hot' and 'cold' racist name-calling. The latter referred to situations in which children deliberately teased or harassed other pupils as part of a game. In contrast, 'hot' name-calling occurred during the heated disputes, often between friends. 'When you get angry it just slips out.' The circumstances eliciting, and the motivations underpinning, racist name-calling are varied. One of them is its use by pupils as a defence strategy when someone is seen as 'picking on' another person. One girl with parents of Afro-Caribbean origins said 'I don't like people calling me things about my colour. I feel strong about my colour.' Her white friends, secure in the belief that their 'whiteness' does not present problems of the same magnitude, are less concerned about being called reciprocally racist names. White pupils acknowledged that racist names were particularly offensive when used against black peers. Listen to the words of a white pupil, Adam: 'It's like if you called them a different colour, it's like saying "You don't belong here, you belong somewhere else with your colour". Like that, you're sending them away'. Irrespective of whether racist name-calling originates in 'cold' or 'hot' contexts, it is perceived as offensive and damaging by the non-white recipients. In that it expresses a white (majority) child's views on race, it reinforces the racist assumptions that are present in British society, in schools and in families. Racism in mainly white primary schools is more prevalent and complex than many educationists, parents and governors would like to admit. 'The curriculum need not only address the real experiences that children bring with them to the classroom, it needs to offer them the conceptual tools to interpret it' (Troyna and Hatcher, 1991). A strength of their book is that it provides strategies for helping achieve this end.

Equally disturbing findings have been found at the secondary-school level. It has been demonstrated that the frequency with which racist name-calling was used by pupils increased between the first and fourth years of secondary schooling (Kelly, 1990). The power of language is often insufficiently recognized. The adage that 'sticks and stones may break my bones but words can never hurt me', is patently suspect. In this debate, the distinction between 'prejudice' and 'racism' is important. All individuals are prey to the former, to holding beliefs without a rational basis. Coupled with power, it is asserted that prejudice becomes racism. Minority ethnic groups often argue that, for this reason, they cannot be racist as they are (relatively) powerless groups. The appeal of this argument is considerable to most ethnic groups. Is it valid? Are the 'thought police' hiding somewhere in the background? The challenges of 'what should schools do, and how?' must be faced.

The above examples could, without difficulty, be greatly extended. They are presented to underline the point that interethnic group antipathies and hostilities are occurring regularly in society and in schools. This is not a recent occurrence, nor is it peculiar to Britain. Indeed, on the positive side, this country has a long tradition of providing sanctuary to individual suffering from political and religious persecution. On the darker side, in common with the vast majority of countries, Britain has a long history of hostile attitudes to immigrants, refugees and minorities (Holmes, 1991). In the interests of all members of society, the situation demands action both to acknowledge and address the tensions and also to capitalize on the potential benefits of a multicultural society. In this, schools, teachers, governors, parents and pupils have crucial roles to play. That is why both the content of the National Curriculum and its modes of delivery are so important.

To date, the NCC has not given adequate guidance to teachers on how a full, balanced and broadly-based curriculum can be made available to all pupils, including those from ethnic-minority backgrounds. As this has never been achieved in this (or any) country, even for pupils from any single cultural background, the lack of guidance is hardly surprising. Equally, ensuring that all pupils learn through their school experiences to understand and respect the varied cultural traditions of the different minority ethnic groups comprising the school, its community, the nation and the world, is an equally great challenge.

In education, as in life, when the pain of not changing becomes greater than the pain of introducing curricular change, change occurs. The key objective is to ensure that the moves that take place enable progress to be made towards an explicit state accepted as an improvement on the current situation by a society's citizens. In addition, the cost-to-benefits ratio of educational change must be perceived as acceptable in the medium and longer term. Confusing 'change' with 'progress' is easily done, unless the evaluation of educational change is systematically carried out.

An NCC Newsletter, published in February 1991, included the advice that teachers should take account of their pupils' cultural diversity by:

- valuing their cultures by drawing on their knowledge and experience in the learning process;
- acknowledging their competence in different languages and dialects;
- offering positive images and role models from all cultures.

'Permeation' of the various core and foundation subjects, cross-curricular themes and dimensions with multicultural and antiracist approaches is one key strategy advocated. Translating this suggestion into practice is an educational horizon facing the profession. Fortunately, there are many promising policies and practices being developed in various settings (Pumfrey and Verma, 1990). This is not to deny that the topic remains both sensitive and controversial.

The National Union of Teachers is the largest teachers' union in the UK. In 1989 it published a paper setting out the union's view that antiracist education represents sound educational practice for all pupils and teachers (NUT, 1989). The formulation, establishment and evaluation of school policies and practices leading to an ethos in which all pupils felt equally valued, was at its centre. Developments towards this end require the involvement of all parties to the endeavour. In any system of compulsory education, this is not easily achieved. There is no 'top–down' solution that can be imposed. The guidance given in 1989 remains pertinent today. The NUT has also published a short resource list of books that have been found helpful in teaching particular National-Curriculum subjects from an antiracist and multicultural perspective. It is available from the NUT Education and Equal Opportunities Department.

At its Annual Conference held in 1991, it called for the following:

- advice to members on safeguarding anti-racist and multicultural approaches throughout the whole curriculum, including national curriculum subjects and cross-curricular themes [and]

- advice on assessment methods including records of achievement which do not disadvantage black, ethnic minority and bilingual pupils (NUT, 1991).

An advisory committee for Equal Opportunities (Race) was established by the NUT. With Mr Elam Singam as chair, it first met in the autumn of 1991 and has produced a fourteen-page pamphlet in which suggestions concerning an antiracist and multicultural curriculum are presented for each aspect of the National Curriculum, for the cross-curricular themes, assessment issues and INSET (NUT, 1992). The tenor of its content is indicated in the following quotation.

> In our view, an emphasis on British, European and Western cultural achievements which excludes the contributions made by the rest of the world distorts reality and would be misleading for pupils. Therefore we would advocate using every opportunity to bring into the content of all syllabuses material which widens pupils' knowledge about the contribution made by non-Europeans and black people to the world's store of knowledge, culture and achievement. (ibid.)

Reactions to this approach, and to certain subject-specific suggestions, were extremely hostile from some sections of the national press. On 18 June 1992, the *Daily Mail* education correspondent (R. Massey) wrote an article entitled 'Now class, we'll teach you not to be racist'. It began 'plans to make school lessons "anti-racist" were condemned as politically-correct claptrap yesterday'. A member of the Campaign for Real Education is quoted as commenting that 'It smacks of the sort of political correctness which has now replaced the old discredited Marxist ideologies . . . It is quite frightening'. The Parliamentary Under-Secretary of State for Schools, Eric Forth, is reported as considering that the union is out of touch with parents and that 'It has forgotten, or ignores, the fact that we are British, European and Western. It is in danger, yet again, of inviting ridicule or distrust when it should be concentrating on providing children with a balanced education of quality and credibility . . . The NUT seems to forget that the [National] Curriculum provides scope to counter racism and create greater understanding and respect for differences.' In the same article Dr John Marks, a believer in traditional approaches to education, is reported as saying 'It is not a function of the curriculum to seek out racism explicitly and attack it. Such tactics often raise antagonisms. Black parents want their children to be engineers, nurses, doctors — they want them to make their way in British society. Much of this anti-racist spouting exacerbates the problems.' Presumably, keeping quiet is seen as a more constructive response. Elsewhere, the director of education of the London Borough of Wandsworth, Mr D. Naismith, is quoted as considering that 'The NUT are being very sentimental, but actually performing a disservice for the very pupils they aim to help. Western values provide the framework of the society into which all ethnic-minority children will take their place. They need an education for their future, not their past'. One cannot help recalling the argument that those who ignore the lessons of the past are condemned to repeat them.

From an educational viewpoint three questions merit serious consideration:

- What type of society do we wish to promote?
- Does education matter?
- How near are we to the time when a situation, with laws and events such as the following, would exist?: The establishment of a racist programme including camps for unwanted immigrants; the ending of the automatic right to citizenship of those born in the country; the review of naturalizations granted since 1974; the creation of a group of second-class citizens; the rejection of the European-Community open-frontiers agreement; the creation of immigrant quotas in the education system; forbidding non-EC foreigners to bring their families to the country, restricting their residence to a period of two years, providing no entitlement to social security, work or council housing; the curtailment of the Islamic religion through a ban on the building of mosques, coupled with laws to control Islamic teaching and social centres.

Taking the above three questions in reverse order, we are quite near to the above situation geographically, if not ideologically. British nationals are members of the EEC. In France the above policies are being expounded by the National Front. Whilst the National Front in France remains a minority group, it has been reported that some 38 per cent of the French electorate back the immigration policies of Jean-Marie Le Pen. Right-wing politicians, such as the former President of France, Valéry Giscard d'Estaing, have warned of the dangers of a large Islamic population. Reactions in Germany to Turkish immigrants and the rise of anti-Semitism in a number of countries are but examples of apparently rising intolerances. Why?

Our era is dominated by the mass media, by materialism and by mobility. The first of these brings regularly to the homes of all our citizens, young and old alike, vivid and recurring evidence of regional, cultural, religious and ideological enmities from around the world. The United Kingdom contributes to this scenario. Which nation does not? Typically, in the power struggles that such animosities represent, opposing sides claim the moral high ground whilst denigration, death and destruction are freely distributed by protagonists. Moderation and compromise are not seen as desirable positions, but are all too frequently deemed contemptible. Slogans replace reflection; rhetoric rules; might is right. The law of the jungle is never far away in any society. In terms of the dominant mass media, events involving collaboration between groups within a society are typically seen as less newsworthy and less dramatically attention-attracting to audiences (Verma and Darby, 1990). This is not to suggest that constructive interethnic group endeavours are never reported, but merely to draw attention to an imbalance in the presentations on which we all depend and on which citizens construct their perceptions of themselves and others.

The simplistic model of the USA as an effective ethnic 'melting pot', with education providing a central unifying influence, has been seriously questioned. Can any other industrialized society claim to have been more successful? To which society can we look for an approximation of social harmony? The balance of 'benefits' to 'costs' of coexistence and tolerance between all ethnic groups within a democratic multicultural society, favour the former. The balance between the perceived rights and responsibilities of members of minority ethnic groups, and other groups, partly determines that balance. It is always in a state of flux. Any state of social equilibrium is dynamic and transitory. We need to recognize that there can be no earthly Utopia acceptable to all, and to address the implications of this assertion. The principle of 'give and take' must remain reciprocal between individuals and groups. It must not be subverted by the egocentric 'You give, I take.'

Few individuals or families migrate to countries where the standards of living and the material prospects are inferior to those existing in the country from which they emigrate. Understandably, materialism is a powerful motivator. The ability to move from one country to another represents far less of a challenge than in the earlier days of this century. Taken together, the mass media, materialism and mobility have produced a marked increase in the rates at which changes take place in virtually almost all societies. Rapid changes in any society produce stresses. Uncertainties breed fears. Ignorance exacerbates intolerance. Scapegoats are sought. As a consequence, minority ethnic groups often suffer. Divisions within a society are exacerbated and harden. Misunderstandings and mistrust between ethnic groups increase. Every action produces a complementary reaction.

In the United Kingdom, we also have a National Front. It is also small, numerically. It thrives on, and exploits, the same fears and ignorance of minority ethnic groups as in France, Germany and elsewhere. Lest it be thought that this is a prerogative of western democracies, the situation is reciprocated in many non-western countries.

What values does the Prime Minister, John Major, encourage when he locates the foundations of anti-immigration sentiments as lying in the 'slums of Algiers and Bombay'? What effects is the debate on immigration and asylum having on the evolution here of a democratic multicultural society? What effects will such pronouncements have in schools? One of the most respected social scientists working in this field, Professor John Rex of the Centre for Research in Ethnic Relations at the University of Warwick, has publicly expressed his fears that this country could, for example, adopt anti-Muslim immigration policies. He considers that these could lead to subsequent unwarranted discrimination against black and Third-World immigrants.

Our second question was: Does education matter? Evidence indicates that school policies and practices can make important and constructive differences in encouraging cultural pluralism. It also follows that the reverse can take place. What can be done in schools to capitalize on the benefits of cultural pluralism? In a tension-ridden pluralistic society, at a time when nationalism is a rising trend in the United Kingdom, in Europe and wider afield, when minority ethnic groups remain the subject of illegal discriminatory behaviours, does the National Curriculum currently being introduced into our schools provide opportunities to develop cultural pluralism? Can teachers in maintained schools, in collaboration with parents and pupils, achieve the following ends:

● Promote the spiritual, moral, cultural, mental and physical development of pupils at the school and of society.
● Prepare such pupils for the opportunities, responsibilities and experiences of adult life. (ERA, 1988, Section 1)

We are convinced that the vision they represent is a worthy one, that it is possible, but that its attainment will not be easy. The enormity of the challenge should not discourage us. We do well to remember that 'No person ever made a greater mistake than he who did nothing because he or she could only do a little.' If the rights and responsibilities of *all* individuals and ethnic groups within a democratic society are to be respectively ensured and accepted, it is crucial that the opportunities afforded by the curriculum to develop the central concept of a common citizenship, be consciously and vigorously pursued. This is not an argument for either the assimilation or integration of minority ethnic groups. It is an argument for cultural pluralism (see Chapter 2 in this volume and Verma, 1990).

Members of the various ethnic groups that comprise the population of Britain differ in numerous significant ways. Culture, creed and colour are but three examples. Each ethnic group has much that is distinctive to contribute towards the construction of a society in which divisions maintained by ignorance, prejudice, fear and hostility are minimized. All groups also have much in common. If, as citizens, we wish to claim the privileges that British citizenship brings, then we must accept the concomitant responsibilities inherent in a democracy. Our educational system, schools, classes and teachers are potent models, for better or for worse. Thus our answer to the second question — Does education matter? — is unequivocal. It does. On the basis of recently published work on improving race relations in urban education, the key educational issues that must be addressed and strategies for so doing, have been identified and described (Pumfrey and Verma, 1990). Relating these insights more specifically to the opportunities inherent in the curricular provisions of the Education Reform Act 1988 is a challenging, but eminently worthwhile task.

Both of the above complex objectives of the ERA are the central focus of the Education Reform Act 1988. The Act requires that these principles be reflected in a balanced and broadly based curriculum to be followed by all pupils attending all maintained schools. 'That curriculum must also serve to develop the pupil as an individual, a member of society and as a future adult member of the community with a range of personal and social opportunities and problems' (DES, 1989, p. 2).

Passing laws is considerably easier than implementing them. The dominant educational challenge in England and Wales for the next decade will be the effective implementation of the Education Reform Act 1988 in general and of the whole curriculum in particular (NCC, 1989, 1990). The whole curriculum includes the basic curriculum, cross-curricular concerns and all other curricular provision. The basic curriculum comprises religious education and the National Curriculum. The National Curriculum consists of three core subjects plus a further seven foundation subjects, their associated attainment targets, programmes of study and assessment. Cross-curricular elements, including themes, dimensions and skills, are 'strands of provision which will run through the National Curriculum and may also extend into RE and provision outside the Basic curriculum'. Religious education continues to be a statutory requirement for all pupils attending county and voluntary schools. The only exceptions are nursery schools, or where parents request otherwise. In county and controlled schools, RE is to be taught according to the local agreed religious-education syllabus. Under the ERA, LEAs are required to establish Standing Advisory Councils on Religious Education (SACREs). The official timetable for implementation of core and foundation subjects has been published. The former will be operative by 1994/5; the latter by 1996/7 (DES, 1989).

This book is the first in a series of four. The series has been planned to consider how cultural diversity can be utilized in the effective delivery of the National Curriculum at the secondary stage (Volumes 1 and 2) and primary stage (Volumes 3 and 4) of education. The focus of the series is on the curricular challenges presented by cultural diversity in delivering each of the National-Curriculum subjects (Volumes 1 and 3), or in covering cross-curricular elements (Volumes 2 and 4). Each of the volumes has a similar structure. Within each chapter in all four volumes, there will be sections headed as follows: 'Context', 'Challenges', and 'Responses'. The present book will consist of two parts. Part 1 comprises the present introductory chapter, plus two others. Chapter 2 concerns cultural pluralism in secondary schools, and Chapter 3 deals with the whole, basic and National Curriculum in secondary schools. Part 2 consists of chapters on religious education and on each of the additional ten foundation subjects in the National Curriculum: English, mathematics, science, technology and design, history, music, geography, the arts, physical education and modern foreign languages.

It is now seven years since the publication of the Swann Committee's report *Education for All* (DES, 1985). That book represented and still represents an important unifying concept in the debate on how the multi-faceted challenge of 'delivering' the National Curriculum can be addressed. It also highlighted problems in society and education that demand attention if the whole curriculum is to delivered.

The population of England and Wales is increasingly characterized by cultural diversity, by both similarities and differences in values, expectations and opportunities linked to various ethnic groups. By virtue of their sheer size, the majority groups' concerns tend, understandably, to be to the fore. A danger in this situation is that the legitimate educational concerns of various minority ethnic groups could be overlooked in the implementation of the National Curriculum.

'The Education Reform Act (ERA) does not require teaching to be provided under the foundation subject headings. Indeed, it deliberately allows flexibility for schools to provide their teaching in a variety of ways' (DES, 1989, par., 3.7). Irrespective of the ways chosen by schools to teach their pupils, a public demonstration of the school's accountability will be required. Programmes of Study (PoS), Attainment Targets (ATs), Statements of Attainment (SoAs), Profile Components (PCs) and the enhanced rights to information concerning pupils' attainments and progress all reinforce this point.

Parents are central to the success of the venture. Booklets for the parents of primary-school and secondary-school children respectively have been published in English, Welsh, Greek, Turkish, Bengali, Gujerati, Hindi, Punjabi and Urdu (NCC, 1990a, 1990b).

In secondary schools the well-established curricular fields, in which considerable professional expertise has been developed, will provide the resource bases from which developments take place. The work of the National Curriculum Council (NCC) and the School Examinations and Assessment Council (SEAC) underline this point.

This series of four books has two major purposes. The first is to describe and discuss cultural diversity and the whole curriculum from various perspectives. The second is to consider how the legitimate educational concerns of minority ethnic groups, and those of larger groups, can be addressed within the framework of the National Curriculum and the equally important aspects of the curriculum subsumed under the broader headings of the 'basic' and 'whole' curriculum respectively. To this end, specialists in the key components of both the whole and the basic curriculum have considered some of the challenges and describe promising practices in a number of specific educational fields. Schools can have profound effects on the nature of the interpersonal and interethnic relationships in society. Schools matter (Smith and Tomlinson, 1989). If Britain is to enter the twenty-first century with a social and cultural cohesion that encompasses its invaluable diversities, education for citizenship must be a central concern of all schools for all pupils of all ethnic, cultural and religious allegiances in the 1990s. School curricula can make an important contribution (NCC, 1990c; Fogelman, 1991).

Finally, we return to our first question: What type of society do we wish to promote? We have argued the merits of a democratic multiculturalism. We consider that the National Curriculum provides many opportunities whereby this goal can be approached. This series is a contribution to that end.

References

COMMISSION FOR RACIAL EQUALITY (1987) *Racial Attacks: A Survey of Eight Areas of Britain*, London, CRE.

COMMISSION FOR RACIAL EQUALITY (1988) *Learning in Terror: A Survey of Racial Harassment in Schools and Colleges*, London, CRE.

DEPARTMENT OF EDUCATION AND SCIENCE (1985) *Report of the Committee of Inquiry into the Education of Children from Minority Ethnic Groups: Education for All* (Swann Report), Cmnd., 9453, London, HMSO.

DEPARTMENT OF EDUCATION AND SCIENCE (1989) *National Curriculum: From Policy to Practice*, London, Department of Education and Science.

FOGELMAN, K. (Ed) (1991) *Citizenship in Schools*, London, Fulton.

GILLBORN, D. (1990) *Race, Ethnicity and Education*, London, Unwin Hyman.

HILL, D. (1990) 'The MacDonald Report: A Report and Commentary', in PUMFREY, P.D. and VERMA, G.K. (Eds) (1990) *Race Relations and Urban Education: Challenges and Responses*, Basingstoke, The Falmer Press.

HOLMES, C. (1991) *A Tolerant Country? Immigrants, Refugees and Minorities in Britain*, London, Faber.

KELLY, E. (1990) 'Use and Abuse of Racial Language in Secondary schools', in PUMFREY, P.D. and VERMA, G.K. (Eds) (1990) *Race Relations and Urban Education: Contexts and Promising Practices*, Basingstoke, The Falmer Press.

NATIONAL CURRICULUM COUNCIL (1989) *The National Curriculum and Whole Curriculum Planning: Preliminary Guidance*, Circular 6/89, York, NCC.

NATIONAL CURRICULUM COUNCIL (1990) *The Whole Curriculum*, York, NCC.

NATIONAL CURRICULUM COUNCIL (1990a) *The National Curriculum: A guide for parents of primary children*, York, NCC.

NATIONAL CURRICULUM COUNCIL (1990b) *The National Curriculum: A guide for parents of secondary pupils*, York, NCC.

NATIONAL CURRICULUM COUNCIL (1990c) *Education for Citizenship: Curriculum Guidance No. 8*, York, NCC.

NATIONAL UNION OF TEACHERS (1992) *Anti-Racist Curriculum Guidelines*, London, NUT.

PUMFREY, P.D. and VERMA, G.K. (Eds) (1990) *Race Relations and Urban Education: Contexts and Promising Practices*, Basingstoke, The Falmer Press.

SMITH, D.J. and TOMLINSON, S. (1989) *The School Effect*, London, PSI.

TROYNA, B. and HATCHER, R. (1991) *Racism in Children's Lives*, London, Routledge/National Children's Bureau.

VERMA, G.K. (1990) 'Pluralism: Some theoretical and practical considerations', in CRE (Ed) *Britain: A Plural Society*, London, CRE.

VERMA, G.K. and DARBY, D. (1990) 'Race relations and the media', in PUMFREY, P.D. and VERMA, G.K. (Eds) *Race Relations and Urban Education: Contexts and Promising Practices*, Basingstoke, The Falmer Press.

Chapter 2

Cultural Diversity in Secondary Schools: Its Nature, Extent and Curricular Implications

Gajendra K. Verma

Context

The patterns and processes of migration, accelerated by improved and more widely accessible means of transport and by the changes in the social, economic and political identities of individuals and groups, are at play in the modern world. That migration — whether forced by political oppression or rejection, whether motivated by the desire to seek a better life elsewhere for oneself and one's family — has contributed to the change in the composition of many so-called 'established' societies across the world. Britain is not an exception in experiencing this phenomenon.

On the other hand, in any large complex society it is rare to find that the population is homogeneous. Most societies are demographically pluralistic, characterized by the presence of two or more distinct groups which are differentiated in terms of language, ethnic characteristics and/or cultural heritages. In spite of such diversity, many nation-states have failed to recognize and support the heterogeneity of its citizens.

In a world of increasing interdependence — economically, socially and politically — the education system has an increasingly important role to play in maintaining, sustaining and, in many cases, changing our conceptions of the world about us and of identities and roles within particular nations in this modern age.

Britain has never been a culturally homogeneous country. There are major differences between social classes and regions, and moreover, the population is made up of people from different ethnic origins. Racial purity in Britain is a fiction. Celts, Angles, Saxons, Scandinavians, Normans, all found home here and contributed to the development of a nation. Later on came Jews, Huguenots and other refugees from Europe, Asia and Africa. After World War II substantial numbers of immigrants came from India, Pakistan, East and West Africa and the West Indies.

Thus, historical and post-war migrations are the antecedents of cultural diversity in British society. The concept of cultural diversity has gained considerable currency since the 1960s and has generated much discussion about the nature of society. It has also become an area of acute controversy within the context of education. For conservative critics, it represents an attempt to publicize education in order to meet minority demands with regard to culture, language, religion etc. For some radicals it is the familiar ideological device of perpetuating the reality of racist exploitation of ethnic minorities by pampering their cultural sensitivities. It should be mentioned at the outset that the term 'ethnic minority' is used in this context for children and adolescents of former colonial immigrants, the majority of whom arrived in Britain during the 1960s. It should also be borne in mind that generalizations about ethnic-minority groups are often unwise and unhelpful. Some of the issues are more pertinent to some ethnic minorities, but less so to others.

In this ongoing process, concern about the education of ethnic-minority children and young people has posed the question as to how they are fitted to the existing educational system and its expectations, and how the education system can be modified to meet the needs and aspirations of a multicultural society. Such a broad question has been on the agenda of all those concerned with education for the last two decades. Such debates have rightly covered much more than educational issues, extending to, for example, prejudice and discrimination in society at large.

The political climate over the past quarter of a century has not been conducive to the development of changed educational policies and practices such as would provide equal opportunities for ethnic minorities or promote cultural tolerance in young people. Even the Archbishop of Canterbury's 1985 report on 'Urban Priority Areas' pointed to a 'growing number of young people, many of them black, excluded by poverty or powerlessness from sharing in the common life of our nation'. The report criticized the lack of political will to tackle the disadvantaged position of most ethnic minorities. Few would disagree that political commitment is a prerequisite for any change in society and there is little evidence of such a commitment up to the present time.

The Swann report (DES, 1985) found much evidence to suggest that many obstacles lay in the path of ethnic-minority pupils and lessened their chances of fulfilling their educational potential. Among those obstacles are ones created by poor interethnic relationships, both inside schools and in the wider society, and by the relative failure of schools to prepare *all* pupils, of whatever origin, for life in a multiracial society. The report recognized that many school practices related to race and ethnicity are harmful and that they reinforce ethnic stereotypes and discriminatory practices in our society. The report also provided evidence of racial prejudice and discrimination against ethnic minorities in society at large.

Challenges

It is now only a few years to the twenty-first century and there is as yet no consensus within the education system, or the wider society, as to how best to educate *all* children and young people growing up in multiracial Britain. Debates and discussions continue as to how ethnic minorities should be fitted to the existing education system and its expectations, and how schools and the curriculum can be modified to meet the issues of cultural plurality in British society. To put it in another way, it is legitimate to ask what contribution education should be making towards creating a society in which life chances of *all* are better distributed. Can this be achieved without detriment or prejudice to the individual, to his/her sense of identity or to that of other individuals?

The ways in which societies respond to such a challenge have been, and still are, subject to considerable study and debate in Britain and elsewhere. The study has been stimulated by a variety of motives. One of the motives has been the intrinsic interest of citizens in the structure of society, the way it adapts to change and the impact it has on individuals, groups and institutions that constitute any given society. Another has been the requirement to find out more about particular situations or problems. Such study would be expressly aimed at gathering detailed information and expert opinion on how to tackle and/or alleviate the disadvantaged position of ethnic minorities within the educational system and in society. Very often the information generated is intended to assist those in our society who are policy makers or decision makers (Pumfrey and Verma, 1990).

Research conducted over the last two decades has clearly shown that ethnic minorities remain the objects of discrimination — conscious and unconscious — and that this discrimination inhibits their life chances. It deprives them and their children of their right to enjoy the economic and social mobility which are taken for granted by many of the white majority (DES, 1985; Verma, 1986, 1988). It would be extremely difficult to question the proposition that the existence of the Select Committee on Race Relations in 1977, the Rampton report (DES, 1981), the Swann report (DES, 1985), the Scarman report (1981), several government and EEC reports testify to the fact that there is something wrong somewhere!

There is also sufficient evidence that the British education system has a deep monocultural and assimilationist orientation (see the section on 'responses'). This can be seen in the kind of curriculum we teach, the assessment techniques we use and the way teachers are expected to present other societies in the classroom. The educational system has also failed to provide an appropriate education to white pupils, which would equip them to understand adequately Britain's post-imperial position in the world and enable them to function effectively in a multiracial society. The advent of the National Curriculum and its associated testing system show little signs of countering the inequalities which exist within the educational system in particular and in society in general (DES, 1988). Some educational commentators are of the opinion that aspects of the Education Reform Act represent a setback to the course of multiracial, multiethnic education. Others see it as an opportunity. An 'entitlement' curriculum for *all* pupils must address some of the current and manifest inequalities.

Responses

Compared with the educational system's responses in the 1960s and 1970s, there were some positive developments in the 1980s. For example, the Swann report, published in 1985, moved the main focus of cultural diversity and equal opportunity debate in Britain from issues concerning the education of ethnic-minority pupils to those concerning the relevant education of *all* pupils for a plural society. It asserted that issues facing ethnic-minority pupils are tied up closely with pupils of the majority group, and therefore could not be solved without changing the basic character of mainstream education.

The Swann report recognized that biases in the educational system contributed to the failure of ethnic-minority pupils to achieve their full potential. It explicitly advocated that the educational system could best perform its task (initially) by replacing the present monocultural education with one that was multicultural and antiracist and which aimed to cultivate equal respect for, and a sensitive understanding of, all cultures. It further argued that the danger of failing to address adequately the question of education for *all* would be a stimulus for certain ethnic groups to set up separate schools. Such a radical analysis of the nature and role of the school cannot be dismissed, if British society is sincere about its core values. Unfortunately, the National Curriculum fails to take proper account of the needs of *all* children as discussed later in this chapter.

Turning to the political stance with regard to the education of ethnic minorities, government education-policy documents since the publication of the Swann report seem at least rhetorically committed to the removal of obstacles that lay in the path of children from ethnic-minority groups and lessened their chances of fulfilling their educational potential. These documents also advocate the elimination of racial prejudice both inside schools and in the wider society. In response to such policies the Council for the Accreditation of Teacher Education, popularly known as CATE, now requires that all student teachers should be adequately prepared to teach pupils from all social, ethnic and cultural backgrounds.

While this strategy may seem pedagogically sound, it has a serious flaw. It does not take account of the fact that its implementation is constantly frustrated by the social context in which any educational system exists and functions. Furthermore, a social structure is not a homogeneous whole, but is composed of different classes, religions and communities. If it is to become homogeneous, it must develop a common public culture, that is, a shared body of beliefs, attitudes and assumptions about people and society. Furthermore, education is not culturally neutral. Its intellectual content and orientation are often permeated by the world-view characteristics of the dominant ideologies and values. Inherent tensions between groups must be identified, analysed and addressed in the interests of all.

In the last three decades or so, generations of white monocultural people have come out of educational institutions. In the main, they look at culturally and racially different citizens with hostility rather than with respect and understanding. Schools have also produced generations of young people of ethnic-minority origins, many of whom have been ill-equipped to compete in a shrinking job market. They also feel that they are not accepted as equal citizens in a country in which most of them were born.

There is evidence to show that ethnic-minority children and adolescents suffer from multiple disadvantages and encounter prejudice and discrimination. Spencer (1987), reporting on a survey of 500 pupils in the London Borough of Barnet, found that racist name-calling was common. This increased with the age of the pupils, and was more frequent than abuse on the basis of sex or other attributes. The study found that some pupils saw teachers as 'condoning the racism which many of them experience daily'.

The CRE (1988) undertook a survey of racial harassment in schools and colleges. This provided copious evidence of poor interethnic relationships in inner-city multiracial schools and colleges, ranging from relatively mild expression of prejudice to physical violence. Its report criticizes the failure of the appropriate agencies to respond adequately to the problem. The report notes that out of 108 LEAs, only thirteen had published clear and detailed guidelines on dealing with cases of racial harassment in schools. Well over half had not given systematic consideration to the issue. Where does your LEA and school stand in this regard?

Cultural Diversity and the National Curriculum

Analysis of the National Curriculum and its associated testing procedures shows that ethnic-minority learners are almost entirely overlooked in the process of the 1988 Education Reform Act. The question is not one of access to the same curriculum but of the responses of the school as a whole to the cultural, linguistic and religious diversity of its pupils. Our schools have a considerable number of Jewish, Indian, Pakistani, Chinese, Bangladeshi, West Indian and other ethnic-minority pupils (see Chapter 3). One would naturally expect them to adjust to the existing structures and rules of their schools. Equally, it would not be unreasonable to expect the schools to respect their pupils' sensitivities in areas that matter to them deeply and which are no threat to the basic objectives of the school (e.g., food habits, religion, dress and language). The schools' response has often been largely negative.

The advent of the National Curriculum may have reduced the freedom on the part of schools to determine the content of lessons but assumptions remain unchanged as to their duty to inculcate standards of behaviour based on justice and mutual respect. Of course, such lessons are learnt, not only through formal studies but also implicitly in the way the schools are organized and conduct their affairs, and explicitly in the policies and priorities which each school adopts. It is interesting to compare the 1988 Education Act with the two main Education Acts of this century: the 1918 Education Act (Fisher) and the 1944 Education Act (Butler). Both these Acts were carried with the support of all parties in the Parliament. In the case of the 1988 Education Act, the government of the day had a large majority in the House of Commons which made it possible for them to get it on to the statute book.

One of the controversial aspects of the National Curriculum is the legislative imposition of testing and assessment for all pupils in maintained schools at the ages of 7, 11, 14 and 16. At the heart of this process are nationally prescribed tests which will be taken by all pupils. These are administered and monitored by teachers, but moderated externally. Many arguments have been put forward in support of testing and the fact that the bulk of testing will be conducted with what are known as 'criterion-referenced' tests. Such a strategy is based on the myth of 'objectivity'. There is no such thing as 'objectivity' or 'objective knowledge' and any delusion that there is becomes more and more pronounced as the knowledge and skills being tested become more sophisticated. Moreover, since the results of the tests are to be one of the bases on which parents are to judge the effectiveness of the schools in selecting one for their children, it appears that the results of criterion-referenced tests will be used normatively. Some would argue that this is scarcely an improvement on previous practice. The efficiency of schools and LEAs in discharging their responsibilities will be similarly graded and judged. 'League tables' of suspect validity will mislead and confuse users of the educational system.

It is disappointing that SEAC (the School Examination and Assessment Council) specifications on assessment do not make any reference to the needs of ethnic, cultural and linguistic groups. Tests and assessment techniques often contain culturally embedded assumptions which unreliably estimate, or discriminate against, cultural and ethnic minorities. For example, if educational policies are to be informed by test results, then, in a democratic society, it must be demonstrated that the instruments and techniques are fair to all those being assessed. On the basis of research evidence it seems likely that ethnic-minority children, particularly bilingual ones, will be further disadvantaged (see Chapter 14; Frederickson and Cline, 1990). The dominant culture and ethos which the National Curriculum reflect are those of the white middle-class Anglo-Saxon. It excludes the significant input from the so-called Third-World countries. It contains a Eurocentric concept of a static Anglo-Saxon culture which no longer exists. It ignores the contributions by non-western civilizations to literature, maths, science, technology, history, music, geography and art, that have helped to shape today's world. There is ample evidence of this. For example, many educators have disregarded the recommendations of their own government inquiry, the 1985 Swann report *Education for All* (DES, 1985).

The National Curriculum appears to most commentators to be the product of a remote, managerially inclined bureaucracy and one lacking any understanding of what 'education' means. Education should be concerned with the development of human abilities and skills, and thereby the acquisition of knowledge — not merely absorption of 'facts' as required in various subjects (e.g., history) in the National Curriculum. It is unfortunate that the terms such as 'motivation', 'identity', 'self-concept', 'culture' and 'ethnicity' are often absent from the National-Curriculum documents. It is also clear that the aims, content and the evaluation in the National Curriculum are not only monocultural and anglocentric but assimilationist in their orientation. Furthermore, there is as yet no formal mechanism for cross-curricular permeation of subjects with a multicultural, antiracist or pluralist orientation. Analysis of earlier reports from various subject working parties suggest that very little, if any, account has been taken of ethnic and cultural diversity and the importance of the curriculum in promoting equal opportunity for all pupils regardless of their backgrounds.

It is not possible within the scope of this chapter to consider all aspects of the content of the National Curriculum. However, a few issues taken from individual subject areas will be instanced here. They illustrate the argument about the National Curriculum's overall character and offer a foretaste of the range of issues raised by individual 'subject' authors in this volume.

Religious education is a contentious issue within the educational system. In the National Curriculum most schools in England and Wales are required to make Christianity the basis of religious education and give pupils a 'broadly Christian' act of daily worship (see Chapter 4). It is unfortunate that the Act has set teachers and minority religious communities on a collision course. In June 1989, The *Times Educational Supplement* carried out a survey of secondary head teachers to find out their views on the new religious requirements. The result showed that 'hundreds of secondary schools are likely to disobey or turn a blind eye to the law on the daily act of collective worship' (Lodge, 1989). The survey did provide evidence that many head teachers are already working out their own ways of 'modifying' this particular requirement of the Act. This clearly shows that many schools are following the Swann recommendations (DES, 1985): 'We are in favour of a non-denominational and undogmatic approach to religious education' (p. 496). This message may seem confusing and uncertain; this may be because our present-day society is confused about the values it seeks to transmit. The Report rightly asserts that: 'The role of education cannot be expected to reinforce the values, beliefs and cultural identity which each child brings to school' (p. 321).

English literature in schools has been dominated by white English and American writers. Many of their works have often perpetuated negative cultural stereotypes of Africans, Asians, black Americans and Chinese (Massey, 1991). A recent report published by Wallen and Dowd (1990) shows that Asian and black authors are largely ignored by A level exam boards when selecting writers for English syllabuses. According to this study five boards offered no texts by Asian or black authors, while the other four offered a total of eighteen. This was based on an analysis of 378 literary choices offered that year to all students in England, Wales and Northern Ireland. Analysis of set book lists for the past four decades revealed that little has changed despite efforts to promote equal opportunity (Chapter 5).

The National Curriculum Council set up to oversee the introduction of the National Curriculum states in its remit that: 'It will be taking account of ethnic and cultural diversity and ensuring that the curriculum provides equal opportunities for all pupils regardless of ethnic origin or gender' (NCC, 1988). Many of the subject working groups ignored this aspiration. For example, the mathematics proposals included statements explicitly against multiculturalism (see Chapter 6). It advocates:

> We are concerned that undue emphasis on multicultural mathematics could confuse young children . . . We have not therefore included any 'multicultural' aspects in our attainment targets. (DES, 1988)

The science group adopted a more positive approach at the time and noted that:

> Science education must take account of the ethnic and cultural diversity of the school population and society at large . . . the international currency of Science is an important force for overcoming racial prejudice. (DES, 1988)

However, it is disappointing that the revised document has given less emphasis to the reality of cultural diversity (see Chapter 7).

Technology offers the potential for a pluralist approach within the framework set out in the National Curriculum. However, much depends on the exploitation of the aims of its syllabus. Here, arguably, too much rests on the resourcefulness and experience of the individual school and teacher. Thus the gap there remains in terms of the in-service training and support offered to teachers to enable them to achieve a truly pluralist interpretation of its aims (see Chapter 8).

The new history curriculum starts with 5 to 7-year-olds but there is no mention of historical personalities outside Britain. In the secondary-school history curriculum, topics cover primarily Britain and, to some extent, parts of Europe. It is only in the final years of compulsory schooling (i.e., 14 to 16 years) that some attention is given to the Indian subcontinent between 1930 and 1964. The history syllabus is designed to proclaim the glory of Britain and largely ignores the great non-western civilizations. It does not foster cultural diversity. Another criticism is centred on the question of balance (see Chapter 9).

In terms of classroom practice, the large number of topics that teachers have to cover by law will leave little time for discussion of many underlying issues and their implications. For example, the unit of study at Key Stage 4, ages 14 to 16, on the British Empire takes primarily a British view of history and does not address the problems from the perspective of colonized peoples. Another Programme of Study on the 'Zenith of the British Empire' examines colonialism in terms of its costs and benefits to Britain. The study of South Africa from 1880–1905 focuses on prominent Whites such as Rhodes and Kruger but there is no mention of prominent Blacks.

Many geography teachers have expressed their concern that the syllabus will make it difficult to relate classwork to fast-changing world events. The curriculum heavily concentrates on Britain and ignores the rest of the world. Concern has also been expressed that requirements to teach the names of specific places in the geography syllabus would reinforce stereotypes, particularly about Third-World countries. It is quite disturbing that the working-party report puts forward a world view which is white, middle-class European and which teachers are expected to teach to pupils of varying ethnic and cultural backgrounds (see Chapter 11).

Since music is a universal experience, one might have expected that its inclusion within the National Curriculum would present no problem in meeting pluralist expectations. However, music is also a very subjective experience and the argument seems largely unresolved as to the 'legitimacy' of what constitutes 'music'. All too often the esoteric values of what is 'culture' overlook the important dimension of the individual experience (see Chapter 10).

Like music, art is another area of subjective experience, since aesthetics tend to be largely cultural-specific. However, in many ways, the productive dimension of art has lent itself to a more liberal interpretation of what is legitimate. On the other hand, the cultural dimension, as in an appreciation of the history of art, still tends to rest on the more monocultural interpretations (see Chapter 12).

Physical education's inclusion in the National Curriculum might suggest an area of activity that was essentially universal since many sporting activities are widely practised across the world, even if western-dominated in their origins. However, a crucial dimension in this field is the range of opportunity open to different pupils. This is not so much because of in-school provision, subject though this is to variations in the facilities available, but because of the out-of-school implications contained in the recommendations. Here the issues of pluralism are allied to the social and other disadvantages experienced by minority groups (see Chapter 13).

The National Curriculum on modern foreign languages had laid two schedules initially. The first contained primarily European languages (Danish,

French, Modern Greek, Portuguese, Dutch, German, Italian and Spanish). Provided schools teach one or more of these languages, they may also offer other languages listed under Schedule 2 (Arabic, Chinese, Hindi, Punjabi, Turkish, Bengali, Gujerati, Japanese, Russian and Urdu). It was obvious that by listing separately ethnic-minority languages they could be seen to be of lower status than European ones. 'It does set up a league table that creates expectations about which languages are valued in society' (*Times Educational Supplement*, 7 April 1989). It should be noted that 70 per cent of the world's population is bilingual. Although the interim report recommended that the two lists should be merged as one, this is simply a cosmetic exercise (see Chapter 14). It is suggested that pupils should be able to study both a European-Community working language and an ethnic-minority community language, but financial constraints on the part of schools will restrict this implementation. The government's view is that schools must be able to offer one of the eight European languages before they should be allowed to offer non-EC languages such as Gujerati, Hindi, Punjabi, Urdu and Bengali and trading languages such as Chinese, Japanese, Arabic and Russian. Furthermore, the government has given no guidance or financial support so far as to how to deal with chronic and growing shortage of modern-language teachers.

Bilingualism is one of the greatest accomplishments one can attain, yet this has received scant attention in the Education Reform Act. 'Teachers often ignore the fact that bilingual children are skilled users of their first language. If teachers of English as a second language do not use or refer to the pupil's mother tongue as an aid to learning, then this may signal a low evaluation of the minority language' ('Linguistic Minorities in England', 1983, pp. 9–10). The current philosophy is that the needs of bilingual children can best be met in the mainstream classroom with additional support (Cline and Frederickson, 1991).

In a very useful analysis of the 1988 Education Reform Act in terms of racial equality Troyna concludes that:

> The proposals for the National Curriculum are likely to discourage overt instances of discrimination and facilitate access of all pupils to the full range of core and foundation subjects, but these advances cannot be seen in isolation. Placed in the appropriate context of opting out, LMS, and open enrolment, these systematic changes will further disadvantage ethnic minority and other disenfranchised pupils in a number of fundamental ways. (Troyna, 1990)

Parental Choice

The Education Acts 1980 and 1988 incorporate clauses on parental choice of schools. No one would deny the importance of such provision. However, recent test cases in Dewsbury and Cleveland have upheld parental rights of choice in a manner that is contrary to the spirit of the Race Relations Act 1976. Under the Act, it is unlawful for local authorities to act in any way that constitutes racial discrimination.

The Dewsbury dispute which resulted in a High-Court ruling that white parents were entitled to send their children to a school of their choice rather than a school attended predominantly by Asian children, set a precedent for parents in other areas wishing to remove their children from racially-mixed schools. The Dewsbury case gave wide publicity to white parental claims that school standards were lowered by a focus on the needs of Asian pupils, although no evidence was ever produced to support this claim.

In Cleveland, in 1988 however, a parent complained that the curriculum was unsuitable and the daughter was 'learning Pakistani'. After taking legal advice Cleveland Council decided that it had a statutory duty under the 1980 and 1988 Education Acts, to comply with the parental request for a transfer. A subsequent investigation by the Commission for Racial Equality high-lighted a potential clash between the 1976 Race Relations Act and the Education Acts. It pointed out that the law needed changing so that the right of parental choice could not be exercised on explicitly racial grounds. Had the same cases arisen in the private sector, the CRE would have been empowered to issue a non-discrimination notice, which would have been binding for five years. In the state sector it is the Secretary of State for Education and Science that has the power to issue such orders. This he has declined to do. There is no doubt that it would be a good thing for education, and for society, if the final outcome of the Cleveland affair were to be a judicial review backing the Race Relations Act. It would do nothing to prevent racist decisions by parents, but it would mean that such behaviour could not be publicly proclaimed with the full backing of the law.

If the long-term objectives of creating a genuinely plural and democratic society are to be met, much sensitivity and understanding will be needed to deal with the delicate balance between individual freedom and social responsibility. In order to keep up with the contemporary world and to prosper in the twenty-first century we need to develop a pluralist style of thinking, talking and behaving.

It is clear from an analysis of the National Curriculum within the context of cultural diversity that its nature, process and the associated assessment system are inappropriate to the diverse ethnic make-up of British society. The level and type of response of the National Curriculum to the social and cultural needs of the British population show that it has failed to take full account of the plurality of cultures which exist in the country. The various British cultural communities expect the educational system to reflect more accurately their cultural presence as well as their economic and social needs. The National Curriculum is narrow and biased in favour of the white, middle-class population.

It is also true to say that no curriculum can cover everything in the world and must by necessity be selective. Selection based on cultural pluralism would aim to ensure that children and young people acquire an understanding of the major representative forms of the subject matter in question. In this process, even though pupils would concentrate on some aspects of the curriculum, their curiosity would be sufficiently stimulated to lead them to follow up the rest on their own. For example, the curriculum on religious studies would include the major religions of the world and aim to enable pupils to appreciate the different ways in which they conceptualize and respond to basic perplexities of human existence.

The curriculum should be taught in ways that are as little biased and dogmatic as possible. Facts are always impregnated with interpretations, and although some are more plausible than others, all interpretations are partial. The curriculum should therefore be taught in a manner that alerts pupils to this point and encourages them to examine various interpretations and arrive at a view of their own. Teachers should adopt a critical approach to cultural bias, prejudice, racism and stereotyping in teaching schemes, curricula, schools and assessment. They should be equipped for their work by learning to recognize cultural diversity as a source of social and curriculum enrichment. 'Schools have a duty to prepare children from the age of 5 for their contribution to a multicultural society, according to Education for Citizenship, a confidential draft report prepared for the National Curriculum Council' (Weston, 1989) (see Volume 2 for further discussion).

Future developments will depend crucially on teachers, school governors, parents and LEAs. A major challenge to plurality in our society is the production of a cohesive national educational system which can offer justice and equal participation to ethnic minorities. If government is sincere about its commitment to justice and the well-being of all citizens, it must adopt the philosophy and strategies to attain cultural pluralism as we move towards the year 2000.

References

CLINE, A. and FREDERICKSON, N. (1991) *Bilingual Pupils and the National Curriculum*, London, University College.

COMMISSION FOR RACIAL EQUALITY (1988) *Learning in Terror: A survey of Racial Harassment in Schools and Colleges*, London, Commission for Racial Equality.

DEPARTMENT OF EDUCATION AND SCIENCE (1981) *West Indian Children in Our Schools*, Report of the Committee of Inquiry into the Education of Children from Ethnic Minority Groups (The Rampton Report), Cmnd., 8273, London, HMSO.

DEPARTMENT OF EDUCATION AND SCIENCE (1985) *Education for All*, Report of the Committee of Inquiry into the Education of Children from Ethnic Minority Groups (The Swann Report), Cmnd., 9453, London, HMSO.

DEPARTMENT OF EDUCATION AND SCIENCE (1988) *The Education Reform Act 1988*, London, HMSO.

FREDERICKSON, N. and CLINE, A. (1990) *Curriculum Related Assessment with Bilingual Children*, London, University College.

LINGUISTIC MINORITIES IN ENGLAND (1983) A Report on the Linguistic Minorities Project, Institute of Education, University of London.

LODGE, B. (1989) 'Reluctant Defenders of the Faith', *Times Educational Supplement*, 30 June.

MASSEY, I. (1991) *More Than Skin Deep: Developing anti-racist multicultural education in schools*, London, Hodder and Stoughton.

NATIONAL CURRICULUM COUNCIL (1988) *Introducing the National Curriculum Council*, York, NCC.

PUMFREY, P.D. and VERMA, G.K. (1990) (Eds) *Race Relations and Urban Education: Promising Practices*, London, The Falmer Press.

SCARMAN REPORT (1981) *The Brixton Disorders*, Cmnd., 8427, London, HMSO, 10–12 April.

SPENCER, D. (1987) 'Racist Names Hurt More Than Sticks and Stones', *Times Educational Supplement*, 18 September.

TROYNA, B. (1990) 'Reform or deform? The 1988 Education Reform Act and racial equality in Britain', *New Community*, 16, 3, pp. 403–16.

VERMA, G.K. (1986) *Ethnicity and Educational Achievement*, London, Macmillan.

VERMA, G.K. and PUMFREY, P.D. (1988) (Eds) *Educational Attainments: Issues and Outcomes in Multicultural Education*, London, The Falmer Press.

VERMA, G.K. (1989) *Education for All: A Landmark in Pluralism*, London, The Falmer Press.

VERMA, G.K. (1990) 'Pluralism: Some Theoretical and Practical Considerations', *Britain: A Plural Society*, Report of a Seminar, London, Commission for Racial Equality.

WALLEN, R. and DOWD, M. (1990) *Black Authors and A-Level Set Texts*, Afro-Caribbean Language and Literacy Project, London, Southwark College.

WESTON, C. (1989) 'Citizenship lessons should start at five', *The Guardian*, 27 December.

Chapter 3

The Whole, Basic and National Curriculum in Secondary Schools: Contexts, Challenges and Responses

Peter D. Pumfrey

Context

Schools matter. Making schools increasingly effective is a national concern. If schools are to carry out successfully the functions expected of them, curricular implications of the cultural diversity characteristic of the school population must be considered. The important cohesive educational and social effects of schools in a rapidly changing world are now acknowledged. The aims, objectives, curricula, methodologies and management of schools are nationally and locally debated. The formative and summative consequences of the education schools provide are increasingly under scrutiny. The accountability of all levels of the educational service to 'consumers', in the guise of parents who pay for the educational system as taxpayers, and to their children, the pupils, is now centre-stage. The introduction of local management of schools gives schools a high and increasing degree of autonomy in the management of their finances. Many decisions concerning educational priorities and resource allocations are dealt with at the school level by governors. Fortunately, a number of national responsibilities continue. Acknowledging and utilizing the resources represented by the cultural diversities within school and communities, is one of these.

It is thirteen years since a study *Fifteen Thousand Hours: Secondary Schools and their Effects on Children* confirmed that schools do 'make a difference' (Rutter *et al.*, 1979). Dependent on the school attended, pupils from similarly disadvantaged socio-economic backgrounds achieved different levels of success in attendance, behaviour, academic attainments and reduced delinquency. More importantly, the processes within school that contributed to beneficial effects were identified. Studies seeking the causes of effective education, and promoting 'good practice', have extended to all levels of education. The first meeting of the International Congress for School Effectiveness was held in London in 1988. It underlined the importance of this field of research and practice (Reynolds, Creemers and Peter, 1989).

A recent major longitudinal study of multiracial comprehensive schools confirms this point. From their entry at the age of 11 years into twenty multiracial comprehensive schools in four LEAs, the progress of 3,000 pupils was studied. Wide variations between even neighbouring schools were found in the availability of subjects now comprising the National Curriculum. Expectations of pupils from working-class backgrounds were often too low. Evidence was found of marked, albeit unintended, social class and ethnic bias when similarly able pupils were allocated to courses and public examinations. Large differences in scholastic attainments were found between comparable children in different schools. The relatively low attainments of British pupils of parents of South-Asian and West-Indian origins at 11 and 13 years of age were less marked at the age of 16. At that stage, differences between ethnic groups were less than differences between schools. There is strong evidence that certain groups of British pupils of parents from minority ethnic groups have caught up with their white peers in terms of school-leaving attainments, provided that they have been attending effective schools (Smith and Tomlinson, 1989; Tomlinson, 1990). Encouragingly, the authors found that there was an absence of racial hostility within the schools studied. However, this point was based on evidence from single interviews with parents and pupils. It would be unwise to generalize. There is unfortunately much evidence of racism and prejudice in schools and society at both individual and institutional levels (Verma, 1989; Pumfrey, 1990).

The existence of distinctive ethnic groupings in this country is a fact. What is done in schools can either capitalize on, or attempt to ignore the cultural diversity of our society. Does the Education Reform Act encourage such developments?

This book considers the implications of cultural diversity for the delivery of the National Curriculum at the secondary stage of education. As legal and professional responsibilities for the delivery of the National Curriculum rest largely on governors, schools and teachers, such considerations must be systematically addressed in relation to all aspects of school life. In this chapter, a background is outlined for the subsequent more detailed consideration of the contribution towards effective cultural pluralism via specific subjects comprising the secondary-school curriculum.

Whilst undoubtedly an oversimplification, the argument that 'power plus prejudice equals racism' has considerable validity. Under the ERA, will majority ethnic groups fail to recognize and utilize the many, varied and valuable cultural and curricular contributions of minority ethnic groups? Will the ERA result in cultural pluralism being put firmly on an educational 'back boiler'?

Conscious and unconscious prejudices and suspicions exist mutually between ethnic groups, whether large or small, in this country. Politicians are well aware of the possibility of racist reactions from the white British public if policies are perceived as unduly favouring ethnic minorities. Suspicions that many ethnic minorities are not a part of the British national identity are fostered by some right-wing politicians and writers. For example, Norman Tebbitt's question concerning which cricket team one supports during a 'test match' is one suspect example. It is suspect because the concepts of national identity and ethnic distinctiveness are not necessarily mutually exclusive.

The point is further illustrated by a quotation from a rhetorical article entitled 'The future for multiracial Britain': '. . . large segments of British cities such as London, Liverpool, Birmingham and Bradford seem to have been transformed into foreign enclaves and incipient casbahs.' Working-class families in such areas have been powerless '. . . as the neighbourhoods in which they have lived for years were taken over by hordes of alien people, often noisy, sometimes gaudy or garish, and not infrequently unkempt and unintelligible' (Mishan, 1988a). The same author subsequently wrote to the effect that it was largely the responsibility of the black community in Brixton that the housing stock had deteriorated and that the environment was bleak and demoralizing. The youngsters of the minority ethnic group were represented as often alienated from mainstream society, aimless, cynical and all too frequently engaged in criminal activities including mugging and dope peddling (Mishan, 1988b).

Scapegoating, harassment and unfair discrimination are the all too common experience of minority ethnic groups in virtually *any* society. In secondary schools in this country, derogatory name-calling occurs and assaults on pupils from minority ethnic groups take place with a worrying frequency. In one extreme case, an Asian secondary-school pupil was stabbed to death whilst at school (Hill, 1990).

Why are there such tensions? What can be done to resolve them during the minimum of ten years spent by our nation's children in the educational system? Can the recently introduced National Curriculum be used to foster interethnic cohesion? If not, there is indeed something rotten in the state of both society and education. Acknowledging the existence of a particular challenge, such as that represented by cultural diversity in a society, is a necessary but not sufficient condition for constructively addressing the challenges. It is important to recognize that all challenges present problems and opportunities. Pessimists tend to see only the former whereas optimists perceive the latter. Realists can accept both perspectives.

In the United Kingdom we have legislation that aims to prohibit individual and institutional manifestations and operations of racism. Teachers and schools must consider the ethical and legal contexts of race relations if they are to understand how the National Curriculum can incorporate cultural diversity. Fortunately, readily available discussions of these issues are available (Kloss, 1990; Lee, 1990). The current controversial debate concerning the Asylum Bill, in the context of moves towards integration under the umbrella of the European Economic Community, underlines the national and international importance of individual and national rights and responsibilities.

Wherever possible, replacing phantasies with facts is a sound strategy. An appreciation of the estimated sizes of various ethnic groups in the population is one starting point. There exists widespread ignorance of such basic information (Cohen, 1989; Pumfrey, 1990). A knowledge of demography is essential. Its interpretation requires considerable care. The following estimates were obtained by the Office of Population Censuses and Surveys (Haskey, 1990, 1991). Table 3.1 estimates changes in the sizes of various minority ethnic groups over the period 1981–8. Currently the annual average increase in the minority ethnic population is estimated at 'just over 80,000 per year' (ibid., p. 35). 51 per cent of the total minority ethnic population is now of Indian, Pakistani or Bangladeshi ethnic origins. Those of West Indian origins comprise about 20 per cent and approximately one in nine is of mixed ethnic origins. The apparent assumption that the white ethnic majority is not of mixed ethnic origins, is intriguing and challenging!

Table 3.2 summarizes the distribution of ethnic groups by age bands. It can be seen that there are great variations between the ethnic groups in the proportions who are children and also those over the age of 60 years. Related analyses have demonstrated that the minority ethnic populations with the oldest age profiles have, unsurprisingly, been resident in the UK for longer than those groups with the younger age profiles. Irrespective of minority ethnic group, the younger the individual, the greater the probability that they were born in the UK. A minimum of 90 per cent of ethnic-minority children under the age of 5 years have been born in the UK. There are marked variations in these proportions between ethnic groups.

In Table 3.3, it can be seen that the proportions of minority ethnic groups born in the UK and elsewhere vary considerably. The effects of policies in Uganda in 1972 and of an exodus of Asians from Kenya during the 1960s and 1979s contribute towards the 18 per cent of Indians who were born in East Africa.

Unsurprisingly, the density of distribution of minority ethnic groups by county across this country is uneven. The reasons for this are important. An overview is shown in Figure 3.1. What have been termed the 'white Highlands' can be broadly identified. This does not mean that education for cultural diversity is the concern of *only* a part of Great Britain.

A more detailed analysis of the information presented in Figure 3.1 is given in Table 3.4. Estimates of minority ethnic populations in various regions of Great Britain are presented. There are great variations from area to area. Within the London boroughs, Brent has the highest concentration estimated at 27 per cent. Gateshead, in Tyne and Wear metropolitan county has the lowest concentration of minority ethnic groups at 1 per cent.

The information contained in the figure and tables is important. The 1991 census results will provide an update on the figures. The patterns will continue to change in predictable ways. Accepting and maintaining ethnic identities, beliefs and values in a culturally diverse democratic society requires tolerance and understanding by all parties. All too readily we claim highly valued rights as members of a democratic society: all too easily we

Table 3.1: Population by Ethnic Group, 1981–1988, Great Britain

Ethnic group	Percentage 1981	Estimated population (thousands) 1981	1986	1987	1988	1986–88 (average)	Sample numbers 1986–88 (average)	Percentages* 1986–88 (average)		Change in population 1981–1986/88 Thousands	%
West Indian†	25	528	526	489	468	495	1,340	19	0.9	− 33	− 6
African	4	80	98	116	122	112	298	4	0.2	+ 32	+ 39
Indian	35	727	784	761	814	787	2,138	31	1.4	+ 59	+ 8
Pakistani	14	284	413	392	479	428	1,169	17	0.8	+144	+ 51
Bangladeshi	2	52	117	116	91	108	289	4	0.2	+ 56	+109
Chinese	4	92	113	126	136	125	343	5	0.2	+ 33	+ 36
Arab	3	53	73	79	66	73	188	3	0.1	+ 20	+ 38
Mixed	10	217	269	263	328	287	801	11	0.5	+ 70	+ 32
Other	3	60	164	141	184	163	429	6	0.3	+103	+173
All ethnic minority groups	100	2,092	2,559	2,484	2,687	2,577	6,994	100	4.7	+485	+ 23
White	—	51,000	51,204	51,573	51,632	51,470	144,745	—	94.4	+470	+ 1
Not stated	—	608	607	467	343	472	1,540	—	0.9	−136	− 22
All ethnic groups	—	53,700	54,370	54,524	54,662	54,519	153,279	—	100.0	+819	+ 2

Sources: 1981, 1986, 1987, and 1988 Labour Force Surveys (Haskey, 1990)
* Derived from grossed-up estimates (column 6)
† Includes Guyanese
Note: averages have been calculated using unrounded figures

Table 3.2: Population by Age and Ethnic Group, 1986–1988, Great Britain

percentages

Ethnic group	Age-group											All ages		Males per 100 females
	Under 1	1–4	5–9	10–14	15–19	20–24	25–34	35–44	45–59	60 and over	Pensionable age*	%	Thousands	
West Indian†	2	8	7	7	10	14	16	9	20	7	5	100	495	94
African	(2)	8	8	8	8	13	20	17	12	3	(2)	100	112	120
Indian	2	9	10	8	9	10	20	14	14	5	4	100	787	100
Pakistani	2	13	15	11	10	9	16	10	11	2	2	100	428	107
Bangladeshi	3	17	14	13	8	7	15	8	13	2	(1)	100	108	124
Chinese	(1)	7	10	10	8	9	23	18	9	5	4	100	125	101
Arab	(2)	8	7	(4)	5	12	28	17	11	6	(4)	100	73	163
Mixed	5	18	17	12	13	10	11	7	6	3	3	100	287	93
Other	2	9	9	7	7	10	20	18	11	6	5	100	163	100
All ethnic minority groups	2	10	11	9	10	10	18	12	13	5	4	100	2,577	102
White	1	5	6	6	7	8	14	14	17	21	19	100	51,470	95
Not stated	3	7	8	9	9	9	14	12	13	18	16	100	472	95
All ethnic groups	1	5	6	6	8	8	14	14	16	20	18	100	54,519	95

Sources: 1986, 1987, and 1988 Labour Force Surveys (Haskey, 1990)
* 65 and over for men, 60 and over for women
† Includes Guyanese
Figures in brackets are based on a sample of fewer than 30

Table 3.3: Population by Ethnic Group and Country of Birth, 1986–1988, Great Britain

Percentages

Ethnic group	All countries of birth	United Kingdom	Total‡	Irish Republic	Old Commonwealth	NCW	East Africa	Rest of Africa	Caribbean	India	Pakistan††	Bangladesh	Far East	Mediterranean	Rem. NCW	Other EEC*	Other Europe**	Rest of World	Not Stated
West Indian†	100	53	46	0.2	0.1	45.0	0.1	0.3	45.0	0.1	–	–	0.1	0.1	0.2	–	–	0.7	0.6
African	100	38	58	0.3	0.1	48.0	7.0	36.0	3.0	0.2	0.2	–	1.0	–	1.0	0.2	0.1	9.0	4.0
Indian	100	37	62	–	–	60.0	18.0	0.2	0.4	39.0	0.5	0.1	0.6	–	2.0	0.1	–	2.0	1.0
Pakistani	100	46	53	0.1	0.1	53.0	2.0	–	0.1	3.0	47.0	1.0	0.1	–	–	0.1	–	0.3	1.0
Bangladeshi	100	32	65	–	–	65.0	–	–	–	0.2	0.5	64.0	0.3	–	–	0.1	–	0.1	3.0
Chinese	100	26	73	0.2	0.7	46.0	–	–	0.4	0.3	–	0.2	44.0	0.9	0.6	0.9	0.3	26.0	0.6
Arab	100	14	85	–	–	2.0	0.3	0.1	0.1	0.4	0.2	0.2	–	0.7	–	1.0	0.3	82.0	1.0
Mixed	100	77	22	0.1	–	14.0	2.0	0.6	2.0	4.0	0.4	–	–	–	3.0	1.0	0.3	7.0	1.0
Other	100	36	62	0.4	0.6	34.0	2.0	0.5	2.0	1.0	0.1	–	7.0	4.0	17.0	1.0	1.0	25.0	2.0
All ethnic minority groups	100	45	54	0.1	0.1	47.0	6.0	2.0	9.0	13.0	8.0	3.0	3.0	0.4	2.0	0.3	0.1	7.0	1.0
White	100	96	4	1.0	0.2	0.6	0.1	–	–	0.1	–	–	0.1	0.2	–	0.8	0.3	0.6	0.3
Not stated	100	68	9	2.0	0.1	4.0	0.6	0.1	0.8	0.5	0.6	0.2	0.4	0.3	0.3	0.5	0.5	2.0	23.0
All ethnic groups (%)	100	93	6	1.0	0.2	3.0	0.4	0.1	0.5	0.7	0.4	0.1	0.2	0.2	0.1	0.8	0.3	0.9	0.5
All ethnic groups (millions)	54.52	50.90	3.34	0.57	0.13	1.52	0.19	0.07	0.26	0.39	0.22	0.08	0.13	0.12	0.06	0.44	0.18	0.50	0.28

Sources: 1986, 1987, and 1988 Labour Force Surveys (Haskey, 1990)

† Including Guyana
* Including Spain and Portugal (12 countries in all)
** Excluding Spain, Portugal and USSR
‡ Excludes Not Stated
†† Pakistan rejoined the Commonwealth on 01.10.89.

Figure 3.1: *Ethnic-Minority Population as a Percentage of the Total Population, by County, 1986–1988.*

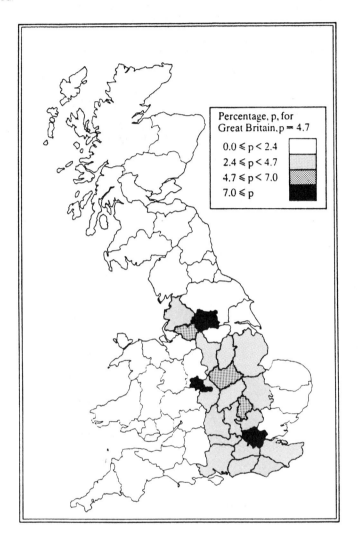

Source: (Haskey, 1991)
Notes: Percentage is estimated — Region instead of county for Scotland

forget our reciprocal and inevitable responsibilities on which such hard-won rights depend.

In all countries, national identity is likely to remain a potent concept. The whole of that identity is much more than the sum of its ethnically distinctive parts. In the UK the dynamic equilibrium between the values, beliefs and behaviours of a wide range of interest groups are dealt with

Table 3.4: Estimated Ethnic-Minority Populations in Various Areas of Great Britain, 1986–1988

thousands

Various areas	Ethnic group									All ethnic minority groups	White	All ethnic groups‡
	West Indian†	African	Indian	Pakistani	Bangladeshi	Chinese	Arab	Mixed	Other			
North												
Tyne and Wear MC	1.8	0.6	5.1	14.2	6.5	4.2	1.6	6.0	1.6	42	2,982	3,042
Remainder of North	0.5	0.3	2.5	5.7	5.6	2.3	1.2	2.2	0.5	21	1,094	1,124
Yorkshire and Humberside	1.3	0.3	2.6	8.5	1.0	1.9	0.4	3.8	1.2	21	1,887	1,918
South Yorkshire MC	24.1	3.7	44.2	86.9	5.7	7.8	5.5	19.9	6.9	205	4,610	4,847
West Yorkshire MC	6.1	0.4	2.5	6.9	0.5	2.8	1.9	4.8	2.3	28	1,247	1,286
Remainder of Yorkshire and Humberside	17.5	2.0	38.0	79.7	5.2	2.1	3.4	10.6	3.9	162	1,856	2,031
	0.5	1.3	3.7	0.2	0.0	2.9	0.1	4.6	0.7	14	1,508	1,530
East Midlands	16.4	1.4	88.0	15.3	3.5	7.0	2.0	17.2	5.9	157	3,708	3,899
East Anglia	3.4	1.0	6.3	10.8	0.3	4.6	0.1	9.3	5.2	41	1,925	1,982
South East	322.8	86.8	418.0	119.5	66.0	71.1	39.8	152.6	118.4	1,395	15,438	16,997
Greater London	288.2	77.4	333.3	72.0	51.2	50.8	31.4	103.5	91.8	1,100	5,462	6,640
Inner London LBs	187.9	57.8	67.6	27.2	42.5	25.1	19.6	55.1	47.6	530	1,876	2,434
Outer London LBs	100.3	19.6	265.7	44.7	8.7	25.7	11.8	48.4	44.2	569	3,586	4,205
Remainder of South East	34.6	9.4	84.7	47.5	14.8	20.4	8.3	49.1	26.6	295	9,976	10,358

Various areas	Ethnic group									All ethnic minority groups	White	All ethnic groups‡
	West Indian†	African	Indian	Pakistani	Bangladeshi	Chinese	Arab	Mixed	Other			
South West	13.5	2.2	10.9	1.0	1.4	6.4	2.9	12.5	3.4	54	4,406	4,494
West Midlands	83.8	3.1	147.6	82.6	17.8	4.1	4.1	26.0	8.1	377	4,729	5,140
West Midlands MC	77.1	3.1	130.4	70.4	17.0	1.5	3.7	17.5	5.0	326	2,256	2,600
Remainder of West Midlands	6.7	0.0	17.2	12.2	0.8	2.6	0.4	8.4	3.1	51	2,473	2,539
North West	24.6	9.7	56.5	75.4	4.9	12.4	7.2	27.7	10.1	228	5,989	6,289
Greater Manchester MC	20.0	2.3	36.0	46.8	3.5	5.2	3.3	13.2	3.5	134	2,397	2,560
Merseyside MC	0.4	5.4	2.8	0.5	0.8	4.0	2.7	8.4	3.0	28	1,395	1,435
Remainder of North West	4.2	2.0	17.7	28.1	0.5	3.2	1.2	6.1	3.6	67	2,197	2,294
England	490.5	108.4	776.6	405.6	106.0	117.5	63.2	271.1	159.6	2,499	43,788	46,690
Wales	3.1	1.3	5.1	5.4	1.2	3.4	5.0	9.6	1.0	35	2,739	2,804
Scotland	0.9	2.3	4.8	17.0	0.9	4.1	4.6	6.1	2.4	43	4,943	5,025
Central Clydeside Conurbation	0.1	0.0	2.4	15.5	0.6	2.4	2.5	1.3	0.1	25	1,609	1,635
Remainder of Scotland	0.8	2.3	2.4	1.5	0.4	1.7	2.1	4.8	2.2	18	3,334	3,390
Great Britain	494.6	112.0	786.5	428.0	108.1	125.0	72.7	286.8	163.0	2,577	51,470	54,519

Source: 1986, 1987, and 1988 Labour Force Surveys (Haskey, 1991)
Components may not add to totals, because of rounding
† Includes Guyanese.
‡ Includes not stated ethnic group.

through democratic processes. The latter are far from perfect, but they appear to have considerable advantages to all concerned over currently available alternatives.

Challenges

The Education Reform Act 1988 (ERA) aims to raise educational standards. With its 238 sections and thirteen schedules, the legislation is complex. Despite this, it is relatively easy to pass a law. Implementing one is much more demanding. Time and effort are required of already extremely busy teachers. The issues concerning cultural diversity in the population, discussed in the previous chapter, represent contextual considerations of the utmost importance.

Objectives of the National Curriculum

Under the provisions of Section 1 of the ERA 1988, all maintained schools are required to provide a balanced and broadly based curriculum which:

- promotes the spiritual, moral, cultural, mental and physical development of pupils at the school and of society; and
- prepares such pupils for the opportunities, responsibilities and experiences of adult life.

The inclusion of the word 'cultural' in the above list of five key facets of development merits comment. It denotes an explicit political acknowledgment of the importance of cultural diversity in our society, and of the complex interactions between all five aims in the context of education.

In addition to the involvement of the Department of Education and Science and the independent inputs from Her Majesty's Inspectorate, two new national organizations have been established. These are the National Curriculum Council (NCC) and the School Examinations and Assessment Council (SEAC). The reasons why these two bodies with clearly complementary functions were not originally integrated remain a mystery that has intrigued both observers in this country and overseas.

The NCC, SEAC and DES have been energetic in their endeavours. There has probably never been a period of such intense administrative activity in education. The departures of the chief executives and other senior staff from both the NCC and SEAC in 1991 indicates that all has not gone smoothly. The retirement of the Chief Inspector for Schools also took place in 1991, but it is not suggested that ERA-related activities were a consideration. 'Did they jump, or were they pushed?' remain issues mainly of historical interest. The central questions left for practising teachers and school governors are: What has been achieved?; What remains to be accomplished?; and How can it be done?

All three official organizations can legitimately be criticized for publication hyperactivity, in which activity has been mistakenly confused with progress. Many forests have been unnecessarily sacrificed on this particular administrative altar dedicated to rapid change without adequate reflection and consultation (NCC, 1990). Before the author today (December, 1991) is a list of 216 recent NCC, SEAC and DES publications spawned as a consequence of the ERA. To keep up with the reading alone would be a full-time occupation.

The secondary-school teacher is faced with heavy teaching and assessment loads. These are top priorities in the interests of the pupils in their care. Where is the time for reading, reflection and reorganization to be found? When and where can the implications of cultural diversity be considered? In such a pressurised situation, it is not surprising that avoidable problems are expensively created rather than efficiently resolved. The sad tale of the standard assessment tasks being developed for use at Key Stage 1 is but one example. It makes other monumental governmental fiascos such as the 'North African groundnuts scheme' pale into insignificance. The relative neglect of the contributions of minority ethnic groups to the effective delivery of the National Curriculum could prove to be even more expensive to the nation in the longer term.

Tensions

In this country, we have a long-established Christian state religion. The Queen is head of the Church and 'Defender of the Faith'. There are numerous Church-of-England voluntary-aided and controlled schools. In addition, many of the 'free churches' have their own schools, as have the Roman-Catholic and the Jewish religions. The government has refused to provide voluntary-aided status to the twenty-six independent Muslim schools that presently exist.

Without doubt, there is considerable dissatisfaction among Muslim parents concerning the integration of their culture and religion within the existing educational provision. Currently, the case for the establishment of Muslim schools is increasingly being heard: Bradford LEA and Newham LEA are two prominent examples in England. A route to the establishment of such Muslim schools exists via the government's opting-out legislation. This approach has been presented by leading Muslim proponents of such religious segregation as a vehicle whereby the specified end can be achieved. Where the appropriate level of parental support can be obtained, schools can present a case for opting out. It is reported that five schools in Newham have been identified as ones where the proportions of Muslim parents are such that a high level of support can be expected in favour of an application for grant-maintained status. If the case is accepted, the law requires that the opted-out school must not change its character within five years. The reported aim is for the schools to follow the work of existing independent Muslim schools in both curriculum and ethos whereby strong links between the school and the Mosque would be established.

A vast majority of Muslims agree with the policy of educational segregation on religious grounds. The dangers of 'ghettoising' the Muslim community, of establishing a form of 'self-imposed apartheid', is seen by some prominent Muslims as counter-productive. They appear to be a minority within a minority. The Muslim-education coordinating committee is based in London at the Regent's Park Mosque. In June 1991, it organized a seminar on opting out. The constitution of the committee requires that it 'help establish separate educational institutions for male and female pupils according to the principles of Islam'. In an article in *Management Today*, a member of the Islamia trust for Yusuf Islam is reported as having written that opting out 'offers the possibility of opting into Islam' and promises that 'the characteristics of "the British School" will be tested in the near future' (Sen and Nurmohamed, 1991).

Coming events cast their shadows before: despite repeated demands the reappraisal of curricular, organizational and pedagogic procedures along multicultural lines has been minimal. The decision by a growing number of black parents and community groups to form their own 'supplementary schools' to provide their children with the skills presumed to be lacking in formal educational institutions was one consequence. 'The DES, LEAs and their individual schools stubbornly resisted any changes at least until very recently' (Troyna, 1984). In 1992 such dissatisfactions remain.

How can the curricular requirements, rights and responsibilities specified in the ERA be used to address these issues? Such issues raise fundamental questions concerning the relationships between ethnic and religious groups in this country. The case outlined in Chapter 1 of Cleveland LEA concerning Mrs Carney and her wish to move her daughter Jenny away from a school attended predominantly by British Asian pupils, is clearly related. Is increased educational segregation between ethnic and/or religious groups a help or a hindrance to the delivery of the National Curriculum? Would such a move foster or inhibit social cohesion in this country? What are the alternatives? There are clearly no easy answers.

A Common Curricular Language

One of the more valuable consequences of the endeavours of the ERA and the organizations it established is that a new educational vocabulary has been created. Its merits are that a terminology now exists in education having a national currency and the backing of law. Teachers from any state school are

Table 3.5: Education Reform Act: Nomenclature for the Years of Education

Chronological age	Description	Abbreviation
5 or younger	Reception	R
5 to 7	Years 1 and 2.	Y1–2 (Key stage 1)
7 to 11	Years 3 to 6.	Y3–6 (Key stage 2)
11 to 14	Years 7 to 9.	Y7–9 (Key stage 3)
14 to 16	Years 10 and 11.	Y10–11 (Key stage 4)
16 to 18	Years 12 and 13.	Y12–13.

required to educate their pupils according to the requirements of the ERA. The tremendous publicity that has accompanied the introduction of the National Curriculum means that the parents of pupils are increasingly familiar with the terminology in use. Communication between teachers, governors, parents, administrators and politicians should become more effective as a consequence. Pupils should benefit from such improved channels.

In order to provide coherence concerning the relationships between the ages of pupils and their description in relation to the stages of the National Curriculum, a new nomenclature has been nationally adopted. Key elements of this are presented in Table 3.5.

The major educational challenge of the 1990s in England and Wales is the effective implementation of the Education Reform Act 1988 in particular and of the whole curriculum in general (NCC, 1989). The whole curriculum includes the basic curriculum and cross-curricular concerns. The basic curriculum comprises religious education and the National Curriculum. The National Curriculum consists of core and other foundation subjects, their associated Attainment Targets, Programmes of Study and assessment. Key definitions are presented in Table 3.6.

It is helpful to know the sequence whereby the various areas of the curriculum are developed. Understanding this sequence of events, knowing the responsible bodies and the consequences of their actions, is important. Such knowledge is a necessary, if not sufficient, condition for contributing to what happens *before* decisions are finalized, rather than merely being reactive to apparently remote events over which schools and teachers can feel that they have virtually no influence. Thus, during the consultation process, representations can be made helping to ensure that the curricular implications of cultural diversity are neither forgotten nor ignored in relation to the particular aspect of the curriculum that is being developed. Such knowledge does not modify the volume of documents flooding into schools, but it does help a school in its forward planning. Forewarned is forearmed.

The stages from the establishment of a working group to the issuing of a statutory order typically take between a year and a half to two years. At any stage, considerable changes in any aspect of the proposals can be effected. The stages are shown in Table 3.7.

Whole curriculum: The full curriculum of a school incorporating the basic curriculum and all other provision.

National Curriculum: The core and other foundation subjects, their associated Programmes of Study, Attainment Targets and assessment arrangements.

Basic curriculum: This consists of the National Curriculum and Religious Education (RE).

Core subjects: English, mathematics and science.

Foundation subjects: English, mathematics, science, technology (including design), history, geography, music, art and physical education. At the secondary-school stage, a modern foreign language is also included.

Programmes of Study: The matters, skills and processes that must be taught to pupils during each key stage in order to enable pupils meet the objectives specified in the Attainment Targets for each subject.

Cross-curricular themes: This refers to strands of provision running through the National Curriculum, RE and curricular provision additional to the basic curriculum.

Attainment Targets: The objectives for each of the foundation subjects, listing the knowledge, skills, and understandings that pupils are expected to develop within that subject area. The Attainment Targets are further defined at each of ten levels of attainment through the use of Statements of Attainment.

Profile components: Groups of Attainment Targets brought together for the purposes of assessment and reporting.

Statements of Attainment: These are more precise objectives than the Attainment Targets. They are related to one of the ten levels of attainment on a single continuous scale. This scale covers all four key stages including pupils from the beginning to the end of compulsory education.

Key stages: These refer to the division of the period of compulsory education into four stages. Each is related to the chronological age of the majority of pupils in a typical teaching group. The stages are as follows:

(KS1) From the beginning of compulsory education to the end of National Curriculum Year 2 (i.e., from the start to the end of infant-school education).

(KS2) From the beginning of National Curriculum Year 3 to the end of National Curriculum Year 6 (i.e., from first to the final year of junior-school education).

(KS3) From the beginning of National Curriculum Year 7 to the end of National Curriculum Year 9 (i.e., from the first year of secondary-school education to the age of about 14 years).

(KS4) From the beginning of National Curriculum Year 10 to the end of National Curriculum Year 11 (i.e., from age of about 14 years to the current end of compulsory education at about the age of 16 years).

Levels of attainment: The ten levels of achievement defined within each Attainment Target.

Assessment arrangements: Arrangements designed to demonstrate what pupils have achieved in relation to the Attainment Targets at the end of each key stage. These arrangements include both testing using standard assessment tasks and continuous assessment by teachers.

Standard assessment tasks: Externally prescribed assessments incorporating a variety of assessment techniques. These SATs are intended to complement teachers' assessments.

Records of Achievement: Cumulative records of pupils' work.

National Curriculum development plan: Each maintained school is required to develop a coherent plan which identifies changes in the curriculum, organization, staffing arrangements and the allocation of non-teaching resources likely to be beneficial. Each school is also charged with producing an action plan to ensure that the changes specified take place, and with evaluating their effects.

Table 3.7:   Developing the National Curriculum: from Working Group to Statutory Order

- The Secretary of State for Education appoints a working group. After about six months, the working group produces an *interim report.*
- The Department of Education and Science (DES) sends the interim report to LEAs and other interested parties for their comments.
- A further six months after receiving and considering representations made concerning the interim report, the DES publishes *proposals.* The National Curriculum Council (NCC) distributes these to some 400 official consultees and to all maintained schools. This consultation document is available free, on request, from the NCC.
- Between four and six months after the NCC has itself received and considered representations, it submits *recommendations* to the Secretary of State and to all consultees. One free copy is sent to each maintained school. Additional copies are available from the NCC at a cost of five pounds per copy.
- Usually within two months, the Secretary of State for Education sends a *draft order* to all consultees and to the NCC for comments. The document is available from the DES in London.
- A month later, two events occur in parallel.
- The *statutory order* is sent free to LEAs, to all maintained-school teachers involved in teaching the subject. Further copies can be purchased from the NCC and from HMSO bookshops.
- The NCC publishes its *non-statutory guidance.* This is sent to all LEAs and to all maintained schools in England to match the number of statutory orders issued. The non-statutory guidance can be purchased only from the NCC.

The official timetable for implementation of core and foundation subjects has been published. The former will be fully operative by 1994/5; the latter by 1996/7 (DES, 1989).

The 1985 Swann report's title 'Education for All' represented, and represents, an important unifying concept in the debate on how this multifaceted challenge can be addressed (DES, 1985). It also highlighted problems in society and education that demand attention if the whole curriculum is to be delivered.

As demonstrated in the earlier tables, the population of England and Wales is increasingly characterized by cultural diversity, by both similarities and differences in values, expectations and opportunities linked to various ethnic groups. By virtue of their sheer size, the majority groups' concerns tend to be to the fore. A danger in this situation is that the legitimate educational concerns of various minority ethnic groups could be overlooked in the implementation of the National Curriculum. If this were to happen, the pluralist democracy advocated in the Swann report could never be approached (Bullivant, 1989). The vision of a pluralist democracy as 'both socially cohesive and culturally diverse', as a society in which it is possible to value and accept the positive aspects of cultural diversity, is not to be discounted lightly.

A warning has been given by a former Secretary of State for Education concerning the educational reforms currently in train. 'The National Curriculum could be a tool of multicultural education, but it could also squeeze out the creativity some schools have demonstrated in eliciting the riches of an ethnically diverse school population. More disturbing are the proposals for "opting out" of a local education authority, which could become an excuse for segregated schooling' (Williams, 1989).

Citizenship is once again receiving considerable attention. In the autumn of 1989, the Citizenship Foundation was launched. Dangerous social fragmentation occurs when indifference to, unawareness of, and misunderstandings about the cultural values and beliefs of ethnic groups within our society, exist. The privileges of citizenship in a democratic society demand an acceptance of the responsibilities that accompany these rights. All individuals, all ethnic groups, all religious groups, whether large or small, are involved (Gundara and Richardson, 1991). To take extremes, schools in the social 'white Highlands' and in the 'multicultural' areas of our country evade such issues at the peril of all our population. The education of pupils, the objectives of the curriculum, the methods and materials used in various subjects are legitimate causes for concern for all professionals, parents and pupils.

Listen to the words of a former head of the State Educational Services in England and Wales concerning the work of secondary schools. 'If those democratic institutions, which we in this country agree are essential for the full development of the individual, are to be preserved, some systematic training in the duties of citizenship is necessary. The conditions in which we live today and the problems that confront us call for a fresh emphasis in the work of education on the social and civic responsibilities which inevitably await the . . . citizen'. In the same book in which these words appear, the aims and theory of 'education for citizenship' are spelled out. In addition, methods that can be used in eleven secondary-school subjects are described. Interestingly, this took place fifty-six years ago (Association for Education in Citizenship, 1936). Some concerns are perennial. The promotion of the parent's charter and the citizen's charter represent contemporary government thinking in this field.

The Speaker of the House of Commons' Commission on Citizenship considered citizenship to be a cultural achievement having its provenance in history. Citizenship can be devalued and destroyed; it can wither or develop. The challenge to our multicultural society is to establish conditions that enable all who wish, to become actively involved in the many levels of decision-making that characterize a democracy. In the making of these decisions, the common good of the whole community is advanced.

'The Education Reform Act (ERA) does not require teaching to be provided under the foundation subject headings. Indeed, it deliberately allows flexibility for schools to provide their teaching in a variety of ways' (DES, 1989, par. 3.7). Thus both the subjects of the curriculum (Volume 1 of the present series) and cross-curricular themes and dimensions (Volume 2) are important at the secondary stage of education. Irrespective of the ways chosen by schools to teach their pupils, a public demonstration of the school's accountability will be required. Programmes of Study, Attainment Targets, Statements of Attainment, Profile Components and the enhanced rights to information concerning pupils' attainments and progress all reinforce this point. In secondary schools the well-established curricular fields in which considerable professional expertise has been developed provide the resource bases from which many, but not all, developments take place. The work of the National Curriculum Council (NCC) and the School Examinations and Assessment Council (SEAC) underline this point.

Responses

Effective educational responses to the challenges represented by ethnic diversity depend, in part, on the availability of adequate resources. Knowing where useful information and ideas can be obtained is always a help. The following sources of information about, and suggestions for, developing policy and practice that capitalize on ethnic diversity, are likely to be of assistance to individuals and groups intent on constructively addressing the challenges identified both here and in subsequent chapters.

Institutions and Organizations

The Commission for Racial Equality (CRE) is a key institution involved in the development and monitoring of policy and its applications in relation to minority ethnic groups. Amongst its activities, the CRE publishes an extremely valuable periodical called *New Community*. Its address is:

Elliot House,
10–12 Allington Street,
London, SW1E 5EH.

The Runnymede Trust is also active in these fields. It has been described as a 'think-tank', established in the late 1960s, to help counter racial discrimination and to encourage understanding and mutual trust between ethnic groups. Its address is:

178 North Gower Street,
London, NW1 2NB.

Most secondary schools would find the list of the publications produced by both of the above organizations of considerable interest and utility.

The Commonwealth Institute represents an important manifestation of multiethnic and multicultural cooperation in many fields. As a founding member of the Commonwealth, Britain continues to play an important role. Fifty independent countries are members. Today, a total of one and a quarter billion people, more than a quarter of the world's population, are citizens of Commonwealth countries.

Whilst acknowledging the importance of enlightened self-interest, the emergence of the Commonwealth from the former British Empire is indicative of the potential for constructive dialogue and action inherent in such a voluntary grouping. Whilst important disagreements between members on various policies exist, the forum provided by the Commonwealth has facilitated solutions to many problems. Whether at the international, national or local level, compromise between ethnic groups in Britain, based on the willingness to accept that no one group has a freehold on righteousness, is a key concept. Any multicultural community striving for mutual acceptance, tolerance and equality of opportunity, needs it. Easy words; difficult decisions! The educational sector is an important field for such negotiations.

The Commonwealth Institute is situated in Kensington High Street, London, W8 6NQ. It is a focus for the cultural diversity that characterizes both the Commonwealth and the country. There is a Northern Regional Centre based in Salt Mill, Saltaire, Bradford. This was established as a joint initiative between the city of Bradford and the Commonwealth Institute. The Commonwealth Institute provides a variety of services of value to teachers striving to make the curriculum reflect the multicultural composition of the UK and the Commonwealth.

- The **Centre for Commonwealth Education and Culture** aims to promote the Commonwealth to people in the UK. Its resources include three floors of permanent exhibitions illustrating various aspects of life in member states.
- The **Commonwealth Resource Centre** can provide a range of current reference materials that can be used in project work in schools.
- The **Education Centre** arranges INSET courses for teachers, including conferences and seminars related to GCSE and 'A' level studies.
- In addition, there is an **Outreach Service** designed to collaborate with LEAs in introducing the Commonwealth to schools, teachers and pupils throughout the UK.
- Working on materials arising from the National Curriculum, a **Curriculum Development and Resources Office** undertakes a variety of activities aimed at enhancing knowledge and understanding of the Commonwealth. Amongst its publications, it produces packs and handbooks for use in schools.
- Finally, an **Educational Resource Centre** exists to provide a specialist loan service to teachers and others working with young people in the UK. Materials that can be supplied include books, posters, slides, records, maps, audio-visual cassettes and wallcharts.

Information and advice concerning various multicultural issues affecting the rights and responsibilities of all citizens can be obtained from a number of other organizations. These include the following.

The Institute of Race Relations,
2–6 Leeke Street,
Kings Cross Road,
London, WC1X 9HS.

National Council for Civil Liberties,
21 Tabard Street,
London, SE1 4LA.

National Association of Racial Equality Councils,
8–16 Coronet Street,
London, N1 6HD.

The Joint Council for the Welfare of Immigrants,
115 Old Street,
London, EC1V 9JR.

Standing Conference on Racial Equality in Europe,
Brixton Enterprise Centre,
444 Brixton Road,
London, SW1 8EJ.

A valuable bibliography and resource base for antiracism and multi-culturalism has been compiled by an educational psychologist having a long-standing and active involvement in this field. Teachers addressing issues of cultural diversity and its implications for any particular subject within the curriculum will find the bibliography a valuable resource. The document comprises listings of references and resources across nineteen categories. As can be seen from the categories summarized in Table 3.8, a number are highly relevant to multicultural education and the National Curriculum. The document was originally published by the Division of Educational and Child Psychology of **the British Psychological Society** in an edition of *Educational and Child Psychology* entitled 'Educational Psychologists Working in a Multicultural Community: Training and Practice' (Wolfendale, 1988). The document is now in its third revision and comprises an update and addition of seventy references across the nineteen categories since the first edition (Wolfendale, 1991). Updating of the list takes place regularly.

Lessons concerning how education can function effectively in a multi-cultural society can be learned from many countries. Drawing on their experiences in Canada, Australia, the Netherlands, India and Japan, fourteen experts have considered ethnic diversity, the challenges these pose to various educational systems if 'education for all' is to be achieved, and constructive suggestions concerning what can be done at various levels of policy and practice (Verma, 1989).

A national conference on race relations and urban education was organized around topics initially selected by attending informed and involved

Table 3.8: Resources 'A'

1. Bilingualism and multilingualism; community languages; mother tongue; language matters (47 entries).
2. English as a second language, including teaching materials (10 entries).
3. Race relations; antiracism, equal opportunities; positive discrimination (all with specific reference to education) (36 entries).
4. Antiracism, racism-awareness training including materials (11 entries).
5. Multicultural education (37 entries).
6. Multicultural education: materials for teaching and curriculum (6 entries).
7. Assessment (17 entries).
8. Achievement (16 entries).
9. Policy; guidelines; statements (18 entries).
10. Home–school links (7 entries).
11. Child services in general and with specific reference to educational psychologists' training and practice (14 entries).
12. Child development; child-rearing; under-fives (7 entries).
13. 'special needs' of ethnic-minority children; special provision (7 entries).
14. Journals (9 entries).
15. Centre; units; resource centres (22 entries).
16. Video materials (12 entries).
17. Research, including trainee educational psychologists' projects and school psychological-service projects (6 entries).
18. Psychology and race; psychology and culture; black psychology (12 entries).
19. Miscellaneous:
    (a) Literature and art (5 entries).
    (b) Information on cultures (2 entries).
    (c) The socio-political dimensions (2 entries).

Table 3.9: Ethnic Diversity: Professional Concerns

1. The multicultural curriculum
2. Racism-awareness training
3. Underachievement in schools
4. LEA and SSD policies and practices
5. Mother-tongue teaching
6. The media and race relations
7. The Swann report: What next?
8. Religious diversity in schools
9. Transition from school to work
10. The police and youth

Source: (Pumfrey and Verma, 1990)

professionals. The topics identified represent concerns that have curricular implications both within subjects and in cross-curricular themes. No claim is made that the list is either exhaustive or representative. Despite this, the topics identified were, and are, of serious concern. The topics are listed in Table 3.9 in rank order based on 224 selections. Are these issues taken into account in current National-Curriculum development work in *your* school?

The requirement by **the Council for the Accreditation of Teacher Education** (CATE) that initial teacher-training courses must include a multicultural approach, is an important advance. In sensitizing entrants to the teaching profession to the challenges presented by both ethnic diversity and the National Curriculum, some of the earlier unawareness of such matters can be reduced (Cohen, 1989). 'Britain has always been a multiracial, multicultural society; what Daniel Defoe describes a "mongrel race". It is only in the last thirty-five years, however, that Britain has become a nation with a large visible minority of black and Asian people.The debate about multicultural education is centred on this fact' (Farrell, 1990).

Acknowledging the importance of the multicultural aspects of the messages embodied in a school curriculum, both the Rampton and Swann reports recommended that teachers should review the books and materials used in schools (Department of Education and Science, 1981, 1985). This objective is easily stated, but less readily accomplished by many practising teachers. The changes taking place in education as a consequence of the Education Reform Act 1988 are themselves extremely time-demanding, and the ongoing and inexorable demands of educating pupils must not be neglected. The flood of materials produced within LEAs, by other statutory bodies, quasi-autonomous non-governmental, and by many other voluntary organizations continues to grow (Pumfrey and Verma, 1990, Wolfendale, 1991).

The AIMER Project

The establishment of a clearing house for such materials was proposed in 1982. With the support of the Commission for Racial Equality, a project was mounted at Bulmershe College. It is known by the acronym 'AIMER' (Access to Information on Multicultural Education Resources). It offers 'students, teachers, advisers and others information on multicultural anti-racist teaching materials'. By virtue of the interest shown by teachers and others in the project, the Department of Education and Science made a three-year grant covering the period 1987–90. This enabled a full-time resource-development officer to be appointed. In 1989 the amalgamation of Bulmershe College with the University of Reading Faculty of Education and Community Studies took place. Eighty-six LEAs were the major users of the service.

The AIMER database is available on the National Educational Resources Information Service (NERIS). NERIS itself was established in 1987 to help teachers, and others, efficiently locate information about teaching materials and other resources. It is an electronic database, run by a non profit-making trust and funded by the Department of Trade and Industry through its industry–education unit. NERIS is also supported by the DES, NCC, SEAC, CCW (Wales) NICC (Northern Ireland), SCCC (Scotland) and the Training Agency. NERIS is based at:

1.	Professional issues
2.	Language/communication
3.	Humanities
4.	Personal/social education
5.	Science/mathematics/technology
6.	Arts — performing/creative
7.	Religious studies
8.	Home economics
9.	Business studies
10.	Games and sport
11.	Other enquiries

Maryland College,
Leighton Street,
Woburn,
Milton Keynes,
Buckinghamshire.

The AIMER database is available to institutions with access to NERIS either on-line and/or by CD-ROM.

AIMER itself provides a postal enquiry service. It can be contacted at the following address:

AIMER,
Faculty of Education and Community Studies,
The University of Reading,
Bulmershe Court,
Earley,
READING, RG6 1HV.

AIMER's postal-enquiry form covers the fields listed in Table 3.10 (At the time of writing, the AIMER postal enquiry form is being revised).

As from 1992 an additional service is offered. Resource lists, updated twice yearly, will be published on a wide range of different topics. These are likely to include the subjects outlined in Table 3.11.

The continuing updating of the AIMER database is labour intensive. Currently, although it continues to receive many requests for information on multicultural teaching materials, the service is under threat because of lack of resources. Its future as a self-funding system will depend on the income that it can generate from subscribers and users. It would be a national tragedy if the service did not continue.

Conclusion

A central challenge faced by schools is to ensure that the benefits of the multicultural composition of the population, not merely of their particular

Table 3.11: Resources 'C': AIMER 1992 Topics

History	Geography	Environmental studies
Economics	Careers	Health education
Race awareness	Materials in Bengali	Materials in Gujarati
Materials in Punjabi	Materials in Chinese	Materials in Italian
Home–school links	Assessment and testing	Physics
Chemistry	Life sciences	Maths
Technology	Music	Dance
Arts and crafts	Oral and written literature	
Religious studies	Home economics	Business studies
Games, sports and toys	English for adults	English for beginners
Language support	Professional development and in-service	

school, are explicitly utilized in delivering the curriculum of each subject. Responses will vary. The contributors to this book point to promising practices in their respective subjects. We are not arguing for perfection. The ideal can often be the enemy of the better. No person, school or society ever made a greater mistake than one which does nothing merely because only a little appears possible.

> The development of education is certainly not conflict-free, but it is one in which people with a very broad range of opinion and outlook can engage. Debates and decisions have to be at government level, of course, but need also to take place within every school, both secondary and primary. The focus needs to be not only upon the content of the curriculum, extremely important as this is, but also upon how each school, and each classroom, can itself be a pluralist democracy in miniature, teaching about justice, rights and responsibilities through example as well as through precept. (Gundara and Richardson, 1991)

We now turn to consider what can be done in relation to religious education, the core and foundation subjects in the National Curriculum.

References

ASSOCIATION FOR EDUCATION IN CITIZENSHIP (1936) *Education for Citizenship in Secondary Schools*, London, Oxford University Press.

BULLIVANT, B.M. (1989) 'The Pluralist Dilemma Revisited', in VERMA G.K. (Ed) *Education for All: A Landmark in Pluralism*, London, The Falmer Press.

COHEN, L. (1989) 'Ignorance, not Hostility: Student Teachers' Perceptions of Ethnic Minorities in Britain', in VERMA, G.K. (Ed) *Education for All: A Landmark in Pluralism*, London, The Falmer Press.

DEPARTMENT OF EDUCATION AND SCIENCE (1981) *West Indian Children in Our Schools: Interim Report of the Committee of Inquiry into the Education of Children from Ethnic Minority Groups* (Chairman; Rampton), Cmnd., 8273, London, HMSO.

DEPARTMENT OF EDUCATION AND SCIENCE (1985) *Education for All: Report of the Committee of Inquiry into the Education of Children from Minority Ethnic Groups* (Chairman: Lord Swann), Cmnd., 9453, London, HMSO.

DEPARTMENT OF EDUCATION AND SCIENCE (1989) *National Curriculum: From Policy to Practice*, London, DES.

FARRELL, P. (1990) *Multicultural Education*, London, Scholastic Publications Ltd.

GUNDARA, J. and RICHARDSON, R. (1991) 'Citizenship is taught, not inherited', *Times Educational Supplement*, 3935, 29 November.

HASKEY, J. (1990) 'The ethnic minority populations of Great Britain: estimates by ethnic group and country of birth', *Population Trends*, 60, pp. 35–8.

HASKEY, J. (1991) 'The ethnic minority populations resident in private households — estimates by county and metropolitan district of England and Wales', *Population Trends*, 63, pp. 22–35.

HILL, D. (1990) 'The MacDonald Report: A Report and Commentary', in PUMFREY, P.D. and VERMA, G.K. (Eds) *Race Relations and Urban Education*, London, The Falmer press.

KLOSS, D.M. (1990) 'The legal Context of Race Relations in England and Wales', in PUMFREY, P.D. and VERMA, G.K. (Eds) *Race Relations and Urban Education*, London, The Falmer Press.

LEE, K. (1990) 'Race Relations in Education in the UK: An Ethical Perspective', in PUMFREY, P.D. and VERMA, G.K. (Eds) *Race Relations and Urban Education*, London, The Falmer Press.

MISHAN, E.J. (1988a) 'What future for multi-racial Britain? Part I', *The Salisbury Review*, 6, 3, pp. 18–27.

MISHAN, E.J. (1988b) 'What future for multi-racial Britain? Part II', *The Salisbury Review*, 6, 4, pp. 4–11.

NATIONAL CURRICULUM COUNCIL (1989) *Booklet 3: The Whole Curriculum*, London, DES.

NATIONAL CURRICULUM COUNCIL (1990) *Publications in print Autumn Term 1990*, York, NCC.

PUMFREY, P.D. (1990) 'Improving Race Relations in Urban Education: Lessons from a National Conference', in PUMFREY P.D. and VERMA, G.K. (Eds) *Race Relations and Urban Education: Contexts and Promising Practices*, London, The Falmer Press.

PUMFREY, P.D. and VERMA, G.K. (1990) *Race Relations and Urban Education: Contexts and Promising Practices*, London, The Falmer Press.

REYNOLDS, D., CREEMERS, A. and PETERS, T. (Eds) (1989) *School Effectiveness and Improvement*, Groningen, RION Institute for Educational Research.

RUTTER, M., MAUNGHAN, B., MORTIMORE, P. and OUSTON, J. (1979) *Fifteen Thousand Hours: Secondary Schools and their Effects on Children*, London, Open Books.

SEN, P. and NURMOHAMED, A. (1991) 'Signing up for pupil segregation', *The Guardian*, 5 November.

SMITH, D. and TOMLINSON, S. (1989) *The School Effect: A Study of Multiracial Comprehensives*, London, Policy Studies Institute.

TOMLINSON, S. (1990) 'Race Relations and the Urban Context', in PUMFREY, P.D. and VERMA, G.K. (Eds) *Race Relations and Urban Education*, London, The Falmer Press.

TROYNA, B. (1984) 'Multicultural Education: Emancipation or Containment?', in BARTON, L. and WALKER, S. (Eds) *Social Crisis and Educational Research*, Beckenham, Croom Helm.

VERMA, G.K. (1989) *Education for All: A Landmark in Pluralism*, London, The Falmer Press.

WILLIAMS, S. (1989) 'Foreword' in VERMA, G.K. (Ed) *Education for All: A Landmark in Pluralism*, London, The Falmer Press.

WOLFENDALE, S. (1988) 'A bibliography and resource-base on anti-racism and multiculturalism: Foundations for a categorised system', *Educational and Child Psychology*, 5, 2.

WOLFENDALE, S. (1991) *A Bibliography and Resource-Base on Anti-Racism and Multiculturalism: Foundations for a Categorised System*, London, Psychology Department, Polytechnic of East London, (3rd version).

Part 2

The National Curriculum Subjects

Chapter 4

Religious Education: Equal but Different?

George Skinner

Context

The unique position of religious education in British schools cannot be understood without reference to the historical role of the churches in education. Popular education grew out of the Christian Sunday school and church-funded school movements of the eighteenth and nineteenth centuries. Christian instruction was at the heart of the curriculum and an essential aspect of the inductive function of church schools. By the middle of the nineteenth century there were some radicals who were advocating a totally secular education system. However, the main religious issue concerned the practical monopoly of educational provision held in any district by a particular Christian denomination and the questions of conscience this raised for parents from other denominations — a situation not unlike that faced by religious minorities in inner-city areas today where a church primary school is the only option. The 1870 Education Act, which sought to fill the gaps in the education system left by the voluntary agencies by establishing local-authority 'Board Schools', addressed this issue. The Act allowed for denominational teaching in the church schools to continue but, in order to avoid denominational tensions, required those new board schools which chose to include religious teaching in the curriculum to do so in line with the 'Cowper Temple clause'. This stated that 'no religious catechism or religious formulary which is distinctive of any particular denomination shall be taught in any school provided by a school board'.

The partnership of Church and State in education continued into the twentieth century, despite the ever-increasing financial problems faced by the churches in maintaining denominational schools. By 1944 the churches were still well placed to have a major influence on the new Education Act. The degree to which the Act was primarily a compromise between Church and State or a response to more widely felt national needs and concerns is debatable. Whatever the motivation, the Act effectively strengthened a dual system which has continued until the present day. In addition to confirming government support for voluntary schools, the Act made the provision of religious instruction compulsory in all county schools and required every local education authority to draw up a suitable syllabus in consultation with local churches and teachers. Thus, until the 1988 ERA's requirements for a national curriculum, religious instruction (RI) remained the only compulsory subject in the school curriculum. Despite the fact that RI was not allowed to 'include any formulary which is distinctive of any particular denomination', the right of parents to withdraw children was reaffirmed and the inclusion of 'conscience clauses' for parents and teachers meant that, in practice, RI was the one subject on the school timetable from which parents could withdraw their children and teachers could, by right, refuse to teach.

In the forty years following the Act, religious instruction was transformed by a wide range of social and educational influences (Cox, 1983; Skinner, 1990). Among these were the gradual erosion of the civic function of Christianity in British society, the increasing presence of children from minority faiths in school, the post-war academic interest in the study of world faiths, the establishing of a thoroughly professional approach to RE teaching and the desire to respond to multicultural and antiracist models of education. Inductive and confessional models of RI were largely abandoned. Religious instruction (in Christianity) became religious education (of the child). Drawing widely (though often superficially) on phenomenological approaches to the study of religion, schools emphasized the shared dimensions of world faiths. Although the RE world vigorously debated methodology (including the strengths and weaknesses of implicit or explicit approaches to RE, thematic versus systematic schemes of study, detached or experiential learning methods) there was usually agreement that RE was more about helping children to understand religious commitment than promoting it and that teachers of RE should draw on several world faiths rather than Christianity alone. LEAs adopted these aims and promoted them through new-style agreed syllabuses which were generally short policy documents rather than detailed programmes of study (e.g., Manchester, 1985; Salford LEA, 1987). It should not be assumed, however, that these developments went uncriticized. The House of Lords debate on the RE clauses in the Education Reform Bill illustrates the concern felt by some that multifaith RE reflected a secular educational philosophy and tended to squeeze out teaching about Christianity (House of Lords, 1988).

The Swann report welcomed the multifaith approach to RE and argued that it could make a valuable contribution to 'challenging and countering the influence of racism in our society' (Committee of Inquiry, 1985). Indeed, Swann went as far as saying that if the place of RE is 'acknowledged and accepted on *educational* rather than religious grounds, then we feel that the legal requirement for provision to be made, the legal provision for withdrawal and the requirement for agreed syllabuses, are no longer justified' and called on the government to consider changing the law accordingly. In the event, the designers of the Education Reform Act chose a very different course.

It is worth noting in passing that the Swann report also raised questions about the continuing influence of the churches in education and argued that one solution to the possible proliferation of 'separate' schools would be a full review of the existing dual system. Whatever the educational arguments might be (and some members of the committee were so strongly in disagreement that they issued a minority statement) such a move was always likely to be politically unacceptable, as the subsequent Act demonstrated. In fact, by the time the Education Reform Bill was being debated, more than a third of primary and middle schools were still associated with the Anglican or Roman Catholic Church. The church's stake in education remained high.

Multifaith Britain.

While the case for including the study of world faiths in RE does not depend simply on the presence of a range of faiths in British society, this presence has had a crucial impact on both the debate about RE and the practical responses of schools, particularly those in multifaith towns. Before the present century, religious diversity in Britain mainly took the form of different denominational groups within the Christian Church. A more complex mixture of cultural and denominational characteristics was to be found in the Orthodox Church, members of which have been present in Britain since the seventeenth century, although the main period of growth has been in the last twenty-five years. Post-war immigration brought large numbers of Afro-Caribbean Christians to Britain, as well as smaller numbers from the Indian subcontinent, China and Africa. While accurate statistical evidence is hard to come by, today the percentage of the population deemed to be regularly practising members of Christian churches is between 5 and 10 per cent. Many more families are involved in churches during celebrations of Christian festivals or rites of passage (such as christenings and weddings). Evidence from recent surveys indicates that although in general church attendance has been in decline in recent years, there have been a number of growth points, not least among the 'black-led' Christian churches and fellowships.

In addition to the Christian Church, there has been a Jewish presence in Britain since the times of the Norman conquest and despite recurring antisemitism, some Jews remained throughout the Middle Ages. A small community of Sephardic Jews was established in Britain in the seventeenth century after their expulsion from Spain. Towards the end of the last century this established and prosperous community grew substantially with the immigration of mainly poorer Ashkenazim Jews fleeing from the tsarist Empire. During the present century the communities have been further supplemented with refugees from Europe. Today the size of the Jewish community in Britain is about 350,000 with the vast majority of Jewish people living in London, Manchester, Leeds or Liverpool.

Sikhs arrived in Britain in small numbers in the 1920s and 1930s and many took up door-to-door selling. In post-war immigration, the Sikh community grew substantially and now is about 500,000 strong. Indian 'Hindus' have been present in Britain in small numbers throughout the eighteenth and early nineteenth centuries. As with Sikhs, post-war immigration established large communities in many industrial towns. In addition, 'Hindu' Indo-Caribbeans settled mainly in London. Today this 'hidden' migrant community (Vertovec, 1992) is possibly as large as 30,000 with the total number of Hindus in Britain of the order of 350,000. During the same period, Muslims from India, Pakistan, Bangladesh and East Africa began to settle in Britain. Muslims now constitute Britain's largest minority with something of the order of a million. There are, in addition, smaller numbers of Buddhists, Zoroastrians and Rastafarians.

Crude statistics tend to camouflage the complex nature of religion and religious practice. For example, the traditional way of establishing numbers of Christians by formal church membership or regular attendance at services has little meaning when considering the Hindu community where there is a much greater emphasis on individual and home-based worship. The complex relationship between religious belief and culture makes distinguishing between cultural and religious identity difficult if not impossible for many members of religious faiths. Religions are complex and dynamic. Degrees of practice will vary substantially among those who identify with a particular faith. All religions live with the tension between orthodoxy (the desire to conserve) and radicalism (the need to reinterpret). Faith, no matter how firmly rooted in the past, has to make some response to modernity, whether it be reinterpretation or retreat to separatist religious enclaves. Within all religions there are structural variations in the form of denominations or sects, and movements which cut across such formal groupings. Members of a faith who identify with a particular movement or interpretation may have more in common with similar-minded members in other formal subgroups than with people of their own group — as is illustrated by the 'charismatic movement' in Christianity or the Sufi movement in Islam. Indeed, a shared view of the nature of religion or spirituality may draw people together across different faiths as they find more in common over a particular understanding, issue or practice than they have with other members of their own faith who see things differently. The so-called separate schools movement often unites members of different faiths whose views about the relationship between religion and education have more in common with each other than with others in their own faith communities.

RE and ERA

The Education Reform Act defines at the outset that the basic curriculum should consist of a National Curriculum of core and other foundation subjects together with 'religious education for all registered pupils'. Thus RE is given equal status with other subjects, but is not included in the foundation subjects. The detailed provision for RE in ERA largely confirmed the 1944 Act, including the compulsory provision of RE, the right of parents to withdraw children (and to make alternative provision for religious education) and the requirement on LEAs to provide an agreed syllabus. However, the Act contained three important modifications. Firstly, the requirement that all new agreed syllabuses should take into account both Christianity (as the main religious tradition in Britain) and other minority faiths. Secondly, the requirement on all LEAs to provide Standing Advisory Councils on Religious Education (SACREs) to define and to resource RE and to report annually. Thirdly, that minority religious 'denominations' (which presumably is to be interpreted as 'faith communities') should be represented on such SACREs and RE syllabus councils.

Challenges

The Role of Agreed Syllabuses

The function of the Education Reform Act was essentially to centralize the control of the curriculum through the foundation subjects. In the case of RE the reverse was the case. Local control of the RE curriculum via agreed syllabuses was confirmed and strengthened. Unlike other 'compulsory' subjects, RE does not have national guidelines or National Attainment Targets. 'RE is basic but it is not national' (Hull, 1989a). However, the balance of such syllabuses is determined by the requirement that any new agreed syllabus should 'reflect the fact that the religious traditions in Great Britain are in the main Christian while taking account of the teaching and practices of the other principal religions present in Great Britain' (DES, 1988).

A superficial reading of the Act's requirement with regard to teaching about Christianity (particularly when taken in conjunction with the school worship clauses) might presume a return to a confessional model of RE — induction into Christianity for the majority or into another religion for those who exercise their right to withdraw children in order to receive instruction in their own faith. Indeed, many members of religious minorities interpreted the Act this way and some responded with centralized calls to remove pupils from RE (Sarwar, 1988). However, DES Circular 3/89 made it clear that 'the Government believes that all those concerned with religious education should seek to ensure that it promotes respect, understanding and tolerance for those who adhere to different faiths' (DES, 1989a). Hull (1989a) argues that, when the RE clauses are considered in the light of earlier sections of the Act about a broad and balanced curriculum, a quite different interpretation might be made:

Here we have a starting point from which the religious provisions of the 1988 Education Act are to be interpreted. Religious Education is to be more educational and less instructional. It is to be broad and balanced, not narrow and authoritarian. It is to be developmental taking spiritual and cultural factors into account.

Furthermore, local agreed syllabuses, while reflecting local religious traditions, need also to take account of other religions in Britain. As Hull points out, local control does not necessarily mean local in content. The content should be 'what is typical of Britain'.

The Role of Standing Advisory Councils for Religious Education

Standing Advisory Councils for Religious Education are not new. The 1944 Act allowed for their provision. What is new is the compulsion on LEAs to establish them and the requirement that they publish annual reports on their work. They must also include representatives of such 'Christian and other religious denominations as in the opinion of the authority will appropriately reflect the principal religious traditions of the area' (DES, 1988). Although SACREs are not under the direct responsibility of the NCC, a professional RE appointment has been made to the council and a first survey of SACREs was published in January 1991. The report is largely descriptive, highlighting key issues raised in SACRE reports. It makes no comment on how effective SACREs have been in enlisting the support of local minority religious groups or including representatives on the councils. If RE is to reflect something of the religious diversity present in Britain locally and nationally, and if it is to win the confidence of religious minorities, it will be essential that LEAs ensure full representation not only from minority-faith communities but from the range of traditions and practices within them. With very few SACREs receiving budgets for their work, it is difficult to see how they can provide the kind of development and support required to ensure that standards in RE do match expectations set by the National Curriculum (NCC, 1991a).

Teaching about World Faiths

It has been noted already that professional interpretations of the Act see it as supporting rather than challenging the established world faiths approach to RE. The expectation is that a multifaith approach to RE can promote intercultural understanding and sustain tolerance. In the words of the recent Tameside LEA (1991a) guidelines 'Religious education encompasses a multicultural and antiracist perspective. It challenges stereotypes and aims to foster mutual respect in a multifaith society. Religious education can do much to dispel ignorance and irrational fears in which prejudice is often rooted'. Such a view reflects DES circular 3/89 which was issued to clarify the meaning of the RE and worship clauses in the ERA. 'The Government believes that all those concerned with religious education should seek to ensure that it promotes respect, understanding and tolerance for those who adhere to different faiths' (DES, 1989a). While the research evidence about the impact of consciousness-raising and 'culture contact' on attitudes and behaviour is inconclusive (Bullivant, 1987), it is not unreasonable to hope that accurate teaching about the beliefs and practices of British religious-minority communities might at least help to undermine the myths on which prejudice is built.

However, the world faiths movement has not been without its critics. Approaches which assume theological relativism are in their own way 'confessional' and have been accused of 'initiating children into agnosticism' (Taylor, 1976). Preoccupation with the outward forms of religions treats RE as if it were social anthropology and misses the point of the truth claims which lie at the heart of religion (Cox, 1984). The 'phenomenological' approach, popularized through the Schools Council Working Paper 36 (Schools Council, 1971) and endorsed by the Swann report, often in practice fails to take seriously the phenomenologists' quest to go beyond the observed data (Hammond *et al.*, 1990).

Of course to go beyond the largely superficial outward forms of religion is to venture into the realm of theology and philosophy and to raise contentious issues. While it is certainly true that RE can contribute, perhaps even lead the way, in 'promoting intercultural understanding and positive race relations' (Committee of Inquiry, 1985) through teaching accurate knowledge of the beliefs and practices of all faiths, it must go beyond the merely descriptive. At appropriate points RE must raise and consider the implications of the religious convictions and commitments which inform and motivate the practices. This is particularly so at secondary level where pupils are more able to discuss, debate and question religious beliefs and experiences and to evaluate their own world views. Firstly, children need to learn to cope with the diversity of beliefs and practices within particular religions — for example, the tensions mentioned above between orthodoxy and radicalism or the degrees of commitment or ranges of practice within particular faiths. Secondly, RE must help children to appreciate that the truth claims about the nature of God, the meaning of life and the hope of 'salvation', which lie at the heart of religions, may not always be reconcilable. While it would be inappropriate for teachers to emphasize such differences at the cost of the vast range of shared values and beliefs, to adopt approaches to RE which deliberately or subtly disguise truth claims in the name of social cohesion or classroom unity is to do a disservice to both religious faiths and pupils (Hulmes, 1979).

All this demands a great deal of the RE teachers who must have not only knowledge of several world faiths but theological competence in them. They must be able to handle the kind of questions which have challenged humankind through the ages — and make them relevant to children — and do all this with the notorious under-resourcing of RE. The recent survey of

SACREs (NCC, 1991a) confirms the long-held view in the profession that too many secondary-school students are taught RE by non-specialists and true recognition is not given to RE heads of departments. It is perhaps not surprising that the turnover rate among RE teachers is higher than for most other secondary-school subjects (School Teachers' Review Body, 1992). Furthermore, RE, unless taken as an examination subject, is not well provided for in Years 10 and 11 (NCC, 1991a), a time when such discussion is most appropriate. In the words of an earlier HMI survey of fourth and fifth year RE, 'Just when they [the pupils] were reaching a level of intellectual maturity capable of sustaining genuine discussion about basic religious issues they would leave the subject behind' (DES, 1985, p. 3). O'Keeffe's (1986) comparative study of county and church schools confirmed this lack of provision with almost half the fourth and fifth-form pupils in the county schools studied receiving no religious education at all. Of equal concern was the lack of confidence expressed by many teachers of RE in their ability to tackle the teaching of world faiths.

Teaching Christianity

The requirement that Christianity should be named in the Education Reform Act was seen as an important reform for some involved in the parliamentary debate. For many professional RE specialists it was more a confirmation of recent practice which had sought to develop and resource the teaching of Christianity (Hull, 1989b). Approaches such as the Westhill project encouraged teachers to explore the rich possibilities of teaching Christianity as a living and a world faith (Read *et al.*, 1986). Agreed syllabuses published shortly before the Act reflected a multifaith approach but also took special account of the place of Christianity. As the chairman's foreword to the Surrey agreed syllabus states:

> For centuries past the Christian faith has been predominant in this country ... This faith has played a major part in shaping our country's history and traditions, culture, code of morals and laws ... A knowledge and understanding of the story, beliefs and the present form of the Christian religion are thus essential background to other studies at school. (Surrey LEA, 1987)

Of course, there may be little common ground between the RE professionals' concept of the phenomenological study of Christianity as a world faith and certain political aspirations of inducting children into the Christian heritage of Britain.

Christianity is without doubt the faith which has had the greatest impact on the history and culture of British society. But it is in no sense 'the British religion'. It is an international faith with its strongest points of growth in the southern hemisphere. In Britain too, some of the most exciting and challeng-ing aspects of Christianity lie in its rich cultural and racial diversity. In a world where there are more black Christians than white and in a country where the black-led churches have been in recent years the greatest growth point, RE materials and teaching styles need to reflect diversity within unity. The challenge facing religious education as it seeks to respond to Britain's multicultural and multiracial society lies not only in the issue of minority faiths but in the minority presence within the Christian Church.

Such diversity provides valuable material for relevant RE teaching. At one level the varieties of worship, music and theology present in the multiracial Church offer many opportunities for stimulating and creative classroom work. At another level, the black experience of personal and in-stitutional racism within the Church raises fundamental questions about religion, race and culture. Research in the Centre for Ethnic Studies in Education at the University of Manchester has highlighted the complex relationship between race, culture and denomination present in the British Church (Skinner, Talbot and Collins, 1992). The experiences and aspirations of ethnic-minority Christians provide a rich resource for exploring the challenges and opportunities facing the church in the world. The movement reported by many interviewees across cultural, racial and sometimes religious divides in the quest for a spiritual home provide important twentieth century examples of the challenge and cost of discipleship. Such issues are sensitive and are not material for a time-filling idle discussion last lesson on Friday afternoon. They raise fundamental questions about the nature of religion and are often at the heart of the experience of many Christians (and members of other faiths) for whom religion is perceived as having more to do with an encounter with God than an inherited culture.

Spirituality across the Curriculum

The Education Reform Act requires the basic curriculum to promote the 'spiritual, moral, cultural, mental and physical development of pupils'. While it may be assumed that RE has a particularly explicit function in relation to teaching about religious faiths, religious issues are likely to arise through-out the curriculum. The western philosophical tradition has tended to per-petuate an individualistic and pietistic view of the Christian religion which is frequently not found in other faiths, or indeed in other worldwide expressions of Christianity. The dualism of religion and science is not found in Islam. Hinduism has no word equivalent to 'religion' in the western sense. Recent research with Hindu children demonstrates a 'fundamental mismatch between the European word "religion" and Indian concepts such as "dharma" which it sometimes translates' (Nesbitt, 1991). If T.S. Eliot's definition of culture as the 'incarnation of religion' is true, even to some extent, religious issues are likely to arise wherever culture and knowledge are studied (Eliot,

1962). So, for example, the National-Curriculum history working group was quite right to acknowledge the importance of religious issues as part of historical studies (DES, 1989b).

Similarly, spiritual development need not be restricted to religious concepts and experiences. It may be understood as 'transcendence' of the physical world (Grimmit, 1987) and 'the distinctive capacity to rise above the feelings and rhythms of animal life and become conscious of personal identity' (Hill, 1991). In this sense, the whole curriculum has a role to play in the spiritual development of pupils.

Responses

Provision for RE in secondary schools is of two kinds: the externally examined GCSE subject options taken in upper school and the 'basic' RE required by law to be provided for all pupils. While GCSE courses provide opportunities for pupils to study a number of different faiths, research evidence suggests that few pupils choose RE as an option, particularly where schools offer a wide range of choices (O'Keeffe, 1986). For the vast majority of secondary-school pupils it is only in the basic RE lessons, if at all, that they will learn about other faiths.

The professional development of RE in the post-war years sought to establish it as a subject in its own right, justified by educational rather than confessional arguments. Hence the aims and objectives of RE were seen increasingly as similar to any other curriculum subject. RE is about developing knowledge, skills and attitudes. Such aims were espoused by many of the agreed syllabus in the years previous to ERA (e.g., Hampshire LEA, 1978; Dorset LEA, 1979; Manchester LEA, 1985; Surrey LEA, 1987). Post-ERA syllabuses appear to have maintained this line. The recent Derbyshire syllabus speaks of developing religious concepts (such as wonder, mystery, and commitment), necessary skills (such as observation and enquiry) and appropriate attitudes (including awareness and respect) (Derbyshire LEA, 1989).

The specific requirements of ERA for RE outlined above applied only to new agreed syllabuses. By January 1991, eight LEAs had produced new syllabuses and another twenty-five were in the process (NCC, 1991b). Hull's convictions about the Act supporting a multifaith approach appear to be upheld by at least some of these. The Derbyshire agreed syllabus states 'At its outset the Statutory Conference was invited to have regard to the RE recommendations of the Swann Report. This syllabus therefore insists that pupils should be introduced to several world faiths'. The new Oldham syllabus (Oldham LEA, 1989) states 'It would not be possible for a syllabus based only on Christianity, or for a syllabus which does not specifically identify the place of Christianity, to meet both requirements [of the Act]'. Tameside LEA, in a paper circulated to all schools, includes under its definition of RE:

Religious Education does not encourage children and young people to become members of particular faith communities. It is education about religion rather than education in a religion . . . In their lessons [children] explore ultimate questions of meaning and purpose, and issues concerning values and beliefs. They learn about the influence of religious beliefs and consider the different belief systems of world faiths. (Tameside LEA, 1991a)

However, confusion over the precise interpretation of the Act led to a number of complaints being made by parents to LEAs and the DES. In March 1991 the DES sent a letter to all chief education officers explaining their official position:

The fact that the religious traditions in Great Britain are in the main Christian would in most cases be properly reflected by devoting most attention to Christian traditions; however an agreed syllabus which conforms with Section 8 (3) cannot confine itself exclusively to religious education based on Christian traditions, or exclude from its teaching any of the principal religions represented in Great Britain. (DES, 1991, p. 2)

Whatever some early impressions of the intention of the Act may have been, it is clear that agreed syllabuses are expected to take seriously the multifaith dimension of British society. This is not to be seen merely as reflecting local variations but as a recognition of national pluralism. As the Swann report argued, understanding about plural Britain is for *all* children. This is not to deny that children also need to understand about the role of Christianity in society or the particular faith traditions which might exist locally.

It has been said already that there is no consistent pattern of basic RE provision across secondary schools, despite legal requirements. Yet it is in RE lessons that pupils are most likely not only to engage objectively with the beliefs and practices of Britain's faith communities, but also to explore a wide range of issues and attitudes, including racism. Recent research in multiracial secondary schools has shown that it was in RE lessons that pupils were most likely to learn about each other's cultures and religions as well to discuss matters such as building friendships and countering prejudice (Verma, Zec and Skinner, 1992). The research also indicated how sensitive the area of religious studies can be. While many pupils valued what they learnt in RE, others were more critical. Sometimes, pupils from religious-minority back-grounds spoke of the embarrassment they felt when 'put on the spot' and expected to speak about their own faith. Tensions between different minority faiths and even between different factions within a faith in the local community sometimes spilt over into school. International events such as the Salman Rushdie incident and the Gulf war resulted in anti-Muslim feeling in some schools with inevitable impact on attempts at objective study of Islam in lessons. Other pupils became disenchanted with a world-faiths approach. As a Year-8 girl interviewed in the research project put it 'We don't learn about each other in RE. RE deals only with foreigners; with foreign religions'. The hidden curriculum also has an impact on pupils' attitudes to RE. If the dietary needs of Hindus are ignored in the school canteen, the study of Hinduism in RE may be seen by a Hindu minority as tokenism. On the other hand, some of the strongest anti-Muslim feeling encountered in the research project mentioned above came from pupils who felt that giving Muslim pupils 'extra holidays' at festival times was unfair.

Teaching RE to teenagers is no sinecure. If RE is to respond creatively to both the opportunities for interfaith awareness and the prejudice and confusion which often accompanies religious encounters it requires skill, sensitivity, knowledge and patience on the part of teachers, and a degree of openness, trust and maturity among pupils. None of these can be taken for granted. However, as part of a whole-school response to cultural and religious diversity, RE provides the ideal opportunity for the explicit exploration of the values, beliefs and relationships which permeate society.

Attainment Targets and Assessment

RE is not a foundation subject and there are no national guidelines, Programmes of Study or Attainment Targets. However, the NCC has a responsibility under the Act to offer advice to SACREs and LEAs who wish to consider drawing up Attainment Targets and Programmes of Study for RE and has already published a set of guidelines (NCC, 1991b). In addition, there are two national criteria of which SACREs might take note:

Firstly, the recommendation of the DES that LEAs should determine Attainment Targets, Programmes of Study, and assessment arrangements to be included in their agreed syllabus (DES, 1989a). The fact that the NCC (1991a) reports that only about a quarter of LEAs are pursuing these recommendations suggest some doubt about their value. Indeed, the National Association of Head Teachers commented 'The NAHT has grave doubts as to whether the inclusion of such targets, programmes and arrangements would be beneficial or desirable. An undue emphasis on this approach could limit the contribution of RE to moral and spiritual development, which cannot be measured against attainment targets' (NAHT, 1989).

Secondly, some guidelines may also be obtained from the national criteria which govern all RE GCSE syllabuses. These criteria recognize the essentially educational nature of RE and parallel many other subjects focussing on aims, assessment of objectives, contents and techniques of assessment. Specific aims include:

- to promote an enquiring, critical and sympathetic approach to the study of religion, especially its individual and corporate expression in the contemporary world; annd

- to enable candidates to recognize and appreciate the contribution of religion in the formation of patterns of belief and behaviour.

Nationally a number of professional bodies including the Association of RE Advisers and Inspectors (AREAI, 1989) and the Religious Education Council of England and Wales (1989) have been developing manuals and guidelines. The RE advisers conclude 'If RE is to maintain parity with the core and foundation subjects it may of necessity have to devise parallel arrangements to those for National Curriculum subjects and to demonstrate equal concern for standard, quality and achievement' (AREAI, 1989). Westhill College (1989) has also produced a teachers' manual in which the case for assessment is based on the principal that 'there are no educational grounds for separating RE from other subjects'.

Conclusion

The Education Reform Act has strengthened the legal position of RE. Despite some initial confusion, it appears to confirm the value of all pupils learning about the rich religious heritage of British society — the historic Christian tradition as well as the more recent contribution of other faiths. The special position of RE in relation to the rest of the basic curriculum may appear clumsy and unnecessary. However, it does provide unique opportunities for local involvement and flexibility with regard to curriculum content and evaluation. Sadly the frequently repeated recognition of the value of RE, both in terms of the spiritual development of individual pupils and of interfaith understanding, is rarely matched with the resources, human and financial, which would enable it to meet more effectively the high expectations of government and communities.

References

ASSOCIATION OF RELIGIOUS EDUCATION ADVISERS AND INSPECTORS (1989) *Attainment and Assessment*, London, AREAI.

BULLIVANT, B. (1987) *The Ethnic Encounter in the Secondary School*, Lewes, The Falmer Press.

COMMITTEE OF INQUIRY (1985), *Education for All* (The Swann Report), London, HMSO.

COX, E. (1983) *Problems and Possibilities for RE*, London, Hodder and Stoughton.

COX, E. (1984) 'Religion in Schools Today and Tomorrow', *RE News and Views*, 1, 2, London, Inner London Education Authority.

DEPARTMENT OF EDUCATION AND SCIENCE (1985) *A Survey of RE in Years 4 and 5 of the Secondary School*, HMI Report, London, DES.

DEPARTMENT OF EDUCATION AND SCIENCE (1988) *The Education Reform Act 1988*, London, HMSO.

DEPARTMENT OF EDUCATION AND SCIENCE (1989a) *The Education Reform Act 1988: Religious Education and Collective Worship* (Circular 3/89), London, HMSO.

DEPARTMENT OF EDUCATION AND SCIENCE (1989b) *National Curriculum History Working Group Interim Report*, London, HMSO.

DEPARTMENT OF EDUCATION AND SCIENCE (1991) *Letter to all Chief Education Officers*, London, DES, 18 March.

DERBYSHIRE LEA (1989) *Agreed Syllabus for Religious Education*, Derby.

DORSET LEA (1979) *The Agreed Syllabus for Religious Education*, Dorchester.

ELIOT, T.S. (1962) *Notes Towards the Definition of Culture*, London, Faber.

GRIMMITT, M. (1987) *Religious Education and Human Development*, McCrimmon Publishing Co.

HAMMOND, J. et al. (1990) *New Methods in RE Teaching — an experiential approach*, Harlow, Oliver and Boyd.

HAMPSHIRE LEA (1978) *Religious Education in Hampshire Schools*, Winchester.

HILL, B. (1991) 'Spiritual Development in the Education Reform Act: a source of acrimony, apathy or accord?', *British Journal of Educational Studies*, 37, 2.

HOUSE OF LORDS OFFICIAL REPORT (1988) (Hansard), London, HMSO, February–May.

HULL, J.M. (1989a) 'Agreed Syllabuses Since the 1988 Education Reform Act', *British Journal of Religious Education*, CEM, Autumn.

HULL, J.M. (1989b) *The Act Unpacked*, CEM/University of Birmingham.

HULMES, E. (1979) *Commitment and Neutrality in Religious Education*, London, Geoffrey Chapman.

MANCHESTER LEA (1985) *Multifaith Manchester — Manchester City Council Agreed Syllabus for Religious Education*, Manchester.

NATIONAL ASSOCIATION OF HEAD TEACHERS (1989) *Guide to the Education Reform Act 1988*, Haywards Heath, NAHT.

NATIONAL CURRICULUM COUNCIL (1991a) *Analysis of SACRE Reports 1991*, York, NCC.

NATIONAL CURRICULUM COUNCIL (1991b) *Religious Education — A Local Curriculum Framework*, York, NCC.

NESBITT, E. (1991) *My Dad's Hindu, My Mum's Side are Sikhs — Issues in Religious Identity*, Warwick, The National Foundation for Arts Education with the University of Warwick.

O'KEEFFE, B. (1986) *Faith, Culture and the Dual System: A Comparative Study of Church and County Schools*, Lewes, The Falmer Press.

OLDHAM LEA (1989) *Agreed Syllabus for Religious Education*.

READ, G., RUDGE, J. and HOWARTH, R. (1986) *Christianity — Teachers' Manual*, Westhill Project, Mary Glasgow Publications.

RELIGIOUS EDUCATION COUNCIL OF ENGLAND AND WALES (1989) *Handbook for Agreed Syllabus Conferences, SACREs and Schools — the report of a working party*.

SALFORD LEA (1987) *Religious Education — Planning and Practice* (The Agreed Syllabus for the City of Salford), Salford.

SARWAR, G. (1988) *Education Reform Act 1988 — What can Muslims do?*, London, Muslim Educational Trust.

SCHOOL TEACHERS' REVIEW BODY (1992) *First Report 1992*, London, HMSO.

SCHOOLS COUNCIL (1971) *Religious Education in Secondary Schools* (Working Paper 36), London, Evans/Methuen.

SKINNER, G. (1990) 'Religion, Culture and Education' in PUMFREY, P.D. and VERMA, G.K. *Race Relations and Urban Education*, Lewes, The Falmer Press.

SKINNER, G., TALBOT, S. and COLLINS, S. (1992) *Christianity in Britain — a Multi-racial Faith*, (Research Report), Centre for Ethnic Studies in Education, University of Manchester.

SURREY LEA (1987) *Agreed Syllabus for Religious Education*, Kingston upon Thames.

TAMESIDE LEA (1991a) *Guidelines for Religious Education*, Ashton-under-Lyne.

TAMESIDE LEA (1991b) *Tameside Foundations for Religious Education*, Ashton-under-Lyne.

TAYLOR, J.V. (1976) 'Initiation into Agnosticism', *Learning for Living*, 15, 4.

VERMA, G.K., ZEC, P. and SKINNER, G.D. (1992) *Inter-ethnic Relationships in Secondary Schools — a research report*, Centre for Ethnic Studies in Education, University of Manchester.

VERTOVEC, S. (1992) 'Community and congregation in London Hindu temples: divergent trends' in *New Community*, 18, 2.

WESTHILL COLLEGE (1989) *Attainment in Religious Education*, Birmingham, Westhill College.

Chapter 5

English

Dudley Newell

Context

The National Curriculum in English is a document which reflects a number of dominant strands in education today. It is a reflection of the reconsidered roles and prominence given to speaking and listening, reading and writing as well as knowledge about language which has been developing during the past few years. The document is also driven by the publicly expressed need (and statutory duty) for schools to quantify and assess student performance and to report these results to parents and the wider public at large, with the consequent public accountability which this engenders (marketing).

The need for greater public accountability developed from the former Prime Minister James Callaghan's Ruskin College speech of 1976, where he questioned the need for the education service to have a 'secret garden' of the curriculum. The discussion surrounding a curriculum for English in the context of the Education Reform Act of 1988 culminated in the publication of the Programmes of Study and Attainment Targets in English in 1989 (Key Stage 1) and 1990 (Key Stages 2–4).

Challenges

The documents build on the work of the Bullock report (DES, 1975), which defined the importance of language across the curriculum and, more recently, the Kingman report (DES, 1988). Against a background of governmental hostility to teachers and right-wing questioning of 'lower standards' in schools, Sir John Kingman was asked to provide a model of the English language as a basis for teacher education and to consider how far and in what ways that model should be made explicit to pupils during the various stages of their education (ibid.).

One thing the Kingman committee did not produce, perhaps surprisingly from the Government's point of view, was a report which advocated a return to Latinate grammar. It was with some care that Kenneth Baker and Angela Rumbold (The Secretary of State and Minister for Education at the time) selected the members of the new committee which was to devise and detail the Programmes of Study and Attainment Targets for English. Professor Brian Cox, a member of the Kingman committee, known for the 'Black Papers on Education' and a supposed educational conservative, was asked to chair the new group. According to Cox 'neither Mr Baker nor Mrs Rumbold know very much about progressive education, and they did not realize that my Group would be strongly opposed to Mrs Thatcher's views about grammar and rote-learning' (Cox, 1991, p. 6). Among the members of the committee was Michael Stubbs, Professor of Education at the University of London Institute of Education, who was 'deeply concerned about the problems of British ethnic communities and of multicultural education' (ibid., p. 5).

What did the committee produce? The document sought to describe what children should learn about English between the ages of 5 and 16, and in doing so, reflected recent thinking about how reading, writing, speaking and listening should be taught in schools. What the committee produced, therefore, was not what may have been anticipated by Kenneth Baker (and Margaret Thatcher) at its time of commissioning. It is a positive, yet demanding, document. It asks that all children be given access to the processes and structures that many 'native' English speakers, readers and writers unconsciously adopt and pass on. It includes and demands the use of information technology, and study of media texts and language. It asks that the widest use of language in all its forms, for enjoyment, for learning, for reflection, for communicating and for power be encouraged, for the sake of the individual and for the nation.

These views and those of the Cox committee are disputed by Helen Savva, writing in the *Language in the National Curriculum* (*LINC*) *Reader* (Carter, 1990). She accepts that 'Parents want their children to have a good command of English, and one of our jobs as educators is to help children achieve that' (Savva, 1990, p. 249). However, she also feels that to withdraw bilingual materials from children when they become able to use English competently is not 'full bilingualism . . . but the eventual supremacy of one language and the neglect of others' (ibid., p. 256). This leaves teachers, as frequently seems to be the case, in a pedagogic dilemma. They are both driven by the legal requirements of the Education Reform Act (ERA) and fully involved in the day-to-day effort and stress of teaching. By default, they often have a limited view of the issues, limited time and limited resources. These points will be discussed later in the chapter.

What did the proposals suggest for secondary-school aged children? It was anticipated that children studying English at Key Stage 3 might range in ability between levels 3–8 and those at Key Stage 4 be between levels 3–10, (Cox, 1991, p. 115). This huge range from infant to sub-A-level standard means that now, more than ever, secondary teachers will have to plan work in such a way that all children can share and benefit from the Programmes of Study. It also will have great implications for the subsequent KS3 and KS4 standard-assessment tasks (SATS). Will the assessments be able to reflect this range, or will pupils with both English as a foreign language (EFL) and English as a second language (E2L) be marginalized? Will such pupils be further restricted, along with the 'less able', in what they study? On what aspects of English will they be assessed? Cox, in dealing with the assessment issue, suggested that all assessment take place in the English language, except for those students using the Welsh language *in* Wales. The feedback from such assessments should, he said, be 'part of a continuing process of recording language development' for E2L speakers (Cox, 1991, p. 96). If this assessment is not completed in a supportive manner, it could very easily lead in a negative direction.

The NC English document is divided into three Profile Components (PCs), each of equal status. Briefly:

- AT1, speaking and listening (worth 33 per cent)
  The Programmes of Study recognize the fact the majority of all communication is through speaking and listening, and can take many forms: working in different situations (solo, pairs, groups), preparing work for different audiences, role play, drama, discussions, etc. A great deal of the work emphasizes the importance of the group: working together, contributing, cooperating, leading, etc.
- AT2, reading: (worth 33 per cent)
  The Programmes of Study at KS3 and KS4 state that 'Teachers should encourage children to read a variety of genres, e.g., autobiographies, letters, diaries or travel books, as well as short stories, novels, poetry and plays, including literature from different countries written in English'. (DES, 1989, p. 31)

The Programmes of Study for secondary-school students include work on contemporary writing, pre-twentieth century literature, 'some of the works which have been most influential in shaping and refining the English language and its literature', including Shakespeare (ibid., p. 31). The current Secretary of State at the Department for Education (DFE), John Patten, has recently endorsed this point. Additionally, the Programmes of Study move beyond what may have been seen as the established range of 'English' by including the study of information texts in a variety of media. The media includes such texts as: instructions and manuals, forms, brochures, publicity materials, and electronically stored information.

Through all of this should run a consideration of knowledge about language, focusing on the characteristics of literary language and how English is constantly changing.

Much of this study, up to levels 5/6 (the average level for 14-year-old children) can be accomplished through discussion and talk. Writing does not have to be the main source of the teacher's information about the student's knowledge of language and ability to use it.

- AT3/4/5, writing/spelling/handwriting: (worth 33 per cent)
  Writing is worth 70 per cent of the above, spelling 20 per cent, handwriting 10 per cent. After level 4 is reached, the last two are merged to form 'presentation'. Once again, the Programmes of Study offer a much more explicit and potentially fuller experience for students in the secondary school than in pre-ERA days. As well as specific teaching about the uses of the comma and the functions and structures of the paragraph, students are expected to (among other things) 'write in a range of forms, including . . . notes, diaries, personal letters, chronological accounts, pamphlets, book reviews, advertisements, comic strips, poems, stories, and playscripts'. (DES, 1990, p. 39)

As well as the strand of knowledge about language, the National Curriculum for English addresses in a very explicit way the issue of standard English. For example:

Teaching about language through speaking and listening . . . should focus on regional and social variations in accents and dialects of the English language . . . the forms and functions of spoken Standard English. (DES, 1990b, p. 25)

Children should 'have increasing opportunities to develop proficiency in spoken standard English, in appropriate contexts'. 'Pupils should be encouraged to respect their own language(s) or dialect(s) and those of others.' (DES, 1990b, p. 25).

The Cox proposals of 1989 emphasized the comments of the Swann Committee (DES, 1985). Swann stressed the need for all members of the community to have a 'good command of English'. Cox recognized that bilingual learners were not to be seen as those with a language deficit, but as who were an asset in the classroom, rather than a problem. 'Bilingual children offer opportunities to explore language in a novel context' (Cox, 1991 p. 98). Nevertheless, Cox wanted to make sure that the teaching of standard English was an entitlement for all children *because Standard English serves as a language of wider communication for such an extensive and important range of purposes that children must learn to use it competently* [my emphasis] (DES, 1990, p. 27).

The Programmes of Study guide the teacher's planning, and the Attainment Targets can be used to report summatively and formatively on the student's progress. What the National Curriculum orders lack, in contrast to the Cox proposals, is any adequate consideration of the multicultural context. In the original report, clear and explicit statements were made about the importance of bilingual learners and the reasons for the inclusion of standard English. These are now missing and without them the documents lack the detail, explanation and justification for their use in multicultural contexts.

If the statutory orders lack the context and explanation given in the proposals, then it is left to teachers, acting individually and collectively as departments, to interpret and develop the Programmes of Study in the context of their school's needs and the needs of their students. Whilst it might be thought that the DES (now DFE) supports the intention of the documents, it has acted in ways that have tended to lessen its impact. This, in particular, relates to the educative and supportive role of the LEA and its in-service provision for schools.

It is the role of the LEA to inspect and advise; to be the quality-control mechanism for those who use the schools and live within the LEA's boundaries. If this role is diminished, through having a minimal form of advisory and inspection service or perhaps abolishing LEAs altogether, then there can be no way in which cultural diversity and provision for bilingual learners can be provided for in any coherent way. It appears that the view of the school as an 'island' separated from others in the area, perhaps as an opted-out school, is one which most ministers favour. Recent statements by the Secretary of State and by his ministers that they 'would not lose sleep if the LEAs disappeared' would suggest that, in their view at least, the role of the LEA in assisting and coordinating a school's approach to cultural diversity is dispensible.

This could lead to a variety of approaches which might only reflect the local interests of the departments and schools. There is a very real danger that curricular development, if left entirely to an individual school, may not be as effective as it could be when placed in an LEA context. So much pressure has been generated by the changes in schools due to the ERA that staff may well feel able only to attempt the statutory aspects, leaving the non-statutory areas to be dealt with by default, or when 'more time becomes available'. English itself is being squeezed for time on the curriculum. With science gaining 20 per cent of time and with the addition of more subjects, the percentage available for English has dropped to around 10 per cent or less. English literature has suffered a similar fate, although it is still to be taught within English. This has led to a variation of approach to curricular issues in schools, together with a consequent unevenness of curricular coverage.

Schools, of course, try to be responsive to the members of their communities. This can create pressures of another sort. Many parents have no means to assess their children's education other than by comparison with what they experienced when they were at school. For some, this experience was largely negative; as a result, they rarely visit the school, and appear to be uninterested. For others, the experience was rooted in a colonial education, where a disciplined education was linked to an acquisition of the 'mother' tongue, an education which focused largely on the canon of English literature, possibly including Byron, Shelley and Keats — a trio of lyrical treats, as this writer experienced in a Canadian classroom in the 1960s (A colleague studying in England also read these three, but never encountered a Canadian writer!). The status, appropriateness and, indeed, relevance of the material was unquestioned. Many West Indians studied and memorized Wordsworth's poetry without ever having seen a daffodil, let alone 'fields of golden daffodils'. This is not unique. Many parents bring to their assessment of their children's education a heritage which leads them to question 'informal' lessons and the need for any recognition of languages other than standard English. This means that the department has to be able to demonstrate that the school experience will develop and educate the children more adequately than were, perhaps, their parents. In one way, the legal force of the documentation could be helpful to departments and parents alike because it describes the Programmes of Study and Attainment Targets. Both parents and teachers can 'see' where the English curriculum is leading. The regular, formal and public assessment of standards and progress will indicate more clearly than hithertofore what is being achieved.

Responses

What resources do schools have on which to build? Many LEAs have policy statements which reflect their interest in a multicultural society; some have not. In many areas of the country, where there is no apparent need to recognize cultural diversity, schools may well find it difficult to accept, let alone address the challenges.

Support for development can be found in a number of ways. The National Curriculum Council (NCC) has a responsibility for informing schools about curricular development and change. Its Circular Number 11 'Linguistic Diversity and the National Curriculum' was published in March, 1991. It is difficult to see how three and a half pages of general advice, with notes headed by the titles 'access', 'language support', 'planning' and 'summary' (only two points in this section!), which includes such prompts as: 'pupil's skills in their community or home language can be used as the basis for planning tasks to support English . . .', will be enough to generate curricular change on its own.

The Education Reform Act (ERA) places the responsibility for curricular change and movement at the level of the school. All schools, primary, secondary and special, are now responsible for preparing and disseminating school-development plans in order to address, in the context of national and local priorities, the concerns of the school and its departments over a period of three years. This coincides with the period of Grants for Education Support and Training (GEST). In theory, then, if school development plans are properly constructed and executed, every school should be determining the issues inherent in the challenge of cultural diversity in the context of the whole school's development. Such matters are often more clearly and specifically addressed in schools with a racially mixed intake but, in this writer's limited observation, less likely to be given more than a cursory reference in schools where minority ethnic group pupils are not present.

As much as it should be the responsibility of the whole school to determine a policy for cultural diversity, it has to be said that any school and staff, given the notional '1265 hours' of contact and non-contact time, will find this difficult. In addition to marking and setting work, writing records of achievement and undergoing an annual appraisal programme, few staff will be able to find the time to determine a policy whilst new Attainment Targets in science and maths, history and geography, among others, are being introduced. One would be unlikely to find very many schools developing such policies whilst burdened with the weight of change at this point in time. Time for consolidation is required. Following the 1992 General Election, the new Secretary of State for Education has acknowledged this point.

It is at the departmental level that teachers are best placed to respond, to plan and prepare for cultural diversity. There are a number of reasons for this. Firstly, the introduction of the National Curriculum in English has provided a structure, flawed perhaps in some respects but nevertheless a structure for discussion, debate and planning. It has often been the case with English that departments and teachers worked around a generally accepted, but little discussed idea of what constituted 'English', moving to the more explicit, and possibly carefully planned approach in the final two years of compulsory schooling in response to the needs of the GCSE. In general terms, this often focused on the class novel and other forms of literature, together with some wider exploration of language derived through a variety of topic work.

As a subject, English has great scope for open discussion concerning beliefs, attitudes and feeling underpinning racism in a range of media (NUT, 1992). The distinction between assertions and evidence can be highlighted. The power of visual images can be explored. Such work can help to make explicit the often unconscious, unchallenged and implicit assumptions that are held by individuals concerning other cultural, ethnic and religious groups comprising the school and community. The literatures of all cultures address in many ways the questions, dilemmas and unknowns that have continued to perplex individuals and societies throughout the ages. Such (metaphorically) universal themes, when identified and explored, can help individuals and groups to understand each other's communalities, as well learning to accept differences.

In relation to English, the importance of including materials from a range of cultures is stressed. Inviting storytellers, poets and writers from various minority ethnic groups into schools, has much to commend it. The curriculum can be enriched (NUT, 1992). 'Books chosen for school use should be checked for racist and sexist language and assumptions, and the school policy should be clear on how this matter is dealt with to ensure a common approach' (ibid.). In effect, censorship is advocated. For some citizens, this issue presents a considerable ethical dilemma.

LEA resource centres and local library services can provide a great deal of advice and information concerning books pertinent to multicultural work in schools. So too can LEA officers and teachers involved in Section 7 funded work (see Appendix 3). In addition to the extensive services of the Commonwealth Institute (see Chapter 3), two further sources of information concerning multicultural books merit the consideration of schools.

Letterbox Library is based at:
Leroy House,
436 Essex Road,
London, N1 3BR.

It is an organization which specializes in multicultural and antiracist children's books.

The Book Trust is located at:
'Book House',
45 East Hill,
London, SW18 2QZ.

It provides an excellent book information service and also has a range of specialized book exhibitions that can be hired at very reasonable rates.

The National Curriculum in English presents at least one form of statutorily acceptable good practice. By 1994, as children move up from the primary school and into the secondary school, they will bring a record (albeit limited, if it is restricted to the numbers of Attainment Targets reached without any written explanation) of their successes in language and the areas in which there is room for improvement. No longer will some schools and departments be justified in delivering a battery of tests which can only reveal, at best, a limited picture of the child's performances. The 'imposition' of this curricular continuity has made teachers much more conscious of what the children have attained and what is required to take them forward. All departments need to be sure that they not only agree on what to teach, but when, so that there is no needless repetition.

Together with the National Curriculum's impact on departments, has been added the departmental reconsideration of their schemes of work in the light of the new demands about the knowledge of language that all children must now consider and acquire, through talking and writing. The three-year Language in the National Curriculum (LINC) project was set up to produce materials and 'to conduct activities to support implementation of English in the National Curriculum in England and Wales in the light of the views of language outlined in the Kingman and Cox reports' (*LINC Reader*) (Carter, 1990, p. 2). The materials so produced were to be used for in-service work with teachers and LEAs and, in the long-term, for general in-service and teacher training.

At the time of writing, the DES has determined that the LINC units, which exist in draft form, are not to be published on the grounds that the materials would be an additional burden on schools and departments already having difficulty coping with an acknowledged avalanche of paper from the DES. Additionally, the materials, whilst acceptable for in-service, might be used for teaching purposes! Some LINC materials deal with specific issues of language and power and the effect that this can have on individuals and on groups of people. These were thought to be too 'political' and not suitable for discussion, at least not in the classroom.

It is perhaps fortunate, that much of the LINC material has been disseminated and discussed through the DES supported 'cascade' system. Although the cascade in-service process ensures coverage, it is not able to provide the opportunities for discussion and debate that fuller, more comprehensive, in-service work might take. The units in draft form exist, together with a set of video recordings and the LINC reader, which contains a selection of articles designed to support the now non-existent units in their 'final' form.

LINC has brought members of departments together to develop and explore language, its nature, uses, teaching and learning. In doing so, it has led them to consider the wider uses of language as they exist in our schools today. Teaching units have been written that explore the range of languages available to children in today's classrooms: dialects and languages other than English. LINC encourages teachers and students to recognize and celebrate the variety of languages that can be used at home, in school and in the playground. It does so in the context of continuity and a lifetime of continuing language development.

Additional support for departments has come in the form of the 'National Oracy Project'. In a booklet *Teaching Talking and Learning in Key Stage 3* (NCC, 1991) the positive role of bilingualism and linguistic diversity is emphasized, with a number of useful classroom examples. In a preface to a chapter on this aspect of oracy, the late Andrew Wilkinson is quoted as saying that the skills of oracy 'will need to be in several languages. To be monolingual will be to be linguistically deprived' (Open University, 1990). LEA support for schools will need to focus on the LINC material, in whatever form it remains, and the work of the 'National Oracy Project' to ensure that linguistic diversity is addressed by all departments and teachers.

There is little doubt that due to a combination of governmental disinterest and a work overload, together with a less than approving public (rightly or wrongly), teachers will have to work very hard to build into their own Programmes of Study and schemes of work, material that accurately reflects cultural diversity in English. Added to this will be the individual response and understanding of what cultural diversity means, both to the majority culture and to those in the minority cultures. There are many different perceptions of the issues. Whilst it is understandable for Helen Savva to argue that the National Curriculum is a means of emphasizing the

Table 5.1:   National Curriculum English

Challenges:	Responses:
1. Broader, wider approach to English that encompasses *oracy* as well as reading and writing (but no multicultural context given)	Reconsideration of the role of English within departments and across schools Development of closer links between primary and secondary schools to ensure greater understanding and smoother transition
2. Recognition of the positive value of bilingual and second-language students (but not mentioned in the Programmes of Study)	Emphasized in the work of LINC and the 'National Oracy Project'; and other materials, e.g., *Language and power* ILEA, Harcourt, Brace Jovanovich (requires positive LEA/school support)
3. Wide range of performance expected: Levels 3–8 (KS3), levels 3–10 (KS4)	Student–teacher discussion and review can be used to back up and reinforce progress not clearly recorded. Assessment by the key-stage assessments and Records of Achievement must be sensitive to variations in mother tongues
4. Limited and restrictive forms of assessment available at the end of both key stages, but particularly for those with less than a full command of English	LEA offers alternative forms of accreditation, possibly linked to 'vocational' or other forms of modular study
5. New relationship emerging between schools and LEAs	School-development plans and departmental planning extended over a period of years enable schools to make detailed and considered responses to cultural diversity LEA initiates policies designed to support linguistic diversity and prompt positive school responses
6. Parental views of what should be taught in English and the place of community languages	LEA policy statements, initiation of LEA-supported parental involvement groups, advice centres and adult-education classes in local schools

supremacy of English, it would be misguided to deny children the opportunity of growing, developing and feeling part of the mainstream culture, however it may be defined, and however much they might wish to participate. Both Swann and Cox argue strongly that cultural diversity is a strength, not a weakness. Sadly, the arguments for this do not appear in the statutory orders.

The responsibility for implementing the orders has been left to schools and to LEAs; but the LEAs' ability to guide and support schools has been considerably threatened by the cash limitations on local government and the prescriptive format of local authority Grants for Educational Support and Training (GEST). Forms of training, either through working with departments in clusters or with individuals, are limited by the amount of time and finance available. There is, at the time of writing, no large-scale project for English in a multicultural society, as there was for arts (Gulbenkian Foundation).

The LINC programme, which offered widespread training for teachers in knowledge about language, albeit on a limited scale using the cascade model of training, has been curtailed. For those teachers who have been involved with it through first-hand work, LINC has given many teachers a chance to reconsider the role of language and how it 'fits' with current practice. LINC, with its emphasis on the varieties of language, has allowed a consideration of the importance of community languages. There are many challenges and obstacles to overcome. Taken as a whole they may seem to be insurmountable. However, the National Curriculum for English *is* an *entitlement* curriculum; everyone has the opportunity to be involved. It is a *common* curriculum; it is available throughout the country. It offers continuity of study, from the age of 5–16. It has demanded that all schools consider what they have been teaching and how they have been teaching it. Every school, every department, every individual teacher and individual will respond to it in a different way. For the first time, *all* languages are a subject for legitimate study and appreciation. For this, in a cold climate, we should be grateful.

References

CARTER, R. (Ed) (1990) *Knowledge about Language and the Curriculum: the LINC Reader*, London, Hodder and Stoughton.

COX, B. (1991) *Cox on Cox, An English Curriculum for the 1990s*, London, Hodder and Stoughton.

DEPARTMENT OF EDUCATION AND SCIENCE (1975) *A Language for Life* (The Bullock Report), London, HMSO.

DEPARTMENT OF EDUCATION AND SCIENCE (1985) *Education for All, the Report of the Committee of Inquiry into the Education of Children from Ethnic Minority Groups* (The Swann Report), London, HMSO.

DEPARTMENT OF EDUCATION AND SCIENCE (1988) *Report of the Committee of Inquiry into the Teaching of the English Language* (The Kingman Report), London, HMSO.

DEPARTMENT OF EDUCATION AND SCIENCE (1989a) *English for ages 5 to 16*, London, HMSO.

DEPARTMENT OF EDUCATION AND SCIENCE (1989b) *English in the National Curriculum*, London, HMSO.

DEPARTMENT OF EDUCATION AND SCIENCE (1990) *English in the National Curriculum No. 2*, London HMSO.

NATIONAL CURRICULUM COUNCIL, (1991) *Linguistic Diversity and the National Curriculum*, Circular No. 11.

NATIONAL CURRIULUM COUNCIL (1991) *Teaching, Talking and Learning in Key Stage 3*.

NATIONAL UNION OF TEACHERS (1992) *Anti-racist Curriculum Guidelines*, London, NUT.

OPEN UNIVERSITY (1990) *Spoken English Illuminated*, Milton Keynes, Open University Press.

SAVVA, H. (1990) 'The rights of bilingual children', in CARTER, R. (Ed) *Knowledge about Language and the Curriculum: The LINC Reader*, London, Hodder and Stoughton.

Chapter 6

Mathematics

Julian S. Williams

Context

The National Curriculum for mathematics now legally obliges state schools to teach a common curriculum of objectives for mathematics to all our children between 5 and 16 years of age (DES, 1989). The curriculum is arbitrarily divided into a number of Attainment Targets (ATs), namely using and applying mathematics (AT1), number (AT2), algebra (AT3), shape and space (AT4) and handling data (AT5). Most of the ATs have several Statements of Attainment (SoAs) at each of the ten levels. Consequently, objectives for algebra appear even at levels 1–3, which 5 to 7-year-old children are expected to tackle.

One must immediately distinguish between AT1 and the others. AT1 is concerned with the processes of applying or using mathematics in real-world situations and problems. It also concerns the ability to solve problems within mathematics: to explore and investigate mathematics itself. The SoAs contain phrases such as 'select the mathematics to use', 'explain work being done', or 'make and test generalizations'. Some of the processes described are similar to those in the design and technology curriculum, and also to those in the investigation (AT1) of science.

The other four targets are concerned with knowledge of, skills in, and understanding of the content of mathematics. The statements contain such phrases as read, write and order numbers up to . . .', 'recognize and understand everyday fractions' and 'use addition and substraction facts up to ten'. These objectives are relatively well defined and understood. Examples of children's behaviour which demonstrate attainment of the objectives are provided in the document, though they are non-statutory and so subject to amendment by teachers or organizations such as the NCC. To say that these objectives are relatively well understood is not to deny that they are problematic. One can 'understand everyday fractions' at many levels, and the achievement of such an objective is strongly dependent on the context in which the fraction is placed, the mode of presentation of the test and structural form in which the fraction is represented. Nevertheless, short questions (such as the examples given in the document) assessed in traditional tests are familiar to the profession as a means of assessing these targets.

However, AT1 provides a problem of interpretation. The examples given in the earlier documents were mostly examples of tasks which might be set, rather than behaviours demonstrating successful attainment of a target, and many problems remain in the latest version. It is clear from the non-statutory guidance that these targets are often expected to be attained through practical work involving longer pieces of work or investigations (NCC, 1989). This reflects good practice generally accepted since the Cockcroft report, codified by HMI in reports and in the compulsory implementation of coursework in all assessment schemes at GCSE level (DES, 1982, 1985). It is now widely accepted that there are essential strategic skills in mathematical problem-solving, in applied mathematics and in communicating with mathematics. And these skills can only be learnt and assessed through more extended pieces of individual and group work. Nevertheless, this is a problematic area. The Statements of Attainment and examples given are still a mystery to most of us and a consensual interpretation will have to be reached before the ATs become useful. There is some evidence that comparison with the Statements of Attainment (SoAs) for science, technology and English might help (Maughan *et al.*, 1990).

So far the Programme of Study (PoS) for mathematics has not been discussed. A Programme of study is supposed to describe the programme of work the pupils need to undertake in order to attain the targets described in the National Curriculum's Attainment Targets. In fact, the PoS was originally defined in the National Curriculum for mathematics by exactly the same statements as the ATs! This contrasts with the other subject documents in which some guidance is given as to the programme needed at each key stage. Since then the redrafting of the curriculum has distilled the original fourteen ATs to five by generalizing groups of Statements of Attainment. The new Programmes of Study are now broadly the same as before, i.e., the same as the Statements of Attainment in the initial drafts of the curriculum. This somewhat bizarre history can only be explained by the fact that of those involved no one really understood the distinction between objectives and Programme of Study in the curriculum or their role, particularly where process objectives are concerned.

This provides schools with a challenge and an opportunity. There will be much non-statutory guidance to help schools to elaborate a comprehensive Programme of Study, but no law. A school therefore has some flexibility to implement a Programme of Study which it believes is most appropriate to helping its pupils achieve the objectives. As with the ATs for technology, AT1 for mathematics is abstractly defined in terms of process skills or problem-solving strategies which might be achieved in almost any open investigation or problem. The other ATs are defined in terms of concepts and skills, and might be demonstrated in a wide variety of contexts. There is therefore scope for designing an imaginative and vigorous programme . . . or else a narrow and dull one!

The most important factor in developing this programme is the world of the child. Our focus here is the secondary-school pupil or student, aged 11–16. From the very beginning there have been criticisms of a National Curriculum defined essentially through a hierarchy of assessment objectives organized on a scale from one to ten. Particularly one must question the validity of providing the same programme for low-attaining 16-year-olds as for bright 9-year-olds (i.e., level 3/4.) The source of motivation of the youngster changes dramatically between these ages, and it is vital that this is taken into account. The maturing teenager increasingly looks outward to other people in society, to their peers, to the adult world of work, sex, entertainment, and even politics. The contexts chosen for applications of mathematics and the teaching styles adopted can address this problem, and there is some support for such considerations in the examples given in the documents and in the non-statutory guidance.

However, there is no direct reference in the National Curriculum to the cultural or historical context of mathematics. Reference to mathematicians occurs twice, once to Pythagoras and once, implicitly, in the term Cartesian! One can hardly accuse the document of being biased towards one culture when it provides virtually no cultural context at all. And yet, the traditional lack of cultural context is a statement about mathematics itself with possibly unfortunate implications about the nature of the subject and how it is learnt. A failure to provide a cultural context may even leave students labouring under the misapprehension that mathematics is essentially a western product (Joseph, 1987). Whilst this might be understood as a further challenge and opportunity to the teacher to embed the curriculum in a cultural context, there are ambiguous indications from the mathematics working party.

> Many of those who argue for a multicultural approach to the mathematics curriculum do so on the basis that such an approach is necessary to raise the self-esteem of ethnic minority cultures and to improve mutual understanding and respect between races. We believe that this attitude is misconceived and patronising. (DES, 1988, par., 10.22, p. 87)

This statement might be interpreted as cutting the ground from underneath the feet of multicultural mathematics. In a sense, it is an augmentation of Margaret Thatcher's widely publicized comment to the Conservative Party's Conference in 1987: 'Children who need to count and multiply are being taught antiracist mathematics, whatever that may be'.

Challenges

The challenge is to implement the National Curriculum in such a way as to optimize all our children's achievements. This must be done in the context of a culturally diverse society, through the design and implementation of an appropriate Programme of Study. The purpose of this chapter is to explore the multicultural dimensions of this challenge.

One can usefully draw a distinction between education of a multicultural society and education for a multicultural society. The former concept asks the profession to recognize the cultural and ethnic diversity of its clients, the pupils and their parents. It is clear that the background of the pupils, their age, gender, maturity, interests, locale, class, culture and ethnicity will influence their learning and should critically influence the Programme of Study needed to optimize their individual attainments. It is the last two of these which will concern us in this chapter. On the other hand, even a purely theoretical class of white British youngsters must be educated to live in a plural society. The mathematics curriculum should draw from and contribute to their understanding of society at large, and of other areas of the curriculum. This is how one might interpret AT1. It is also the principal reason for placing mathematics in the core curriculum in the first place, i.e., because mathematics forms an essential discipline for the individual who wants to successfully negotiate adult life in our (multicultural) society.

Responses

Eliminating Bias

It is elementary, in theory, that teaching materials should avoid stereotyping. Examples of books in which ethnic minorities are unrepresented or even devalued are still not uncommon. A large collection of such examples still in frequent use has been published (ILEA, 1985). Even though most publishers are now committed on paper to progressive policy, one finds examples and contexts used which may not be as appropriate to ethnic-minority children as those of the indigenous majority culture. If these are still being written and published now, this is probably a matter of ignorance rather than poor intentions.

This presents contemporary classroom practitioners with a methodological issue. Faced with using materials which are of dubious quality on grounds of 'racism', such as a school's scheme, should they abandon them and use other materials or invent their own, which may be of inferior quality on other grounds? The response of the more committed antiracist teacher may be different from the majority: they may actually be able to put to good use the more virulent racism as examples to a class. Older secondary students may value such a social dimension being introduced into their classroom dialogue. Yet many mathematics teachers see their role exclusively as teachers of mathematics, and feel either out of their depth or unprofessional if they involve themselves in discussion of racism with their pupils. There is widespread suspicion that antiracism involves indoctrination (Jeffcoate, 1984, 1985), a point of view challenged rather effectively by Mullard (Mullard, 1985).

Even in the writing of new examination and textual materials, an anti-racist commitment is not unproblematic. The accepted policy in regard to gender involves, for instance, only using 'girl friendly' contexts in questions. Logically one should look to a similar policy toward ethnic minorities. Many statistics questions, in an effort to relate to children's experience, deal with pet ownership, which is rare in some cultures. Yet it may be unrealistic and impractical to deal with this effectively for any but the best-represented minorities.

More important factors in gender discrimination involve methods of assessment and teaching styles. It seems likely that these factors will be more critical to minority cultures too. Yet little is known about these factors and how the teaching of mathematics should take them into account. If one observes in traditional Chinese culture a notable respect for one's elders and a stress on memorization and practice, what can one deduce about an optimum teaching style for mathematics to Chinese pupils? (Hirst and Hirst, 1988). A possibly critical factor in both race and gender discrimination lies in teacher expectation (Good and Brophy, 1987). Expectations that children of West-Indian origin will make strong athletes may even allow teachers to believe they are being optimistic about their pupils' potential while actually diverting them into less valuable training and qualifications!

Ethnomathematics and the Multicultural Dimension

Good mathematics teaching often starts with the personal experience of the children, and an ethnically diverse class can provide a rich resource to be exploited. The religious calendars yield interesting mathematics, for instance in the calculation of Easter, Ramadan, or the Chinese or Jewish New Years (Brown, 1987). Islamic or Celtic designs on buildings, porcelain or clothing present a context for the introduction of almost the whole geometry curriculum (Joseph *et al.*, 1992). The non-European roots of mathematics provide a complementary perspective that is often ignored, yet provides a valuable resource if the multicultural dimension is to be incorporated in the mathematics syllabus (Joseph, 1991). The international experience of children can provide concrete examples for the understanding of the twenty-four hour clock through time zones or the algebra of functions through currency and exchange rates. And yet all these contexts may not arise directly from the experience of the children in the classroom. Is their use valid just because they are drawn from many cultures? The mathematics working party thinks not:

> It is sometimes suggested that the multicultural complexion of society demands a 'multicultural' approach to mathematics, with children being introduced to different number systems, foreign currencies and non-European measuring and counting devices. We are concerned that undue emphasis on multicultural mathematics, in

these terms, could confuse young children. (DES, 1988, par. 10.20, p. 87)

There has recently been a growth of literature which concerns itself with the ethnomathematics of various cultural groups (Gerdes, 1985). These aimed either simply to document these mathematical social practices or to harness them in the design of appropriate curricula. One might expect, perhaps, that an Angolan algebra curriculum might use the sand-drawings of the Tchokwe as a context rather than those to be found in widely exported British textbooks (Gerdes, 1988). Such attempts to develop the curriculum of schools through the use of appropriate social contexts are obviously valuable. There may be some role for using some of these foreign curriculum materials without modification in this country with ethnic-minority children from the appropriate cultures. This is rare at present but may be a natural extension of the language-support strategy in the future. But transplanting these materials without modification into the mainstream UK classroom would be generally inappropriate.

The ethnomathematics of most secondary-school pupils in the UK is that of the disco, the supermarket, the dart board and the television: certainly not that of Angolan sand patterns, Chinese rod numerals and Vedic mathematics. Nevertheless, there may be a role for such exotic mathematics in the curriculum. In general the principle should be that children are first introduced to mathematics through a context which is familiar, perhaps through their own 'ethnomathematics'. Subsequently it is important that the mathematics become generally operational in other contexts. Finally, children should learn to use mathematics in new, unfamiliar contexts. It is now generally accepted that it is madness to learn about different number systems before learning about the denary system. But the latter can only be completely understood, in the end, by contrast with its alternatives. In general it can be seen from research into secondary pupils' understanding of concepts that insufficient attention is paid to the critical role of the counter-example in the formation of a concept. Learning about the mathematics or number systems of other cultures and times can be very helpful in providing such an experience. Furthermore, in some cases, cultural products such as Islamic designs are universally understood by children because they are concrete and visual, or because they have been disseminated into the indigenous culture from their original sources. In fact, in many such cases, the cultural sources are actually lost in antiquity. In such instances there may be a strong argument on cultural grounds as well as on grounds of good practice in learning mathematics for including them in the curriculum.

The Historical Approach

Most authors and reports which have considered the matter do seem to conclude that mathematics teaching should involve an historical dimension.

'Some attention to the history of mathematics could show the contribution to the development of mathematical thinking of non-European cultures' (DES, 1988 par., 10.20).

There are two reasons. First, the historical development of mathematics does, to some extent, mirror the learner's psychological development. Thus, a historical study shows that the number zero developed only very slowly. Initially it arose not as a 'real' number *per se* but as a mark to indicate a gap between digits. The Egyptians, it may be a comfort to many school children to know, resisted the use of almost all fractions other than those in the form 1/n, i.e., 1/2, 1/3 . . . When negative numbers were first used, they were considered an invention of the mind rather than 'real'. And, of course, complex numbers like $\sqrt{-1}$ were invented for solving equations, and are still called 'imaginary' today. The historical development not only reflects the logical development of the number system, but also the psychological development underpinning its learning and teaching. At each stage children have to invent or construct a new universe of numbers, which they will not initially 'believe in'. Teaching adolescents about the history of the invention of numbers may, perhaps, help them to tolerate their own difficulties, and persist (Green, 1976).

Second, a historical approach emphasizes the role of persons and societies in the invention, application and dissemination of mathematics. It is important that children learn to feel in control of mathematics, in the sense that it is theirs to play with, to use, even perhaps to invent. Knowing that others have gone before and have invented or used mathematics in interesting ways may be important in helping to establish this ownership. For instance, one would like to teach that the first recorded artifacts demonstrating counting skills date back over 30,000 years, that formal mathematics as we know it was born in Africa (Euclid in Alexandria) and that Pythagoras' theorem was actually well-known some years before his birth and demonstrated in China in a book called the *Chou Pei* (Needham, 1959). It may be a very small step to acquaint teachers with such facts, and yet peppering one's teaching with such incidental information may provide a powerful antidote to our pupils Eurocentrism.

The development of notation, of number systems and of algebra also embeds much school mathematics in a cultural context. An important strategic skill in solving problems is a willingness and ability to introduce or invent an appropriate notation in a problem. It may help children if they appreciate that numbers have been recorded in different ways by different cultures at different times. The rod-and-bar numerals of the ancient Chinese and the Egyptian hieroglyphics are a case in point. The adverse comment, referred to previously by the working party for mathematics, about studying different number systems can only be understood in terms of the inappropriate use of so-called 'modern' multibase arithmetic materials by primary schools in the 1960s and 1970s. It would be unfortunate if the study of different cultures' number systems was extinguished because of this. The history of the number π, (the ratio of the circumference to the diameter of a circle) may be very helpful in making the concept meaningful to pupils. Historically one finds the use of $\pi = 3$ (the Bible), $\pi = 22/7$, $\pi = 31/8$ (Babylonian), $\pi = 3.142$ (Is it a variable or can't the teachers make up their mind?). The progress in calculating the constant to increasing degrees of accuracy over the millennia provides a concrete reference point for understanding the irrational nature of π, i.e., the idea that it is a limit of an infinite sequence of fractions.

A different approach to the history of mathematics is taken by French curriculum innovators (Fauvel, 1990). They use original texts as sources for teaching material (alongside modern French translations). This appears to have motivational value for older students of ages 16–19. Unfortunately much early mathematics has no documented history of this kind. The more recent the mathematics, in general, the more advanced the student needs to be to appreciate it. Perhaps this approach would find its most natural home in the undergraduate and postgraduate mathematics curricula, which certainly seem to stand in need of an injection of humanity.

The historical approach is, logically, a cultural approach; it is also a multicultural approach, since school mathematics was invented or discovered by cultures largely from Africa and Asia, i.e., India, China, the Middle East and North Africa. Although there are clearly merits in adopting a historical and cultural approach to teaching mathematics wherever realistically possible, such an approach does not claim to, and will not in itself, provide an effective antidote to racism.

Applications of Mathematics

The curriculum gives considerable weight to the application of mathematics. The Cockcroft report went so far as to declare that:

> We believe it should be a fundamental principle that no topic should
> be included unless it can be developed sufficiently for it to be applied
> in ways in which the pupils can understand. (DES, 1982, p. 133)

Contexts for applications should be various. Daily life and scientific contexts are not uncommon in most texts. The criterion is generally that of finding a context which will motivate, one which is regarded as significant or important. Motivation must be considered more than any other problem in the teaching of secondary-school pupils, particularly those who find mathematics difficult and for older secondary pupils (Larcombe, 1985.) It is important for older children that their individual tastes and interests are recognized and valued. A diversity of applications and materials that support them are therefore desirable, and they should not be cursory or trivial. The mature pupil is not easily fooled!

One area which has a growing literature is that of mathematics applied to art (see references in Joseph *et al.*, 1992). Mathematics, with the aid of drawing instruments or computer software, can be motivated as a powerful tool in understanding and even generating artistic designs and patterns. This may provide a valuable antidote to the public perception of mathematics as a scientific (and one might add, dry and dull) subject, and may also prove a promising route to encouraging 'arts' students to participate in mathematics.

The growth of applied research into fractals and chaos theory testify to the fact that such areas of mathematical investigation are serious as well as recreational. A most important, well-concealed fact about mathematics can be revealed through such work, i.e., that the dual criteria of elegance and rigour seems to ensure the validity and future utility of mathematical theory.

Other important applications, for statistics in particular, arise in the social sciences. Many of the targets for data handling might be practised or demonstrated through social contexts such as the economics of inequality or the arms race (Hudson, 1987a, 1987b). Projects in such areas can be motivating for some older and more aware pupils. Issues of conservation and ecology are also very relevant to modern teenagers, and curriculum innovators are exploiting this interest through applications of data-handling and computer modelling.

Both the above examples might be undertaken by pupils through, or with, other disciplines, or within the 'thematic' approach typical of the primary school. Certainly many secondary-school teachers of mathematics would benefit from help from, or collaboration with, art or humanities specialists. There is a danger that lack of expertise may allow cross-curricular work to promote good mathematics but bad social science and art (or, God forbid, vice versa!). At a local conference organized to discuss collaboration on GCSE coursework, a craft teacher commented that full marks were given in mathematics for the design of a bookcase which involved cutting unacceptably across the grain. But this will always be an occupational hazard for mathematics which tries to make itself useful, unless the teamwork between the disciplines is impeccable!

These developments of application approaches may be significant in extending the multicultural approach currently accepted in the humanities and arts curriculum, and even the technology curriculum, into mathematics. The more one connects mathematics with a cultural context, the more one is obliged to ask: Whose culture?

Conclusion

In conclusion, the principal areas of concern in the future will be:

- the identification and eradication of inequality of treatment of ethnic minorities in materials, methods of assessment, teaching methods and teacher expectations;

- the rational development of an ethnomathematical approach to teaching in an ethnically and culturally diverse classroom;
- identifying appropriate historical approaches to certain topics in the curriculum, taking appropriate account of the global development of elementary mathematics; and
- developing applications of mathematics in other areas, such as the arts and social sciences, which can positively contribute to 'multicultural education'.

References

BROWN, A. (1987) *The Shap Handbook on World Religions in Education*, London, Commission for Racial Equality.

DEPARTMENT OF EDUCATION AND SCIENCE (1982) *Mathematics Counts*, London, HMSO.

DEPARTMENT OF EDUCATION AND SCIENCE (1985) *Curriculum Matters 3: Mathematics for Ages 5–16*, London, HMSO.

DEPARTMENT OF EDUCATION AND SCIENCE DES (1988) *Mathematics for Ages 5–16*, London, HMSO.

DEPARTMENT OF EDUCATION AND SCIENCE (1989) *Mathematics in the National Curriculum*, London, HMSO.

FAUVEL, J. (1990) 'History in the Mathematics Classroom,' *The IREM Papers*, 1, Leicester, The Mathematical Association.

GERDES, P. (1985) 'Conditions and Strategies for Emancipatory Mathematics Education in Underdeveloped Countries', *For the Learning of Mathematics*, 5, 1, pp. 15–20.

GERDES, P. (1988) 'On Possible Uses of Traditional Angolan Sand Drawings in Mathematics', *Educational Studies in Mathematics*, 19, 1, pp. 3–22.

GOOD, T.L. and BROPHY, J.E. (1987) *Looking in Classrooms*, London, Harper and Row.

GREEN, D.R. (1976) 'History in Mathematics Teaching', *Mathematics in Schools*, 5, 3, pp. 15–17.

HIRST, A. and HIRST, K. (Eds) (1988) *Proceedings of the Sixth International Congress on Mathematics Education*, ICMI Secretariat, Budapest, Janos Bolyai Mathematical Society.

HUDSON, B. (1987a) *Global Statistics*, York, York University.

HUDSON, B. (1987b) 'Multicultural Mathematics', *Mathematics in Schools*, 16, 4, pp. 34–38.

INNER LONDON EDUCATION AUTHORITY (1985) *Everyone Counts*, London, ILEA.

JEFFCOATE, R. (1984) *Ethnic Minorities and Education*, London, Harper and Row.

JEFFCOATE, R. (1985) 'Anti-racism as an Education Ideology', in Arnot M. (Ed) *Race and Gender*, Oxford, Pergamon Press.

JOSEPH, G.G. (1987) 'Foundations of Eurocentrism in Mathematics', *Race and Class*, 28, 3, pp. 13–28.

JOSEPH, G.G. (1991) *The Crest of the Peacock: Non-European Roots of Mathematics*, London, Tauris.

JOSEPH, G.G., NELSON, R.D. and WILLIAMS, J.S. (1992) *Multicultural Mathematics*, Oxford, Oxford University Press.

LARCOMBE, A. (1985) *Mathematical Learning Difficulties in the Secondary School*, Oxford, Oxford University Press.

MAUGHAN, C., STEEG, T. and WILLIAMS, J.S. (1990) *Bouncing Balls at Trinity High School*, MAP, Manchester University Department of Education.

MULLARD, C. (1985) *Race, Power and Resistance*, London, Routledge and Kegan Paul.

NATIONAL CURRICULUM COUNCIL (1989) *Mathematics Non-Statutory Guidance*, London, HMSO.

NEEDHAM, J. (1959) *Science and Civilisation in China*, 3, Cambridge, Cambridge University Press.

Chapter 7

Science

David Reid

> Science for all is not yet a reality . . . and much remains to be done if it is to be equally accessible to all pupils, irrespective of their gender, ethnic background and intellectual ability . . . It is a matter of some regret to us that . . . we have not been able to address [these issues] as thoroughly as they deserve, much less to resolve them. (DES, 1988a)

Context

The Science National Curriculum

The quotation that introduces this chapter is taken from the science working party's report to the Secretary of State in August 1988 (DES, 1988a). Its explicit message is that the Science National Curriculum (SNC), now encapsulated in law through the Education Reform Act of 1988, is inadequate for the majority of children in our schools. The corollary to this is that changes to the SNC were clearly envisaged as necessary by the working party even at the time of its publication. This chapter is written in the context of what must be a continuing debate about the future of the SNC (Reid and Ryles, 1989), with a focus on a culturally diverse society.

Indeed, we have already witnessed the first major revision of the SNC. In December 1991 the Original Attainment Targets (OATs) were revised and new ones published (DES, 1991). There are just four Attainment Targets in the new SNC (often referred to as 'NATs', to distinguish them from the 'OATs'), and each of them is divided into a number of 'strands'. These strands each represent a main scientific idea, and the Statements of Attainment attached to each of the strands reflect how these scientific ideas progress in complexity as the children move up through the school from levels 4 to 10. Table 7.1 shows the four National Attainment Targets (NATs) which will be taught in schools from September 1992.

Table 7.1:   Science ATs in the National Curriculum: Differences between Single and Double Components of the SNC at Key Stage 4

			Double	Single
AT1 Scientific investigation	strand 1 strand 2 strand 3	Ask questions, predict, and hypothesize Observe and manipulate variables Interpret results and evaluate scientific evidence		
AT2 Life and living processes	strand 1 strand 2 strand 3 strand 4	Life processes and organization of living things Variation and mechanisms of inheritance and evolution Populations and human influences within ecosystems Energy flows and cycles of matter in ecosystems		
AT3 Materials and their properties	strand 1 strand 2 strand 3 strand 4	Properties, classification, and structure of materials Explanations of the properties of materials Chemical changes Earth and its atmosphere		
AT4 Physical processes	strand 1 strand 2 strand 3 strand 4 strand 5	Electricity and magnetism Energy resources and energy transfer Forces and their effects Light and sound Earth's place in the universe		

At Key Stage 4 children may opt to take either a double-science course (resulting in the equivalent of two GCSE passes at 16+) or a single-science course. The single-science award will lead to the equivalent of a single GCSE award at 16+. Already then, in the context of multiethnic education, we are faced with an unfortunate anomaly. Single science offers only half the remuneration in terms of GCSE-equivalent award as double science. Reference to Table 7.1, however, shows that it demands expertise in all of the four NATs. There are 138 Statements of Attainment (SoAs) attached to double science at Key Stage 4, and eighty-four to single science. Thus, in terms of quantity, single science demands nearly two-thirds of the content of double science. It follows that the science achievement of single-science-award children is devalued as compared to double-science-award children. It is reasonable to suppose that those children most likely to opt for the less demanding science timetable will be those who find science difficult, and these will include children with language difficulties, including those from some ethnic-minority groups. Not only is the science education of this group devalued in terms of examination results, it is also devalued in terms of the quality of curricular provision, since some of the potentially most important SoAs relevant to ethnic-minority children are missing from the single-science Programme of Study, namely strands S3 and S4 in NAT2, 'human influences' and 'cycles of matter'. We shall return to this point in more detail later.

Science for All — A Hierarchy of Needs

If 'science for all' is not to become part of the rhetoric of the ERA, then it is vital that the science education of those children known to underachieve in the subject is systematically confronted. As we have seen, the working party usefully alerts us to three major groups of children who have a tendency to fall into this category: girls; the less able; and those from ethnic backgrounds. A great deal has usefully been said about the science education of girls (Bentley and Watts, 1986) and the less able (Reid and Hodson, 1987). What is unique about the children who form the subject matter of this chapter is the sheer variety of personal perspectives they may hold about the relevance of science and technology in their lives, and the very nature of science itself. It is now widely accepted that the ordering of science-curriculum priorities must be based on the experiences that children bring with them into the classroom, whether these be socially (Solomon, 1983) or cognitively deduced (Driver and Oldham, 1986).

> Only by refocusing our attention to take account of children's personal and affective needs can we begin to raise levels of attainment in the cognitive domain . . . We need to re-orientate the science curriculum to prioritise personal development, perhaps best expressed as heightened personal awareness. (Hodson and Reid, 1988)

'Prioritizing the affective' means that such learner-centred aims as 'the communication of feelings', the 'establishment of a sense of personal adequacy' and 'the attainment of self-esteem' have to take precedence over more familiar sounding science-centred aims such as 'the attainment of knowledge and understanding of a range of scientific facts, concepts and theories'. Such a model of science education reflects Maslow's (1970) 'pyramid of needs', in which needs lower in the hierarchy must have been thoroughly met before any significant progress in the higher order needs can hope to be achieved (Figure 7.1). The application of such a model in the school laboratory has far-reaching implications for the science curriculum and for the day-to-day activities of the science teacher.

Challenges

The Affective Domain

This is the first and greatest challenge to the science teacher. John Head, in his book *The Personal Response to Science* (1985) argues that 'people are likely to pay attention and get involved in activities which they expect to be interesting, rewarding and worthwhile in some way. Previous experience . . . will serve as a basis for such beliefs'. This being so, the science teacher needs

Figure 7.1: A Hierarchy of Priorities for the Culturally Diverse Classroom

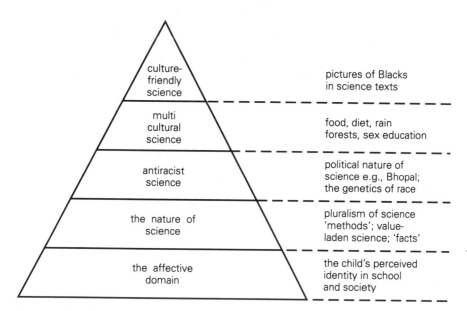

to be aware of some of the different perspectives that children from ethnic minorities have of the natural world and their place in it, since not to understand these perspectives will act as a barrier to the preparation of appropriately differentiated Programmes of Study.

Children reared in the western tradition have, for example, experienced the efforts of the scientist to control the environment to his or her own benefit. They will have seen the effects of this in everyday living: transport systems, heavy industry, intensive farming, the control of disease, and so on. But for some West-Indian children the word 'science' may connote a quite different world of 'spirits and spirit-dominated practice, beliefs and superstitions' (George and Glasgow, 1989). In common with many societies, the African tradition takes a holistic view of man's place in the universe. Children with this perspective will 'know', for example, that the persistent violation of ecological rules they perceive happening in the West is a recipe for societal disaster (Green, 1987). Muslim children too see a serious conflict between the western view of science and the view promulgated by the Koran and by the prophetic traditions. Muhammad is reported to have said 'to listen to the words of the learned and to instil into others the lessons of science is better than religious exercises' (Sardar, 1980). Nevertheless, muslim children will feel uneasy about the 'spread of the teaching of a science of nature without reference to God' (Nasr, 1988). Nor should science teachers assume that all indigenous white children will be at ease with a purely secular view of science. The Christian ethnic embraces many beliefs and values not dissimilar from those of Islam and Judaism. For many children, be they black or white, it is still God and not chance that orders the universe. Poole (1990) asks:

> Does secondary science education somehow kill the wonder of the primary-school pupil, so that awe is made to appear babyish and based on ignorance? It seems that for some people scientific explanations of the amazing world around us has the effect of banishing wonder.

This is the secular equivalent to the theological argument put by Coulson (1955) who warned Christians about separating their Christian beliefs from their scientific understanding of the universe and thereby creating the danger of an ever-diminishing 'God of the gaps'.

The Nature of Science

For many of us in the West conventional science has come erroneously to be seen as value-free. Its processes are engaged in by disinterested, neutral, unbiased observers, whose function it is to amass a body of incontrovertible facts. Upon these facts have been built the great predictive laws of science which we have come to associate with such names as Einstein, Galileo, Lavoisier, Mendel, Newton and so on. This view of science, arising by a process of inductive reasoning and giving rise to a means-end, determinist view of the nature of science and scientific method, goes a long way back in western traditional culture. Manthorpe (1982) suggests that it developed as a way to survive the re-establishment of the Church as the source of knowledge of authority during the Counter Reformation. Later the situation was compounded by the achievements of the Industrial Revolution, where empiricism, reason and experience were seen to underpin the increasing power and authority of science. It is not surprising, therefore, that such a view of the nature of science is often held by science teachers (Kimball, 1967; Anderson *et al.*, 1986). As we have seen, this is not the intuitive view of the nature of science held by many children brought up in African, Asian and Caribbean cultures, or certain western subcultures. It is suggested that this is an important element in the disaffection shown by many children towards science in secondary schools in this country, a disaffection which is often reflected in underachievement.

However, the process by which human beings make observations is not fully understood. It was William James (1890) who noted that, in order to make an observation, some conscious control was necessary. The process of observation can only take place after a person has selected the object to observe. But the selection of the object in the first instance must be influenced by the experiences which the observer brings to the task, i.e., it will always be, to some extent or other, culturally induced or biased. Thus it is that, despite the best efforts of scientists to remain 'neutral', the ideas, concepts, hypotheses and theories which they subconsciously bring to the observation task will affect what it is they choose to observe. Not only that, but how they interpret a particular phenomenon will also depend upon their existing thought patterns. Lewis Thomas, observing scientists at work, believes that a great deal more than a purely intellectual exercise is going on in the process of science itself:

> Scientists at work . . . seem to be under the influence of a deeply placed human instinct. They are, despite their efforts at dignity, rather like young animals engaged in savage play. When they are near to an answer their hair stands on end, they sweat, they are awash in their own adrenalin. (Thomas, 1988)

The Association for Science Education puts it like this:

> An integral part of science is the use of man's imagination. Because of this science can never be completely objective but must be tentative and uncertain and influenced by numerous social and cultural factors. (ASE, 1979)

Science is a human construct in just the same way as are other areas of human endeavour such as literature and music, for without human beings there would be no such thing as science. And whilst science might legitimately attempt to employ a more overtly rational methodology in its search for 'truth' than some of the other areas of human endeavour, that in no way negates its essential subjectivity. When we understand this about scientific methodology, it becomes less difficult to realize that scientists from differing cultures will bring to the study of science elements of their own idiosyncratic belief systems, which will influence not only the methods they use, but the very questions they choose to study and the interpretation they put on their findings.

This is why the inclusion of the 'nature of scientific ideas' into the Programme of Study for both single and double science is so important. It appears in strand S3 of NAT1, and recognizes the essentially ambiguous nature of scientific evidence in these terms:

> Pupils should be given opportunities to develop their knowledge and understanding of the ways in which scientific ideas change through time and how their nature and the use to which they are put are affected by the social, moral, spiritual and cultural contexts in which they are developed. In doing so, they should begin to recognise that whilst science is an important way of thinking about experience, it is not the only way.

At attainment level 5 children are required to 'evaluate the validity of their conclusions by considering different interpretations of their experimental evidence'. We can probably go further than that. Not only are such different interpretations possible, but each may be as legitimate as the other within the context of the interpreting cultures. It is this ambiguity, that there is not always a 'right' answer, which many science teachers will have difficulty in living with. Yet the media present us with examples of it on an almost daily basis. The use of human embryos in researching genetic engineering, extolling the virtues of forms of birth control in Third-World countries that are unacceptable in our own, nuclear power stations, bovine spongiform encephalopathy (BSE), acid rain, Amazonian forests, the ozone layer and so on. To none of these problems facing the human race today is there one answer which will satisfy everyone concerned. Unfortunately, none of this is made very explicit in the 1991 SNC, and it is left to the teacher to provide examples which are appropriate and relevant to the children.

It is necessary to distinguish here between the nature of the 'fact' itself, and the interpretation of the fact. Sometimes the 'facts' are only the best evidence available so far. This is why BSE is causing such debate — we simply do not know what beef is now safe to eat. But there are also 'facts' which, one day, will prove to be incorrect. The history of science is replete with examples. A Victorian child suffering from asthma was coddled in bed with a feather mattress and pillow. Today we know that one of the habitats favoured by the house mite, to which asthma sufferers are allergic, is the feather mattress. As far as the interpretation of scientific 'facts' is concerned, that too may be legitimately idiosyncratic. The Muslim and the devout Catholic will argue against a case for genetic engineering based on human-embryo research. Equally, the humanist will argue the opposite. It is not the 'facts' that are in dispute.

Responses

Antiracist Science Education

Antiracist science education is not just about helping individuals of different cultures to like each other better. The unpalatable truth is that racism is part of our own cultural inheritance. Racism is embedded in history (the slave trade), catalyzed by our economy (Bhopal), manipulated by politics (sanctions against South Africa), justified by science (evolutionary racism), permitted by education (inefficient differentiation), reinforced by social conditions (housing and unemployment), and stereotyped by the media (black muggers). It is so deeply disturbing to come to terms with the thought that some of our own teaching might be 'racist in nature and could be used to reinforce racist beliefs and stereotypes' (Pugh, 1990), that many of us prefer not to question ourselves too deeply on the subject. Whilst we may be alert to perceiving Blacks as good dancers, Asians as quiet and well-behaved, and Chinese as good at science, it is more difficult for us to deny that one major cause of starvation in Ethiopia is due to that country's over population.

So, the first step in any antiracist science education must be for science educators to sensitize themselves as to how their own attitudes have been influenced by the culture in which they have been reared. It must be a matter of some concern then, that the explicit requirement that all entrants to the profession be provided with this opportunity (DES, 1989b, Section 6, pars 3 and 4) has been removed from the new criteria for the initial training of teachers which were announced by the Secretary of State recently (DES, 1992).

A second step might be to tackle head-on the scientific basis for the concept of human race itself. The holocaust of Nazi Europe may elicit feelings for the sense of such an approach. NAT2 (strand S2) in the SNC provides a tangible baseline for antiracist science education. The basic Statements of Attainment numbers 5b, 6c, 8c, 9b and c, and 10c ask you to:

- 5b know that information in the form of genes is passed on from one generation to the next;
- 6c know that variation in living organisms has both genetic and environmental causes;
- 8c understand the principles of a monohybrid cross involving dominant and recessive alleles;
- 9b understand the different sources of genetic variation;
- 9c understand the relationships between variation, natural selection and reproductive success in organisms and the significance of these relationships for evolution; and
- 10c understand the basic principles of genetic engineering, selective breeding and cloning, and how these give rise to social and ethical issues.

These SATs give teachers the opportunity to present scientific evidence that the concept of race is pseudo-scientific, and to adduce first-hand evidence that the genetic differences between Africans (and Indians, Pakistanis, Chinese), and Caucasians 'is negligible as compared with the polymorphism within each group' (Rose, Lewontin and Kamin, 1984). The statement in the Programme of Study (for both single and double science) 'explore the basic principles of . . . how some diseases can be inherited' offers further scope for enabling the science department's written antiracist policy by introducing such examples as sickle-cell anaemia. Unlike the OATs, however, the NATs do not specify examples, and it is again left to the teacher to search them out.

Multicultural Science Education

Troyna (1989) argues that antiracist and multicultural education are quite different in their ideological approach to the problem. Antiracist education 'deliberately seeks to make a connection between institutional discriminations and inequalities of race'. Multicultural education, on the other hand, focuses on issues relating to culture. It is at this higher level of the hierarchy in Figure 7.1 that this section of the chapter is concerned. Here we shall consider just three issues: those of the content of the secondary-school science curriculum itself, the process of communication in science, and teaching about science.

Multicultural Science Content and the SNC

The most obvious examples of multicultural science content tend to be biological. Gill, Singh and Vance (1987) give a list of topics such as diet and the testing of a wide variety of foods including yam, sweet potato and pasta; medical care disease and oral hygiene. But each science department will need to make a systematic search of the SNC in order to alert itself to all the possibilities of multicultural exemplification. A few of the more obvious examples are given in Table 7.2.

Communication in Secondary-School Science Lessons

It is almost impossible to exaggerate the importance of language issues in the context of the teaching and learning of science in secondary schools. Researches have consistently shown that it is not only the technical jargon of science which is the cause of the problem (Reid, 1984a), but the entire linguistic register within which we, as science teachers, work (Barnes, 1976; Lunzer and Gardner, 1984). That communication in science should involve more than the written word (Hoyle, 1987) was explicitly recognized by the working party, which originally allocated an entire Profile Component (communication) to the SNC. The definitive document (DES, 1991) relegates communication to part of NAT1, and although it appears regularly throughout the levels of NAT1 it does not play the central role originally allocated to it.

One of the Secretary of State's reasons for demoting the importance of communication is that it would prove difficult to assess progress in communication skills. This in itself is unfortunate, suggesting as it does that the only worthwhile teaching is that which can be measured by quantitative techniques. But in any case the Secretary of State's assertion is not true.

In recent years there have been two highly relevant researches which provide the science teacher with the opportunity to set about systematically improving the communication skills of reading and writing in science. As far as reading skills are concerned, Davies and Greene (1984) have provided a series of what they call 'Directed Activities Related to Texts' (DARTs), which have been specifically devised for use in secondary-school science lessons. The aim is to develop the skills necessary for the reading of expository (as opposed to narrative, i.e., those that tell a story) texts. DARTs do this by providing a situation in which the child has to read information-rich texts in a reflective way. DARTs pose questions which force the child (working cooperatively with one or two other children) to stop reading and look

Table 7.2: Examples of Topics Appropriate to Multicultural Exemplification

KEY: DS = In the double-science curriculum only

Attainment Targets (NATs)	Attainment level and strand	Statement of Attainment (SoA)
NAT1	L5 S3	Evaluate the validity of conclusions on different interpretations of evidence
	L9 S3	Analyse and interpret data in terms of uncertain evidence and tentative conclusions
NAT2	L4 S3	Understand that the survival depends on competition for scarce resources (DS)
	L5 S3	Know how pollution can affect the survival of organisms (DS)
	L6 S2	Know that variation in living organisms has both genetic and environmental causes
	L7 S2	Understand how selective breeding can produce economic benefits and improved yields
	L7 S3	Know how population growth and decline is related to environmental resources (DS)
	L8 S3	Understand the impact of human activity on the Earth (DS)
	L8 S4	Understand the role of microbes and the cycling of nutrients (DS)
	L10 S2	Understand basic principles of genetic engineering: social and ethical issues
	L10 S4	Understand that food production demands care in the management of ecosystems (DS)
NAT3	L4 S4	Know that weathering and erosion lead to different types of soil (DS)
	L5 S4	Understand the water cycle (DS)
	L6 S4	Understand how airstreams affect weather over land and sea (DS)
	L8 S4	Understand how the atmosphere has evolved and how its composition remains constant (DS)
	L9 S3	Evaluate social, economic, health, and environmental factors associated with manufacture (DS)
	L9 S4	Explain changes in the atmosphere causing weather phenomena (DS)
NAT4	L5 S2	Understand the difference between non-renewable energy resources and need for fuel economy
	L6 S2	Understand that the sun is the major energy source for the Earth
	L8 S5	Use data on the solar system to speculate about elsewhere in the universe (DS)
	L9 S2	Evaluate economic, environmental and social benefits of different energy sources

back over the text in order to extract specific types of information. These DARTs can be graded according to the difficulty of the reading task or the inexperience of the readers. Thus, in the simplest examples, the children might be required to replace lines of a fixed length with an appropriate missing word in a type of cloze test. The teacher has previously removed certain words from the text, so that the small group of children is forced to search for syntactic and semantic clues in order to arrive at the correct word. For very naive readers it is possible to put the list of words to choose from at the bottom of the passage. Later, as the child progresses in its reading skill, the DARTs can be made more difficult. Perhaps the child will be required to underline in blue all those phrases which refer to the function of a particular scientific process, and in red those parts of the text which relate function to structure. There are a number of other useful features attached to the use of DARTs. In the first place it ensures that the teacher has a good grasp of exactly what it is she or he is asking the child to do! In the second place it provides an opportunity for small groups of children to work cooperatively together in a fun task. In the third place, the children have the positive feedback of knowing how well they have done and how they are progressing. Such an approach to reading eliminates vague hopes on the part of the teacher that appropriate reading skills will somehow osmose into the learner as more and more reading takes place.

One of the DARTs activities involves the use of pictures and diagrams by children learning science. The majority of secondary-school science texts are replete with pictures, presumably on the assumption that pictures will help the child's learning and understanding (Barlex and Carre, 1985). This effect of pictures has been called the 'picture superiority effect' (Reid, 1984b). However, recent research has produced evidence that the learning of science by less successful children can actually be inhibited by the addition of pictures to the text (Reid and Beveridge, 1986). Furthermore, the strategies which less successful secondary children employ when learning from illustrated texts indicate that special care needs to be taken to train these children how to use such pictures (Reid and Beveridge, 1990).

If reading can be problematic for children whose first language is not English, then writing can prove even more difficult for them. In a project funded by the Northern Universities Joint Matriculation Board, an approach to the systematic development of writing skills in secondary-school science has been developed (JMB, 1987), called 'Staged Assessments in Literacy' (SAIL). It is not as well known as it deserves to be. Many of my overseas postgraduate students have found it invaluable as a teaching aid in their own countries where the language of education is English but the mother tongue is not. On a recent INSET course in Africa, Malawian teachers also thought it would be useful (Brown and Reid, 1990).

In essence SAIL suggests that all writing can be identified by reference to three parameters: the focus, use, and organization parameters (Table 7.3).

The model in Figure 7.2 describes the system in diagrammatic form. In terms of the focus parameter, a child writing about himself or herself is reckoned to be easier than writing about a subject, and this is easier than writing for a third person. Again, it is easier to relay specific facts than it is to expand on these facts involving additional research or exemplification. The most difficult writing task within the 'use' parameter is examining the

Table 7.3: Parameters Identifying Writing Difficulty

Parameter	Description
Focus	What the writing is about: self, the subject, or the reader
Use	What is the writing for? To specify things about a topic, to expand a topic or to examine a topic in wider context
Organization	What is the principle which determines how the material is to be organized? Is it to be ordered in a time sequence? Are like things to be put together in a group? Or is a more abstract principle to be employed, based about a theme?

Figure 7.2: A 3-dimensional Model of Writing Difficulty

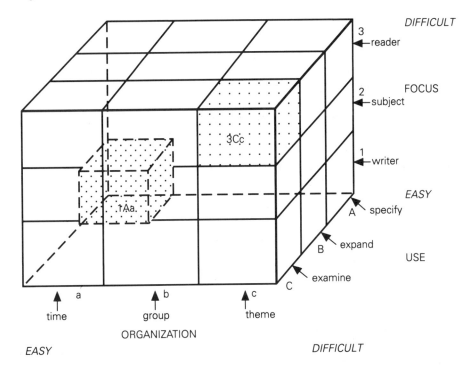

issues involved in an analytical way. Again, organizing one's writing chrono-logically is thought to be easier than comparing or contrasting issues around groups, and this is easier than discussing an issue in the context of an abstract theme. There are twenty-seven cells in the model. The easiest form of writing is denoted by cell 1Aa. We can take a simple example of how this might be used by poor writers in a science lesson on, say, diet. The children might be asked to write a sentence in their diary about what they ate for their main meals on one day of the week. Here they themselves are the focus of the exercise; they are specifying items of food on a chronological basis. At the opposite extreme children able to write within the parameters laid down by cell 3Cc would be highly literate. They might, for instance, be asked to write a report (focus; another reader) discussing the problem of malnutrition (use; examining) in underdeveloped countries (organization; theme). Such an exercise would involve a careful interplay of facts and substantiated opinion about the scientific basis of malnutrition (of different kinds) and how it might be influenced by the political and social conditions prevailing in Third-World countries. It is not, of course, intended that a child should move systematically from cell 1Aa by twenty-seven stages to cell 3Cc. Rather, that teachers be alerted to the fact that various levels of writing difficulty exist, and that by judicious selection of writing tasks they can encourage improvement in children's scientific literacy.

Teaching about Science
It is most unfortunate that OAT17 (the nature of science) has been entirely subsumed within NAT1. This devalues its importance in the eyes of teachers. Even the most multiculturally aware teacher will find it more difficult to justify the inclusion of cross-cultural science in their everyday teaching under the NATs than under the OATs. Nevertheless, a cross-cultural approach should be encouraged and it is regrettable that a major revision of the SNC has resulted in a curriculum with less of a flavour for a multicultural exposure than the original. In the 1989 version there were three Statements of Attainment that specifically referred to cross-cultural science.
They were SATs 6b, 7a and 8a, i.e., to:

- 6b be able to describe and explain one incident from the history of science where successful predictions were made to establish a new model;
- 7a be able to give an historical account of a change in an accepted theory or explanation, to demonstrate an understanding of its effect on people's lives — physically, social, spiritually and morally; and
- 8a be able to explain how a scientific explanation from a different culture or a different time contributes to our present understanding.

In the new version there are none. The only reference, and that tangential, is in the Programme of Study (Key Stage 4) for NAT1: 'Study examples of scientific controversies and the ways in which scientific ideas change'. No examples are provided. Some encouragement is to be found in the non-statutory guidance to the OATs, which it is still intended should be read for information on the teaching of the NATs. Here we are told that 'examples and stories are still more appropriate than philosophical principles', and that teachers should support the development of 'an empathetic understanding of science as a human activity'. There are plenty of such stories, for instance the Chinese roots of modern astronomy, where modern astronomers can still learn from the records made by Chinese star-gazers 2,000 years ago (Stephenson, 1980).

Conclusion

This chapter strives to achieve three goals: to provide a theoretical model for thinking about the problems of teaching the SNC in our culturally diverse society, to identify some of the contents of the SNC which offer possibilities for a more overt multicultural approach to its teaching, and to look briefly at some pedagogical devices through which such an approach might be facilitated. We can be optimistic that we have come some way in our thinking since 1985, when a conference at the London Institute on 'science education in a multicultural society' produced a number of guidelines useful for teachers developing their own materials (Brandt, Turner and Turner, 1985). The guidelines included such advice as 'avoid line drawings that caricature', 'show ethnic peoples in positive, high-status roles', and 'avoid link drawings that are obviously European figures coloured black'. Such practical advice is not to be ignored, but it is essentially cosmetic (Figure 7.1). Facing up to the underlying issues is not easy and there remains a strong case for sensitive INSET and initial training provision:

> Strategies must be employed which challenge all teachers to examine their own views on our multicultural society and the implications for their practice. Teachers must then be supported in developing their teaching from the personal starting point they have identified. (Carter, 1985)

Initial teacher-training requirements can provide new entrants to the profession with ideas as to how best to approach the teaching of science in our culturally diverse society, but it must be said that the criteria laid down by Clarke in January 1992 are not so explicit as those laid down by his predecessor in 1989. We have to face up to the fact that antiracist science education is political. In a recent article in *the Economist* (1990) the 'gobbledegook' of the teacher-trainers' trade was lampooned. Many students, it claimed, 'have to sit through workshops on anything from gay sexuality to antiracist science teaching' and concluded that 'If low salaries do not put bright graduates off the profession, the prospect of teaching antiracist mathematics certainly will'. It seems that to make a stance is to invite criticism.

But fundamental differences in world views do legitimately exist between a largely secular British teaching force and religious cultures. As Jenkins (1990) points out, perhaps the concept of scientific literacy itself is so value-laden that it cannot cross national or cultural boundaries 'Different social contexts impose different priorities upon the various meanings that might be given to scientific literacy'. A corollary of Jenkins' thesis is that to have the same aims of the science curriculum for all children in a pluralistic society is to 'burden such education with responsibilities it cannot hope to meet'. At the moment we do not know. Perhaps the identification and celebration of such cultural differences represent a more optimistic scenario, and might turn out to be a catalyst in helping 'to enrich the quality of science education for all pupils' (DES, 1988a).

References

ANDERSON, H.O., HARTY, H. and SAMUEL, K.V. (1986) 'Nature of Science, 1969 and 1984: Perspectives of pre-service secondary science teachers, *School Science and Mathematics*, 86, 1, pp. 43–50.

ASSOCIATION FOR SCIENCE EDUCATION (ASE) (1979) *What is Science?* ASE Studies Series,15.

BARLEX, D. and CARRE, C. (1985) *Visual Communication in Science*, Cambridge, Cambridge University Press.

BARNES, D. (1976) *From Communication to Curriculum*, Harmondsworth, Penguin.

BENTLEY, D. and WATTS, M. (1986) 'Counting the positive virtues: A case for feminist science', *European Journal of Science Education*, 8, 2, pp. 121–34.

BRANDT, G., TURNER, S. and TURNER, R. (1985) 'Science education in a multicultural society', Report on a conference held at the University of London Institute of Education.

BROWN, M. and REID, D.J. (1990) 'Black for the people, green for the land, red for the blood of the martyrs: A case study of INSET in Malawi', *Research in Education*, 44, pp. 93–107.

CARTER, A. (1985) *Teachers for a Multicultural Society*, York, Longman (for SCDC).

COULSON, C.A. (1955) Science and Christian Belief, London, Collins.

DAVIES, F. and GREENE, T. (1984) *Reading for Learning in the Sciences*, Edinburgh, Oliver and Boyd.

DEPARTMENT OF EDUCATION AND SCIENCE (1988a) *Science for ages 5 to 16: Proposals of the Secretary of State for Education and Science and the Secretary of State for Wales*, London, HMSO.

DEPARTMENT OF EDUCATION AND SCIENCE (1988b) *National Curriculum: Task Group on Assessment and Testing*, A Report, London, HMSO.

DEPARTMENT OF EDUCATION AND SCIENCE (1989a) *Science in the National Curriculum*, London, HMSO.

DEPARTMENT OF EDUCATION AND SCIENCE (1989b) *Initial Teacher Training: Approval of courses, Circular* 24/89, London, HMSO.

DEPARTMENT OF EDUCATION AND SCIENCE (1991) *Science in the National Curriculum*, London, HMSO.

DEPARTMENT OF EDUCATION AND SCIENCE (1992) 'Reform of Initial Teacher Training: A consultation document', London, HMSO.

DRIVER, R. and OLDHAM, V. (1986) 'A constructivist approach to curriculum development in science', *Studies in Science Education*, 13, pp. 105–22.

THE ECONOMIST (1990) 'Stuck at the start', 12 May.

GEORGE, J. and GLASGOW, J. (1989) 'Some cultural implications of teaching towards common syllabi in science: A case study from the Caribbean', *School Science Review*, 71, 254, pp. 115–23.

GILL, D., SINGH, H. and VANCE, M. (1987) 'Multicultural versus antiracist science: Biology', in GILL, D. and LEVIDOW, L. (Ed) *Anti-racist Science Teaching*, London, Free Association Books.

GREEN, M. (1987) 'Kenya: The conservationists' blunder' in GILL, D. and LEVIDOW, L. (Ed) *Anti-Racist Science Teaching*, London, Free Association Books.

HEAD, J. (1985) *The Personal Response to Science*, Cambridge, Cambridge University Press.

HODSON, D. and REID, D.J. (1988) 'Changing priorities in science education, Part I, *School Science Review*, 70, 250, pp. 101–8.

HOYLE, P. (1987) 'Science education in and for a multicultural society: Some language issues', in DITCHFIELD, C. (Ed) *Better Science: Working for a Multicultural Society*, SSCR Curriculum Guide 7, London, Heinemann Education Books/ASE.

JAMES, W. (1890) *Principles of Psychology*, New York, Dover.

JENKINS, E. (1990) 'Scientific literacy and school science education', *School Science Review*, 71, 256, pp. 43–51.

JOINT MATRICULATION BOARD (1987) *Staged Assessment in Literacy*, Manchester, JMB.

KIMBALL, M.E. (1967) 'Understanding the nature of science: A comparison of scientists and science teachers', *Journal of Research in Science Teaching*, 5, pp. 110–20.

LUNZER, E, and GARDNER, K. (1984) *Learning from the Written Word*, Edinburgh, Oliver and Boyd.

MANTHORPE, C.A. (1982) 'Men's science, women's science or science? Some issues related to the study of girls' science education', *Studies in Science Education*, 9, pp. 65–80.

MASLOW, A. (1970) *Motivation and Personality*, London, Harper and Rowe.

NASR, S.N. (1988) 'Islam and the problem of modern science', *Muslim Education Quarterly*, 5, 4, pp. 35–44.

POOLE, M. (1990) 'Beliefs and values in science education: A Christian perspective' (Part I), *School Science Review*, 71, 256, pp. 25–32.

PUGH, S. (1990) 'Introducing multicultural science to a secondary school', *School Science Review*, 71, 256, pp. 131–5.

REID, D.J. (1984a) 'Readability and science worksheets in secondary schools', *Research in Science and Technology Education*, 2, 20, pp. 153–65.

REID, D.J. (1984b) 'The picture superiority effect and biological education', *Journal of Biological Education*, 18, 1, pp. 29–36.

REID, D.J. and BEVERIDGE, M. (1986) 'Effects of text illustration on children's learning of a school science topic', *British Journal of Educational Psychology*, 56, pp. 294–303.

REID, D.J. and BEVERIDGE, M. (1990) 'Reading illustrated science texts: A micro-computer based investigation of children's strategies', *British Journal of Educational Psychology*, 60, pp. 76–87.

REID, D.J. and HODSON, D. (1987) *Science for All: Teaching Science in the Secondary School*, London, Cassell Education.

REID, D.J. and RYLES, A.P. (1989) 'Balanced Science, the National Curriculum and Teachers' Attitudes', *Research in Education*, 42, pp. 45–57.

ROSE, S., LEWONTIN, R.C. and KAIM, L. (1984) *Not in Our Genes: Biology, Ideology and Human Nature*, Harmondsworth, Pelican.

SARDAR, Z. (1980) 'Can Science come back to Islam?', *New Scientist*, 23 October.

SOLOMON, J. (1983) 'Messy, contradictory and obstinately persistent: A study of children's out of school ideas about energy', *School Science Review*, 65, pp. 225–9.

STEPHENSON, F.R. (1980) 'Chinese roots of modern astronomy', *New Scientist*, 26 June.

David Reid

THOMAS, L. (1988) 'Natural science', in THOMAS, L. *The Wonderful Mistake: Notes of a Biology Watcher*, Oxford, Oxford University Press.

TROYNA, B. (1989) 'Beyond multiculturalism: Towards the enactment of anti-racist education in policy, provision and pedagogy, in MOON, B., MURPHY, P. and ROYNER, J. (Eds) *Policies for the Curriculum*, London, Hodder and Stoughton.

Chapter 8

Technology and Design

Glyn W. Price

Context

When it was announced by the government in 1990 that technology was to hold a place of special importance in the National Curriculum there was no great surprise. Subjects seen as very directly related to the world of work and enterprise were regarded as important. With the three core subjects as mathematics, English and science the positioning of technology (whatever that subject was to become) as the first to be developed of the remaining foundation subjects was in keeping with announced priorities. The surprise was in the nature and content of the technology. There has been much recent debate as to the meaning of technology as a school subject and, in particular, its relationship with design. Both terms boast a wide variety of definitions, and the outcome of the working party chaired by Lady Parkes was awaited with interest.

At the extremes of definitions of technology and design there are two models. The first sees the act of designing, innovating or creating as a key activity in pupils' development. This focus is primarily on creative design; the term 'technology' is reserved to describe the underlying facilities and operations which enable the design to be implemented. In the context it is more usual to talk of 'technologies' rather than 'technology'. The second approach describes technology as the subject area and activity as a whole, with design a subset of technology; the word 'design' is here used to describe the process of solution of technological problems. Between these extremes lies a continuum of alternative models each with its proponents. As a result, various emphases have emerged. Preferences are mainly identified in terms of background, type of training, and experience of the teachers concerned but one important use of the term technology is to indicate a systems-based, problem-solving treatment including modelling concepts. The confusion arising from the different approaches spills over into the delivery of National Curriculum technology and has cross-cultural implications.

Historically the different models come from different traditions, with the design-dominated models reflecting an arts-based tradition and the technology-dominated model having its roots in engineering and science. This is, of course, far too much of an oversimplification for what is a complex issue (Black and Harrison, 1985), but the 'two cultures' reflect influences clearly seen in the National Curriculum. To their credit, the developers of National-Curriculum technology have approached the problem boldly and incorporated aspects of differing traditions in the Statements of Attainment and Programmes of Study, seeing the best of each incorporated. The historical complexity of the internal culture of school technology still creates problems which lie deeper than just those of communication.

Challenges

Various subject areas were brought together to form technology for the National Curriculum (DES, 1990). Of these craft, design and technology (CDT) and home economics were well established with distant historical roots in the 'boys' crafts' and 'girls' crafts' respectively. In both areas the priority given to craft skills has diminished greatly to make way for the intro-duction of new subject matter and the provision of time for the designing and evaluation of products, as well as their production. The extent of the loss of emphasis on craftsmanship is particularly regretted in some cultures where mass production has reduced opportunities for the craftsman.

There is another dimension in the addition of business studies to National-Curriculum technology. For many schools this is new, not in principle but in location. Following the National Curriculum lead, some secondary schools have incorporated business studies within a technology framework, but the new element is written very much in terms of product innovation and management and in terms of a western-style economy and culture. Whilst the writers of the scheme might well disclaim such influence, there are also, in the minds of some analysts, urban and industrial overtones. There is a welcome link developing with art and design in the aesthetic aspects of technology. Finally information technology is to be expected as part of any modern technology scheme in a high-technology environment.

Technological design as an activity to be performed by children in the classroom and workshop is not generally questioned in UK education. It has become central to the technology National Curriculum. This is not so in many other countries where the cultures and educational systems interpret technology differently (Verma and Entzinger, 1992). The particular form which technological design activity takes tends to be dominated by the interests and cultural backgrounds of the teachers in the school. Differences of approach tend therefore to be within national or ethnic groupings, rather than between them, though this is not universally so. The challenge here presented by the National Curriculum in technology is to extend the breadth of technology, even within one school, beyond a narrow model so as to encompass many different approaches and different contents. This gives pupils awareness of the richness and variety of activity possible. A recent publication provides illuminating examples of cross-cultural similarities and differences in the values attributed to, and the use made of, a range of technologies. Through such examples, the interests of minority ethnic groups can be spotlighted and used to enhance the whole of the technology curriculum in British secondary schools (Verma and Entzinger, 1992).

Technology is thus to be seen within the dynamics of ongoing curriculum development in a variety of loosely linked subject areas and in terms of varied theoretical positions. The action of National-Curriculum technology has been to legislate for stronger cooperation between these areas and also in favour of particular directions of development at the expense of others. This is forcing change in schools where there had been curriculum-development inertia, and it is inhibiting or redirecting technology developments in schools where staff were promoting schemes tailored to local needs. The latter is the price to be paid for gaining the former. Cross-cultural issues form one area benefitting from the requirements of Section 1 of the Education Reform Act 1988 (see Chapter 1).

The technological design process is generally seen as being both a holistic operation, and also in structural terms, as a sequence of events in a problem-solving routine. In the field of imaginative thinking the children can, relatively harmlessly, push back against the absorbed boundaries which influence their classroom thinking, and this impinges directly on the theme of this book.

Within the framework, the consideration of business studies should clearly include rural technologies, agriculture and horticulture, struggling economies as well as affluent ones. There is plenty of opportunity here for an international awareness of developing economies, particularly in terms of typical project work facing up to the technological needs of other countries, but very great sensitivity is needed. The danger of patronizing approaches based on the assumption of the superiority of technologies in advanced industrial societies can be seen clearly, and this is at a very important formative stage of children's development. In the UK we have much to learn from technologies of self-sufficiency that do not depend on the consumption of non-renewable resources at an increasing, unsustainable and, in many ways, harmful rate.

The 'art-and-design' dimension of technology stands in an unusual position. Much of art-and-design education is not primarily of a technological nature. Much of fine art is 'pure' art; much of artistic design is not related to the specific problem-solving activity which characterizes technology in the National Curriculum. Yet the contribution of aesthetics to design, in the sense it is used in the National Curriculum, is so very important; it reflects so much of the individual's contribution: age, time, values . . . and culture. It rightly has a key place in the Attainment Targets and Programmes of Study.

Yet care is required. In many technologies we see the international standardization of design styles (so often imposed by the affluent nations on others).

The Attainment Targets are divided into two main capabilities. The use of this term is in itself significant. The 'education for capability' movement of the Royal Society of Arts (1984) has been pervasive in its influence on school technology (Price, 1991; Carter and Jordan, 1990). The first of these is 'design-and-technology capability'. We should be careful not to equate this to the school subject 'craft, design and technology' (CDT) with a diminished craft element, though sadly that is what it is in a small proportion of our schools. Generally nowadays, however, teachers of the subject have wider vision.

The design-and-technology capability has just four Attainment Targets. The comparison with the earlier science Attainment Targets is striking. The original science AT1 emphasized the process of science, which was to permeate all the remaining Attainment Targets and AT17 concerns the nature of science. The remaining fifteen have targets as content elements to be covered, albeit in a well defined and new specification of context. That design-and-technology capability should have four process specifications provides indication of the differences of approach of the members of the science and technology working parties. It changes very substantially the nature of the cross-cultural challenges presented by the two subjects. In the revision of the science Attainment Targets to reduce the number, the principle has not changed (see Chapter 7).

This is no criticism of the approach of the science National Curriculum developers. Science educators have done much to promote the model of technology education which is now beginning to emerge. As far back as 1983 the Association for Science Education (ASE) was pressing publicly for a clearer view of where we should be going in school technology and of its relationship with science (ASE, 1973). Woolnough in the ASE publication *Technological Education and Science in Schools* reinforces the need for a 'capability' approach.

> In addition to being knowledgeable about different technologies and aware of their implications for society, all pupils should be encouraged to develop their own capability in tackling a technological ... problem ... Such a capability would tackle realistic practical problems, require consideration from a variety of perspectives ... [and] incorporate the ... inherent humanity of trial and error ... (Woolnough, 1984)

- Technology AT1 (identifying needs and opportunities) requires that: Pupils should be able to identify and state clearly needs and opportunities for design and technological activities through investigation of the context of home, school, recreation, community, business and industry. (DES, 1990, p. 3)

There is an inherent requirement in AT1 that pupils will analyse situations, will seek out and develop understanding of the views of others, especially those which differ from their own, will research thoroughly and so on. There is real danger of the development of restricted or caricatured cultural views, but with opportunity for the development of intercultural understandings at a practical level. It needs little imagination to see the opportunities whereby pupils might work together and seek to understand the contribution of each other's views, consulting where appropriate with members of the wider community. The opportunity is there if only it will be grasped clearly. The damage, not least to racial understanding, of handling this issue badly will be severe. Awareness of this issue is strongly underlined in an important collection of papers entitled *Learning Technology in the European Communities* (Cerri and Whiting, 1992). All teachers of technology would be well advised to read it.

- Technology AT2 is 'generating a design'. This requires that:
  Pupils should be able to generate a design specification, explore ideas to produce a design proposal and develop it into a realistic, appropriate and achievable design. (DES, 1990, p. 7)
- Technology AT3 is 'planning and making':
  Pupils should be able to make artefacts, systems and environments, preparing and working to a plan and identifying, managing and using appropriate resources, including knowledge and processes. (DES, 1990, p. 11)

These present great opportunity. Design-and-technology capability requires not only the context of production of artefacts and systems, the traditional areas of design and technology, but also of environments. Note the plural. This is not just a study of the international global environment (though such a study would be entirely appropriate in National-Curriculum technology). The pupils are required to study and design environments on a smaller scale. The aesthetic dimension is important here, as are ergonomics, anthropometrics and safety. The environments might involve domestic, school, industrial or public situations. Insofar as technology involves the adaptation of environment to meet a perceived need of those performing the intervention in the existing environment, or on behalf of a request for intervention , so the outcomes will depend on the perceptions of what would be a desirable world to live in. *This meets cultural values head on.* There is a difference between a classroom exercise seen in isolation for the development of pupils' individual skills and the provision of activity which requires the pupils to think in terms which must be communal.

Sensitivities to the needs of others and their cultural values will emerge. These are not primarily ethnic in origin, though ethnicity and race will contribute to the establishment of appropriate value structures. The intra-ethnic variation in this respect might well be greater than the interethnic variation. This same sensitivity applies in the design of artefacts and systems.

- The final Attainment Target (AT4) in design-and-technology capability is evaluating.

  Pupils should be able to develop, communicate and act upon an evaluation of the processes, products and effects of their design and technological activities and of those of others, including those from other times and cultures. (DES, 1990, p. 15)

Here is the cultural aspect, right at the fore of the specification of an Attainment Target, and in a form which leaves no doubt as to need to implement an understanding of the effect of cultures on the 'processes, products and effects' of technology. It is central to the evaluation aspect of National-Curriculum technology and teachers omitting this are in breach of the requirements of the Act.

The simplicity of specification of information-technology capability is appealing.

> Pupils should be able to use information technology to communicate and handle information; design, develop, explore and evaluate models of real and imaginary situations; measure and control physical variables and movement. They should be able to make informed judgements about the application and importance of information technology, and its effects on the quality of life. (DES, 1990, p. 45)

There is only one Attainment Target (AT5) for information-technology capability. This leans towards 'high' technology, with the computer dominant. The National Curriculum may be open to some criticism for this. Certainly the pupils will respond well to an approach using computers as the main equipment and equally certain this is an emphasis that many future employers would wish to see. But information technology is not a new technology. In its uncomputerized form it has been with us many years, and in parts of the world continues to be so. Some of the non-microelectronic solutions are elegant in simplicity of design. High technology has strong cultural links and bias. It is very much a product of the technologically developed world, with major implications for redistribution of the prospects of employment.

For the National Curriculum to bring together craft, design and technology (CDT) with the home-economics subject area was no bad thing. Indeed, in very many schools close curriculum cooperation was already emerging, driven by equal-opportunities legislation requiring boys and girls to receive equality of opportunity in all subjects. Generally this was welcomed, and pupils were given a broad base of opportunity, in theory at least.

In many single-sex comprehensive schools, with limited provision of one of CDT or home economics, no merging of departments could take place. Either a new subject area had to be developed or else that area had to be omitted from the subject of technology. This has clearly created a difference of educational opportunity for pupils whose parents or guardians have elected (frequently on cultural or religious grounds) for a single-sex education system. That is not to say all parents and guardians would regard the omission as a disadvantage. For some parents it has become desirable to accentuate traditional differences between boys' and girls' technological subjects on the basis of differing career opportunities and family structures. Separate schools for Muslim girls is an important example. Separate schools for Muslim pupils in general is another with profound implications for the curriculum. Then again, development of specific facilities for delivery of National-Curriculum technology may not necessarily follow the traditional pattern of facilities which grew out of craft subjects. Indeed, by rethinking the environment in which these skills are taught, it may be possible to enhance the opportunities of the girls beyond those available in mixed schools (Price, 1986).

Responses

One important issue is whether there is explicit and implicit racism in National-Curriculum technology. The following example is pertinent to both top-junior and secondary-school work in technology. Zaman is at Key Stage 2. His class will be following three main topics during the year: 'Sound', 'Machines' and 'Other Times'.

> During the Autumn term the class investigates sounds and how musical instruments work. Pupils learn that an orchestra is a system which uses instruments playing different notes to produce music. A group visits the school to perform West Indian music and dance, and this is used by Zaman's teacher to encourage children to find out about the music of other countries. Zaman is encouraged to find out about the music of Arabia, his home area. In a group of six pupils, Zaman plans and organises a drama with accompanying music . . . Zaman uses the computer to make a pamphlet about their play. (National Curriculum Council, 1990a)

The above is taken from the non-statutory guidance for National-Curriculum technology. Is this technology? Is it a token attempt to plant an idea of internationalism, or of multiculturalism, or antiracism in the scheme of things?

The National Union of Teachers established an Advisory Committee for Equal Opportunities (Race) in 1991. It produced a pamphlet containing suggestions whereby NC subjects and cross-curricular elements could provide a multiracial and antiracist curriculum (NUT, 1992). In relation to technology, the study of human activities common to all societies, such as food production and storage, can open up many possibilities. Exploring differing technological solutions to common human needs is a promising avenue. The 'high-technology' solution is not always appropriate. The resources, material conditions, cultural values and the priorities of a community, can lead to differing solutions to the same type of technological challenge.

The Curriculum Development Centre of the Commonwealth Institute has recently produced a most helpful resource pack entitled 'Design and Technology from an Islamic Perspective'. It bridges the primary and secondary stages of the National Curriculum (Commonwealth Institute, 1992). An awareness of Muslim art and design is facilitated by the provision in the teacher's section of a summary of the philosophical underpinnings of Muslim design. The emphasis on 'complementing nature rather than conquering it' is an important theme. Another is the relationships between 'craftsmanship, unity, integration and a respect for nature'. It has been pointed out that the 'British arts and crafts' movement shared many of these philosophical beliefs (Marland, 1992). The latter was but a (relatively) recent manifestation of a longstanding quest engaged in various ways by all cultures. The different 'solutions' and 're-solutions' that they have reached underline the challenges and responses involved in technology and design.

The material provided for pupils in the pack is excellent. It starts with patterns emphasizing the continuing quest for unity with God. Illustrations of Islamic designs in carvings, murals, tiles and carpets are considered bearing on this search for unity. The art of handwriting, interest in which has recently been undergoing a revival here, is also included. In terms of architecture, the relationships between available materials, climate, the environment, and the search for balance and harmony are well illustrated and explored. One need only consider the magnificent church architecture of other religions and cultures both in the past and present, to appreciate that religion has stimulated and inspired excellent architecture in many countries, including our own. Fortunately, it continues so to do. Victorian Gothic is but one example of the unity between religious vision and design (Marland, 1992).

It is easy to be negatively critical, but whatever the limitations of the examples (and it could be suggested that they are quite severe) at least an attempt has been made to propose what may well be a substantial step of new thinking for some school technology teachers. It serves the purpose of suggesting that technology is no longer a very limited subject, confined to craft workshops, cookery rooms or computer suites. It alerts the teachers to opportunities which will enhance their classroom activities.

With older children and within the 'business-studies' dimension the teacher can consider the costing of projects, the alternative methods of payment, and use value analysis to optimize design. But teachers must be aware that not all the children within the class will have the same home framework of values. That is not referring to alternative economic models, important as they are in the present, rapidly changing world economic situation. But, to take one example, the concept of borrowing money (such as for a house mortgage) may have unacceptable moral connotations in the home and religious culture of some pupils. The teacher can do three things here. One is to ignore the differences and assume that the problem will not intrude into the teaching; the second is to use the opportunity for the pupils holding the 'minority' view to better understand the 'majority' view; the third is to allow the alternatives to become open information for discussion and the widening of understandings of the various pupils. The last is not necessarily the obvious answer: pupils' age, experience, ability and familiarity with cultural issues will guide the teacher in such a professional decision.

Within the home-economics dimension many examples are obvious. The preparation of food for export has been a clear problem for parts of the British food industry for some years, mainly due to the cultural misunderstandings involved. Here is an opportunity to meet a particular need identified by the National Curriculum. The multicultural class can provide a ready-made framework for a study of food, for discussion and awareness of export activities that could only be provided with considerable difficulty by other means. Issues related to the preparation of food in this country for use in the school-meals system provide similar opportunities.

As word processing develops as a major element of information technology, schools will be able to use some of the foreign-language packages being developed. Some word processors for Arabic and Asian languages are less simple to use than their European counterparts but well illustrate alternative methods of handling information.

The main plea, however, must be that we take advantage of the opportunities presented by the National Curriculum in technology. The requirements for all pupils in our schools to become involved in active technology is excellent. No longer can home economics, craft, engineering, business studies, micro-electronics, or information technology be separated from the wider view of their contexts. This is good news for intercultural understandings; it is good news for antiracism; and it is good news for children who take part in learning to understand, enjoy and celebrate the cultural diversity of humankind. But it can only move from the printed page to a classroom reality through the ability of the teaching force to implement it. The teachers of technology in the UK have worked hard over recent years to implement changes in the nature of their subjects. They are continuing to do so. Schools need very much more research (of the right type) to optimize teaching strategies and make best use of children's time in a somewhat overloaded curriculum. Teachers are asking for guidance, and they should receive it. Change will not be rapid, though the cross-cultural opportunities of technology are now greater than in most subjects.

We may go further than the simpler approaches of the technology National Curriculum and start asking important questions about children's thinking in technology and culture and the relationship between them. In his book *Mindstorms: Children, Computers and Powerful Ideas* Seymour Papert wrote of his work in developing a new computer language for children. He comments:

And in teaching the computer how to think, children embark on an exploration of how they themselves think. The experience can be heady: thinking about thinking turns the child into an epistemologist, an experience not ever shared by most adults. (Papert, 1980, p. 19)

Technology is about designing, analysing, creating and asking questions. It might help the child start to ponder his or her own values as well as lead to important steps in cultural understanding. The response meanwhile is fairly clear: Let us view the opportunistic taking of any local situation in the delivery of National-Curriculum technology as a source of cultural wealth. In the mutual benefit the subject of technology for all pupils will gain greatly from the cross-cultural elements, perhaps even more than cross-cultural understandings will gain from technology.

References

ASSOCIATION FOR SCIENCE EDUCATION (1973) 'An Association View of School Science and Technology', *Education in Science*, 55, November.

BLACK, P. and HARRISON, G. (1985) *In Place of Confusion*, London, Nuffield-Chelsea Curriculum Trust.

CARTER, G. and JORDAN, T.A. (1990) *Student Centred Learning in Engineering*, Salford, University of Salford Department of Electronic and Electrical Engineering.

CERRI, S.A. and WHITING, J. (1992) *Learning Technology in the European Communities*, Proceedings of the DELTA Conference on Research and Development, The Hague — Oct 1990. Kluwer Academic Publishers.

COMMONWEALTH INSTITUTE (1992) *Design and Technology — the Islamic Perspective*, London, Commonwealth Institute.

DEPARTMENT OF EDUCATION and SCIENCE (1990) Circular 3/90, *National Curriculum: Section 4 Order — Technology: Design and Technology and Information Technology*.

DEPARTMENT OF EDUCATION AND SCIENCE AND THE WELSH OFFICE (1989) *Science in the National Curriculum*, London, HMSO.

DEPARTMENT OF EDUCATION AND SCIENCE AND THE WELSH OFFICE (1990) *Technology in the National Curriculum*, London, HMSO.

MARLAND, M. (1992) 'A planetary culture', *Education Guardian*, 12 May.

NASH, M., ALLSOP, R.T. and WOOLNOUGH, B.E. (1984) *The Factors Affecting the Uptake of Technology in Schools*, Oxford, Oxford University Department of Educational Studies.

NATIONAL CURRICULUM COUNCIL (1990a) *Technology: Non-Statutory Guidance* (Design and Technology Capability), York, National Curriculum Council.

NATIONAL CURRICULUM COUNCIL (1990b) *Technology: Non-Statutory Guidance* (Information Technology Capability), York, National Curriculum Council.

NATIONAL UNION OF TEACHERS (1992) *Anti-racist Curriculum Guidelines*, London, NUT.

PAPERT, S. (1980) *Mindstorms: Children, Computers and Powerful Ideas*, Brighton, The Harvester Press.

PRICE, G.W. (1986) 'The Introduction of School Technology to a Girls' School: A Development Case Study', in HEYWOOD, J. and MATTHEWS, P. (Eds) *Technology,*

Society and the School Curriculum: Theory and Practice in Europe, Manchester, Roundthorn Publishing Ltd.

PRICE, G.W. (1991) 'Enhancement Equals Education for Capability Equals Experiential Learning', *International Journal of Technology and Design Education*, 1, 3.

PRICE, G.W. and REID, D.J. (1990) 'A Preliminary Study into the Development of Craftsmanship Skills in Children', *International, Journal of Technology and Design Education*, 1, 1 Spring.

ROYAL SOCIETY OF ARTS (Occasional Papers commencing 1984) *Education for Capability*.

VERMA, G.K. and ENTZINGER, H. (1992) 'Transferring Knowledge in a Cross-Cultural Perspective', in CERRI, S.A. and WHITING, J. *Learning Technology in the European Communities*, The Hague, Kluwer Academic Publishers.

WOOLNOUGH, B. (1984) *Technological Education and Science in Schools*, Hatfield, Association for Science Education.

Chapter 9

History: Policy Issues

Peter Figueroa

Context

The National Curriculum statutory order for history in England sets out the knowledge and understanding, the matters and historical content, the skills and processes that are required (Department of Education and Science, 1991). Three Attainment Targets, each with its several Statements of Attainment across ten levels of attainment, are laid out. These specify 'the knowledge, skills and understanding' which pupils are expected to attain to (DES, 1991, p. 1). The three Attainment Targets are:

- knowledge and understanding of history;
- interpretations of history; and
- the use of historical sources.

Furthermore, detailed Programmes of Study specifying the matters, skills and processes which are required to be taught to pupils are spelt out. These Programmes of Study 'should enable pupils to develop knowledge and understanding of British, European and world history'. Besides, pupils should throughout have opportunities to:

- explore links between history and other subjects; develop information technology capability; and
- develop knowledge, understanding and skills related to cross-curricular themes (DES, 1991, p. 11).

At Key Stage 1 (Years 1 and 2) the Programme of Study consists of one study unit geared to attainment at levels 1–3. This study unit should give pupils opportunities 'to develop an awareness of the past through stories from different periods and cultures' (DES, 1991, p. 13).

At Key Stage 2 (Years 3–6) the Programme of Study consists of nine study units, of which four are prescribed, a further one or two must be chosen from a pre-specified list of two units, and the remaining three or four must conform to a tight set of requirements. In this Programme of Study, which is geared to attainment at levels 2–5, pupils should:

> be taught about . . . Britain's past, from Roman to modern times . . . investigate local history . . . be taught about ancient civilisations and the history of other parts of the world . . . develop a sense of chronology and . . . learn about changes in everyday life over long periods of time. (DES, 1991, p. 15)

At Key Stage 3 (Years 7, 8 and 9) the Programme of Study consists of eight study units, of which five — focused primarily on Britain — are prescribed, while the remaining three on British, European and non-European history must conform to a specific set of requirements. In this Programme of Study, which is geared to attainment at levels 3–7, pupils should:

> be taught to understand how developments from the early Middle Ages to the era of the Second World War helped shape . . . modern Britain . . . study developments in Europe and the non-European world . . . understand how the histories of different countries are linked . . . be taught about ancient Rome and its legacy to Britain, Europe and the world. (DES, 1991, p. 33)

At Key Stage 4 (Years 10 and 11) one of two alternatives is prescribed. Under 'Model 1' the Programme of Study consists of one core-study unit on Britain, Europe and the world in the twentieth century, 'focusing' on: the development of British democracy; international conflict and cooperation from about 1945; and economic, social and cultural change in Britain, Europe and the world. 'Model 2' consists of this core-study unit plus two supplementary study units, which must also conform to a quite rigid set of requirements. The Programme of Study at Key Stage 4 — which we are expressly told is 'not a course in current affairs . . . [and] should focus on events from the turn of the century to about twenty years before the present day' (DES, 1991, p. 49) — is geared to attainment at levels 4–10. In it pupils should:

> understand how the world . . . has been shaped by developments in twentieth-century history . . . consolidate their understanding of earlier periods of history . . . prepare themselves for citizenship, work and leisure. (DES, 1991, p. 49)

Across all of the key stages pupils should: come to grips with the study of change; 'learn about the past from a range of historical sources' (DES, 1991, p. 13, 16, 34, and 49); ask questions about the past; and have opportunities to communicate their knowledge orally, visually and in writing. Chronology is specifically mentioned in Key Stages 2, 3 and 4. Also, from Key Stage 2 there is specific mention that pupils should 'be taught the concepts and terms necessary to understand the periods and topics in the core study units' (DES, 1991. p. 17). Furthermore, from Key Stage 2 on, political, economic, technological, scientific, social, religious, cultural and aesthetic perspectives should be employed and pupils should be taught about 'the social, cultural, religious and ethnic diversity of the societies studied and the experiences of men and women in these societies' (DES, 1991, pp. 16, 34, and 49). With increasing sophistication they should also investigate historical topics on their own, asking questions about how to find out about the past, choosing sources, and collecting, recording, selecting and organizing historical information.

Challenges

Two sets of interrelated issues will be touched on: issues to do with the nature of history; and issues to do with history within the context of multicultural and antiracist education. Both of these are relevant in developing a rationale for the history curriculum, not only in the sense of a document on paper, but equally in terms of the actual curriculum in operation.

The history non-statutory guidance states that history can mean both 'the past, and the study of the past' (National Curriculum Council, 1991, p. B1). In the first sense history consists of the events, developments, realities, beliefs and values which have preceded our era, and without an understanding of which it is impossible to understand our era in any depth. In the second sense there are at least four aspects to history. The first is knowing and understanding these events, developments, realities, beliefs and values — including their origins, 'causes', patterns, interrelations, 'unfolding', discontinuities and consequences. The second is knowing and understanding how to study the past and what constitutes good grounds for claims to historical knowledge and understanding. The third is the actual practice along such lines; and, closely related to this, the fourth is communicating appropriately the knowledge and understanding which is thereby accomplished. This would include indicating a reflective awareness of limitations.

Three basic aims of school history must, therefore, be:

- to introduce pupils to a knowledge and understanding of the past;
- to introduce them to a critical and reflective knowledge and understanding of what is involved in finding out about, and in interpreting and understanding, the past; and
- to encourage them to a disposition to behave and communicate accordingly, and to give them appropriate opportunities to do so. (Lee, 1991, p. 51)

Knowledge and understanding of the past, and of what is involved in studying it, are interdependent. Furthermore, the issues of 'What knowledge?' and 'From what point of view?' need to be addressed. Closely related to this, one needs to recognize that the past can be viewed from many different perspectives, and that studying the past involves making selections and interpreting (Atkinson, 1978).

Unfortunately, the non-statutory guidance, which is written in a staccato, authoritative style with little of its own reasoning or grounds spelled out (Slater, 1991, p. 15), after identifying the two meanings of history mentioned above, simply asserts that:

There are two main aims of school history:

- to help pupils develop a sense of identity through learning about the development of Britain, Europe and the world; [and]
- to introduce pupils to what is involved in understanding and interpreting the past. (NCC, 1991, p. B1)

Developing a sense of identity is important, and studying history can contribute to this; but an important point here is that in one reading of 'developing a sense of identity' there is a ring of indoctrination. What is intended here? Is it a *British* sense of identity? Or just *a* sense of identity, different for each individual pupil? Identity requires differentiation. Is it a main aim of school history to help black pupils develop a sense of a black British identity, or to help females develop a sense of being female? Would these be examples of what is intended?

In fact there seems implicitly to be a bias towards privileging a narrow British identity. For instance, the final report of the history working group states that, 'an ethnically diverse population strengthens rather than weakens the argument for including a substantial element of British history [the meaning of which is taken as self-evident] within the school curriculum' (DES, 1990, p. 184). This can be read as having an assimilationist ring to it. Furthermore, there tends to be a narrowly British emphasis in the contents of the statutorily prescribed study units. But any privileging of a narrow British identity is problematic for minority ethnic groups, and indeed for the 'majority' population, rather than facilitating and healthy. It is predicated on the assumption that there is and ought to be one homogeneous British identity. This is antithetic to a complex, 'post-modern' society like Britain today, which is characterized by social and cultural diversity. What is needed is not a mechanical form of solidarity, but an organic one, in which the different and differentiated groups and segments of society function interdependently and constructively in an open rather than a closed system.

Another point relates especially to one of the secondary 'purposes' identified in the non-statutory guidance: 'to understand the present in the light of the past' (NCC, 1991, p. B1). Which present and which past? Is there an unspoken assumption here that there is agreement about these? Is it some 'official' view of how things were and are, and of the important issues? This purpose could be meant in a completely open and problematic way; but is that how it is likely to be taken? Knowledge of the present and knowledge of the past, value assumptions about the one and value assumptions about the other, are closely interrelated. The challenging nature of such issues needs to be expressly addressed. But does the non-statutory guidance encourage such an approach? Another example relates to the third of the three 'strands' which the non-statutory guidance identifies in AT1: 'knowing about and under-standing key features of past situations' (NCC, 1991, p. B3). Does this assume that there is consensus about the 'key features'? Or is this again intended in an open and problematic way? The latter interpretation is possible in view of the account given of AT2, which is said, for instance, to have the aim of developing an understanding that 'there is more than one way of viewing the past', and that 'accounts of the past differ for many reasons' (NCC, 1991, p. B6).

Under Programmes of Study, in speaking about 'historical content', the non-statutory guidance introduces the concept of 'the British Isles'. This is not a salient concept in the statutory order. Moreover, the non-statutory guidance seems to identify 'British history' with 'the history of the British Isles'. However, the latter is more easily understood in a narrow sense than the former, that is as referring essentially to history *within* the British Isles. The non-statutory guidance gives as examples that pupils might 'investigate Irish emigration to the British colonies or assess the contribution of the Welsh coal industry to the British economy in Victorian times' (NCC, 1991, p. B10). But what of (virtually forced) emigration from the Raj to the Caribbean, or of Caribbean plantation society and its contribution to the British economy in Stuart or Victorian times?

A central part of British history for the understanding of Britain and the world today, and a central part of British history that is interesting as a study in itself and which illustrates and exemplifies the problematic nature of history and of its methodology, is the British Empire. Yet the British Empire is highlighted only as part of core-study units 2 and 3 at Key Stage 2 and as part of core-study unit 4 at Key Stage 3. Also, the 'reasons for the break-up of the overseas empires of European countries' is only one of many subtopics in the rather wide-ranging core-study unit at Key Stage 4 (DES, 1991, p. 51). A brief mention is also made of 'colonies and empires' as part of one of six themes from which at least one, and not more than two, of the supplement-ary study units at Key Stage 2 must be chosen (NCC, 1991, p. F1). The British Empire features as the focus of an entire study unit only as one poss-ible example out of many competing alternatives for the three supplementary units at Key Stage 3 (DES, 1991, p. 47).

The Caribbean, which was of immense economic and strategic import-ance in British history, and over which wars were fought with other European powers, is virtually absent from National Curriculum history. There seem to be only three explicit references to the Caribbean in the entire National Curriculum history programme. Two of these are subthemes in a unit entitled 'Black peoples of the Americas: 16th to early 20th centuries', which is the last of eighteen examples of possible supplementary study units at Key Stage 3. These two references are as follows: 'slave economies in the Caribbean and the USA', and 'the development of black communities in the Caribbean' (NCC, 1991, p. F36). The third reference is to Cuba from a super-power's perspective. It features within one of many topics from which one of the two supplementary study units are to be chosen at Key Stage 4 for those pupils doing the full course. This topic reads: 'Latin America 1910 to 1962 (from the Mexican Revolution to the Cuba Crisis)' (DES, 1991, p. 53). Two of the other topics that this has to be chosen against are the Indian subcontinent and Africa south of the Sahara.

The Indian subcontinent, the former 'jewel in the crown', really only features as one of many possible examples of a supplementary unit at Key Stage 3 (DES, 1991, p. 48), and as one of eight topics from which one of two possible supplementary units at Key Stage 4 is to be chosen for pupils doing the full course (DES, 1991, p. 53). One of the other eight topics that India stands against is 'Africa south of the Sahara 1900 to 1963'. Apart from this mention of Africa, the only other notable references to that great continent are to 'Benin' as one of several possible options for a supplementary study unit at Key Stage 2 (NCC, 1991, p. F16), and to 'people . . . in . . . Africa', again as one of several possible topics for a supplementary study unit at Key Stage 3 on a 'non-European society' (DES, 1991, p. 48). The possible examples that are given for this supplementary study unit in Key Stage 3 are: 'black peoples of the Americas, Indigenous peoples of North America, Peru, India, Imperial China and Islamic civilisations' (DES, 1991, p. 48). This reference to Islam and that in another possible option, 'the crusades' (NCC, 1991, p. F23), for one of the other supplementary study units at Key Stage 3 provide the only explicit references to Islam in National Curriculum history.

Moreover, virtually no mention is made of the presence and contribution of black people in Britain since Roman times, although, as Walvin says, by the nineteenth century a substantial black population 'permeated most ranks of society, through the length and breadth of the country' (Walvin, 1973, p. 72; Fryer, 1984; Ethnic Minorities Unit, GLC, 1986). The closest one gets is in core-study unit 4 at Key Stage 2 (Britain since 1930), where, among several other themes, 'immigration and emigration' are mentioned (DES, 1991, p. 25), and in the supplementary study unit on local history at Key Stage 2, in relation to which the non-statutory guidance states, among many other things, that pupils could learn about population movements brought about by empire or twentieth-century immigration (NCC, 1991, p, F7). 'Migration' (covering the period from 'at least 1500' up to the 'present' day) is also given as just one of many examples of a possible theme for one of the supplementary study units for the full course at Key Stage 4.

It is remarkable, furthermore, that the statutory order only just about manages to mention cross-curricular 'themes', but nowhere refers to the wider concept of cross-curricular 'elements', and avoids cross-curricular 'dimensions' (see Volume 2). Yet it is under the concept of cross-curricular 'dimension' that the National Curriculum Council tidied away matters to do with equal opportunities and multiculturalism, hardly mentioning antiracism at all (NCC, 1990, pp. 2–3). This concept of 'dimension' is in fact itself inadequate, since it gives little attention to the important knowledge content and skills central to these concerns.

The non-statutory guidance does actually refer to cross-curricular elements, and includes a brief section on 'equal opportunities and multi-cultural education'. It states that:

> National Curriculum history requires pupils to be taught about the cultural and ethnic diversity of past societies . . . Through history pupils acquire understanding and respect for other cultures and values. They should develop . . . the quality of open-mindedness which questions assumptions and demands evidence for points of view. (NCC, 1991, p. C18)

The non-statutory guidance also suggests that: 'pupils might study how women were portrayed in late nineteenth-century literature and art . . . or explore why textbooks contain few references to the role of black troops in World War I — not to mention World War II (NCC, 1991, p. C18)? Furthermore, the non-statutory guidance states that:

> As pupils' ability to understand interpretations of history develops, they will be able to explore conflicting viewpoints. This will help them identify and thus challenge racial or other forms of prejudice and stereotyping. (NCC, 1991, p. C19)

The non-statutory guidance likewise says that through 'the skilful handling of sensitive issues, teachers of history can help pupils develop tolerance and mutual understanding', and that children 'should learn that amicable disagreement is an acceptable outcome' (NCC, 1991, p. C26).

Unfortunately, however, there is a danger of the bland assumption that information and the study of history will automatically engender respect for diversity. Similarly, although being able to identify racism is a precondition to combating it, the challenging of it does not follow automatically from its identification. Moreover, the concept of racial prejudice and stereotyping is wholly inadequate (NCC, 1991, p. C19). 'Race' is a social construction and the term has no scientific validity (Hiernaux, 1965; Figueroa, 1991). More fundamentally, racism is not just a matter of prejudice and stereotyping, nor of ignorance, but of taken-for-granted images, beliefs and values embedded in the group culture, of discrimination and certain other forms of inter-personal behaviour, of certain largely subterranean institutional arrangements and procedures, and of structures of inequality across the society (Figueroa, 1991).

Needless to say, the terms 'racism' and 'antiracism' merit no mention at all either in the statutory order or in the non-statutory guidance. Only the problematic term 'racial' is used occasionally. For instance, in the example of a possible supplementary study unit on the British Empire at Key Stage 3, it is indicated that pupils could learn about 'racial views and attitudes', although this should perhaps be read as in the empire generally rather than in Britain specifically (NCC, 1991, p. 21). Without being specific the non-statutory guidance also mentions, under cross-curricular skills and themes, that in history pupils study 'the development of British democracy and of a multicultural and pluralist society' (NCC, 1991, p. C12). This reference, however, might give the impression of a non-controversial development in the society.

In brief, themes such as black British history, immigration, the Caribbean, the Indian subcontinent, Islam, and even the British Empire, receive relatively little attention in National Curriculum history. Similarly, multiculturalism and especially antiracism tend to be marginal and inadequately conceptualized. Yet, the present, of which history is supposed to contribute to an understanding, is a present that is largely a legacy of empire (an empire that was largely shot through with racist assumptions); a present of a multicultural post-war Britain in which Caribbean, and Indian-heritage people, immigration and Islam, are seen as major problems; and a present in which the experience of racism by minority ethnic groups seems to be pervasive (DES, 1985, pp. 234–5 and p. 761).

Of course, history, and not least school history, must be selective. But on what criteria is the selection carried out and within what, often tacit, frames of reference? Who does the selecting, for whom and to what effect, if not purpose? As Slater (1991, p. 12) points out, of the ten full-time members of the history working group, only three were women, and all were white. Have equity and open-mindedness been seriously considered? Have the multicultural nature of British society and the multiethnic nature of the world been genuinely acknowledged and respected? Has the need in history for polymorphism and sophistication been fully taken on board? The discussion developed, for instance, by Atkinson (1978, pp. 95–187) about historical explanation and causation implies, even apart from the different ways in which different groups might view the same event, that any event can be considered to be a function of many different factors: intentional, rational, social, material, chance and others.

On account of the problematic nature of historical evidence and the unavoidable need for interpretation, the intrinsic criteria of history include such things as: open-mindedness, a questioning approach, the need to provide evidence and to submit it to public criteria of acceptability (DES, 1990, p. 11; NCC, 1991, p. C18). Thus criteria for the history curriculum must include both pluralism and rationality. These criteria tie in with that of respect for other cultural and historical points of view, and with that of justice for all and of equity. Thus the history curriculum must be accessible to all. It must also take on board the experience and history of all sectors of the society, and it must address narrow-mindedness and bigotry.

At the least one alternative approach to the present National-Curriculum history would have been a less rigid and prescriptive framework which gave more cognizance to pluralism, diversity, openness, polymorphism and multiple causality. The historian necessarily stands within a certain contextual web, and his or her perceptions and interpretations are inevitably influenced by that context. They are therefore problematical and must be brought into question. Furthermore, the historical event or person being studied was also located in a complicated context, and would have been open to varying interpretations by different observers and actors at the time. That event or person may likewise not be taken at face value, but must be subject to extensive questioning. Moreover, the relationship between the historian's context and that past context is problematical. They may be closely related historically and culturally, in which case they may share common biases, or they may be quite unrelated. In either case, they may have substantial features in common, or they may not. Hence the relationship of the historian to the event or person under investigation is itself complex, and must not be taken for granted.

The challenge, then, relates to questions such as the following: to what extent does the present National Curriculum history measure up to the criteria identified above? Insofar as it does not, how could that be changed? What support for multicultural and antiracist education can be found within the Education Reform Act, the statutory order and the non-statutory guidance? Even where such support is not manifest, to what extent can the existing requirements of the statutory order be legitimately put into practice in such a way as to meet the requirements of history in a multicultural and antiracist context?

Questions thus arise about:

- incorporating the cross-curricular elements — especially the 'dimensions' of multiculturalism and of equal opportunities, the personal, social and communication skills, and the theme of citizenship — into school history;
- approaching and presenting (even narrowly British) history in ways which would make it accessible to all pupils;
- promoting basic values of a democracy such as: respect, equality, justice and fairness, liberty, autonomy, pluralism, solidarity and antiracism;
- promoting basic democratic procedures permitting all individuals and sectors to participate genuinely in decision-making and in the determination of the society's destiny, and of their own;
- exploring and combating racism and antidemocratic tendencies;
- promoting a deepened understanding of, and providing accurate information about, British society in its diversity, in its strengths and weaknesses, in its positive and negative features: and

- avoiding cultural, linguistic, racist, ethnicist, nationalistic and related forms of bias in the curriculum, the teaching, the books and other teaching materials, and in assessment, allocation and other procedures — as well as in school-wide and more general education policies and practices, such as those relating to staffing.

Additional related questions arise, for instance, about: identity; plural British identities; multiple identities; group identity and nationalism; the history of black people in Britain; the normalcy of migration; the riches of cultural contact through the ages; the crucial importance of empire in British history; Britain in Europe and the world; problems of interpretation and of bias, in particular cultural and racist bias, in history.

Responses

It is not possible to develop a response to all of these questions here. However, the general approach must be to make history accessible to all, to avoid bias, and to exploit to the maximum all hints at multiculturalism, antiracism and equal opportunities, all ambiguities, and all possible openings, in the Education Reform Act, in the statutory order and in the non-statutory guidance. This includes the references to world history, cultural diversity, other countries, equal opportunities, and multicultural education. Context, content, historical method, pedagogy, and assessment, as well as wider issues, such as those of overall school policy and staffing, must be addressed.

Teachers must avoid as far as possible what many of them seem to think is being foisted upon them: a mechanistic implementation of a predetermined curriculum. National Curriculum history is, indeed, more prescriptive than the National Curriculum Council suggests. Nevertheless, it does provide some options, and is open to interpretation. The theme of empire, for instance, offers the possibility of pursuing a critical and rich study of history with a world-wide orientation. It provides, for example, the opportunity of looking, from their point of view, at the history of any of those countries which were brought under the sway of the British Empire, and of doing this for the periods both before and after the impact of empire. It is relevant also to a broad, balanced and in-depth understanding of the post-war world, and Britain's place in it.

At Key Stage 3, both 'The making of the United Kingdom: Crowns, Parliaments and peoples 1500–1750' and 'Expansion, trade and industry Britain 1750–1900' provide many opportunities for multicultural historical discussions. Pupils are required to identify different ways in which past events are construed and interpreted. The ways in which various media such as films, pictures and written accounts transmit perceptions concerning, for example, North American Indians in the nineteenth century, make the point. The book 'Roots', and subsequent film presented a viewpoint often neglected in the UK, despite the endeavours of Wilberforce. It is important that the perspectives of indigenous peoples in other parts of the world towards European exploration and exploitation of resources and labour, be considered.

Key-Stage 4 pupils will be taught the concepts and terms required in an understanding of twentieth-century history. These concepts include liberalism, conservatism, totalitarianism, socialism, capitalism, materialism, welfare state, nationalism, imperialism, decolonization, conservation, equal opportunities and ecumenism. The study of such themes provides opportunities whereby pupils can develop awareness of how the histories of the UK, Europe and the world are linked.

At all Key Stages, teachers are advised to teach pupils about the social, cultural, religious and ethnic diversity of the societies studied and the experiences of men and women in these societies. A specific requirement at Key Stage 4 is teaching how cultural, ethnic and religious differences within and between societies have influenced relations between communities and nations. Whilst the history Programmes of Study keep referring to the British perspective, 'there is ample scope for widening horizons to include the rest of the world, and it would be a very narrow historian who did not take that view' (NUT, 1992).

Consider one example, taken from the work of Hix (1991), of how a National-Curriculum history study unit could have a specifically multicultural or antiracist orientation. Although this concerns a supplementary study unit based on local history, category B, for Key Stage 2, Hix's approach could, as she points out, also be adapted for Key Stage 3, supplementary study unit A. It is thoroughly worked-out and most interesting. To ensure depth of study Hix chooses the option of focusing on 'an aspect of the local community during a short period of time' (DES, 1991, p. 31). Her concern is to address the multicultural dimension (NCC, 1990, p. 2–3), which she takes as 'inclusive of both multicultural and antiracist perspectives' (Hix, 1991, p. 112), and she decides to focus on migration during 1850–1899 into and out of Petersfield and Sheet in the heart of the large shire county of Hampshire (Hix, 1991, p. 113). This may seem an unlikely location for addressing multicultural and antiracist issues, but in fact Hix's study suggests that these issues can fruitfully be addressed via local history in what may seem the most unlikely regions of the country, so pervasive are the phenomenon of migration and the impact of empire. Hix also specifically indicates how the three National Curriculum history Attainment Targets could be met within her model; and that pupils would have ample opportunities to use a variety of methods to communicate their findings (Hix, 1991, pp. 121–3).

First of all she carries out some valuable research into the history of Petersfield and Sheet, thus identifying and collecting together sources and materials useful to the teacher. These were drawn from the censuses for 1871 and 1881, from newspaper evidence, from the papers of the Bonham-Carter family (who lived in the area), and from such environmental evidence as buildings and street names. Some of the concepts and terms (DES, 1991, p. 17) which Hix identifies as necessary for the understanding of the period and topic she has chosen, and which therefore should be introduced to the pupils and explained or revisited are: empire, migration, immigration, emigration, culture, race, racism, ethnic and minority. She also takes care to cover, as required, political, economic, technological and scientific, social, religious, cultural and aesthetic perspectives.

She suggests that pupils could start 'by asking questions about the population of Petersfield and Sheet between 1850 and 1899' (Hix, 1991, p. 115), and provides sample sheets of the 1871 and 1881 censuses for this purpose. Pupils should consider, for example, who left and who entered the community, what evidence there might be of such movement, and where the migrants lived. They could consider what political meetings took place, where and relating to what issues — which in fact included Irish home rule and matters concerning India, Greece and Africa. They could ask questions about the occupations of the in- and out-migrants, which covered a wide range (Hix, 1991, p. 118). They could identify religious activity associated with migrants, and be 'introduced to . . . Hinduism through letter evidence from India' (Hix, 1991, p. 119). Newspaper evidence would show, too, that 'the residents had enjoyed the music and songs of . . . Greece, Africa and possibly India' (Hix, 1991, p. 120). The pupils could furthermore discover 'how the fields of medicine and railway technology provided employment for migrants . . . throughout the British Empire', and that Florence Nightingale had connections with the Bonham-Carter family (Hix, 1991, p. 120).

As Hix shows, National Curriculum history, despite its prescriptiveness, does contain possibilities for open, non-ethnocentric and questioning teaching. However, to exploit such possibilities one has to adopt a creative and interpretative approach. Inevitably, this highlights the restrictiveness of many of the study units and the narrowness of what often seem to be the underlying ideological assumptions. Such assumptions must be brought to awareness and carefully examined, and any restrictiveness and especially any narrow conception of British identity and British history must be questioned.

References

ATKINSON, R.F. (1978) *Knowledge and Explanation in History: An Introduction to the Philosophy of History*, London, Macmillan Education.

DEPARTMENT OF EDUCATION AND SCIENCE (1985) *Education for All: The Report of the Committee of Inquiry into the Education of Children from Ethnic Minority Groups* (The Swann Report), London, HMSO.

DEPARTMENT OF EDUCATION AND SCIENCE (1990) *History for Ages 5 to 16: Proposals of the Secretary of State for Education and Science* (including National Curriculum History Working Group Final Report). London, HMSO.

DEPARTMENT OF EDUCATION AND SCIENCE (1991) *History in the National Curriculum (England)*, London, HMSO.

ETHNIC MINORITIES UNIT, GREATER LONDON COUNCIL (1986) *A History of the Black Presence in London*, London, GLC.

FIGUEROA P. (1991) *Education and the Social Construction of 'Race'*, London, Routledge.

FRYER, P. (1984) *Staying Power: The History of Black People in Britain*, London, Pluto Press.

HIERNAUX, J. (1965) 'Biological aspects of race', *International Social Science Journal*, 37, 1, pp. 71–161.

HIX, P.A.N. (1991) 'Local History in All White Areas: Multicultural and Anti-Racist History Teaching and Learning' Unpublished Master's dissertation, Southampton, University of Southampton.

LEE, P. (1991) 'Historical knowledge and the National Curriculum', in ALDRICH, R. (Ed) *History in the National Curriculum*, London, Kogan Page.

NATIONAL CURRICULUM COUNCIL (1990) *Curriculum Guidance Three: The Whole Curriculum*, York, National Curriculum Council.

NATIONAL CURRICULUM COUNCIL (1991) *History Non-Statutory Guidance*, York, National Curriculum Council.

NATIONAL UNION OF TEACHERS (1992) *Anti-racist Curriculum Guidelines*, London, NUT.

SLATER, J. (1991) 'History in the National Curriculum: the Final Report of the History Working Group', in ALDRICH, R. (Ed) *History in the National Curriculum*, London, Kogan page.

WALVIN, J. (1973) *Black and White: The Negro in English Society, 1555–1945*, London, Allen Lane.

Chapter 10

Music Education: Whose Music?
Whose Education?

Jill Scarfe

Context

The fundamental approach of the National Curriculum music working party to the principles of music education, as outlined in their interim report (NCC, 1991a) was for the most part, enthusiastically received by music teachers and parents, supporting as it did many of the innovative changes which have taken place in classrooms during the last twenty years. When the move from O level and CSE was made, these changes culminated in a very radically altered GCSE, possibly more altered than was found appropriate to any other subject.

It has, however, been vehemently disliked by a body of opinion which sees it as undermining the standards and principles of the European classical tradition.

> On this curriculum, pupils will be able to study music for 10 years without gaining a sound knowledge of either the history or the technique of western classical music, which is surely one of the greatest achievements of our civilisation. (O'Hear, 1991)

Such criticisms are unjustified, and stem from a misunderstanding of the emphasis in the report in favour of a multicultural approach to music education

> Multicultural education has come to be recognised as the entitlement of all pupils, and music provides exceptional opportunities to experience the cultural heritages of others. (NCC, 1991a, p. 53)

Opposition to the National-Curriculum music working-group interim report appeared to stem from both a basic lack of understanding of what constitutes music education and what is meant by a multicultural music curriculum. For example:

> In a classroom with many West Indian or Asian children, there is
> some justification for broadening the curriculum to embrace
> Caribbean and Indian traditions, though it is a rare teacher who can
> enthuse equally knowledgeably about ragas, reggae and Rigoletto.
> (Morrison, 1991)

The insistence upon a Euro-classical music curriculum not only denies the
value of the musics of other cultures, it also ignores the value to each pupil of
his or her own popular cultures. Such a curriculum could mean that many
pupils would be denied access to a successful music education.

Another area or misunderstanding was highlighted by Stevenson.

> Finally on the question of multicultural education, it should be re-
> cognized that Britain is a European state both geographically and in
> its cultural traditions. European music should therefore be seen to be
> the core of our children's education and not a peripheral part of it.
> (Stevenson, 1991)

However, as Britain is to Europe, so is Europe to the world. It is a logical
step therefore to see world music as part of our pupils cultural heritage.
Further, a multicultural music curriculum is worthy of support, not just
because it may be seen in some ways to redress the balance of values afforded
to the music of an individual or cultural group. Surely it makes sound
educational sense to offer to our pupils the range of stimuli without which
they may not achieve success. The interim report made it quite clear that the
inclusion of world music in the curriculum should be for all children.

> All pupils' lives are enriched by an understanding of their own
> cultural heritage, and by seeing that heritage valued in society. We
> believe that schools should therefore reflect in their choice of music
> not only the varied cultural backgrounds of their pupils, but also a
> wide range of those cultures not represented in their schools. (NCC,
> 1991a, p. 53)

At the time of writing, the final orders for music are before Parliament
and have not yet been published. The above criticisms made their mark and
the debate has been fierce and voluble. Musicians of the calibre of Simon
Rattle, Pierre Boulez and Sir Peter Maxwell Davies, to name but a few,
joined ranks with leading music professional and education organizations to
protest about the changes made by the NCC to the working party's report, in
the subsequent consultation report and draft orders (January 1992). Michael
Marland, writing in the *Education Guardian* states:

> The non-statutory examples of the aspects of study for music are
> unexpectedly Eurocentric, with only a single mention of 'calypso' to
> balance 27 western composers. (Marland, 1992)

When asked to contribute an article in *Teaching Today*, the in-house magazine of the teachers' union NAS/UWT, David Pascall, chair of the National Curriculum Council, protested that the media coverage and the resultant criticism of the proposals had been misinformed. A1 question still arises from his statement that:

> the NCC has strengthened the requirements in knowledge and understanding to ensure that pupils appreciate both our diverse heritage and a wide variety of other traditions, and that it is important that these areas are made explicit rather than implicit as in the working groups reports. (Pascall, 1992)

Why is it that references in the draft statutory orders for music, (DES, 1991b) to 'western classical' culture found in the Programme of Study and illustrative examples are prescriptive, whilst 'non-western' references hardly exist?

It is necessary to address these issues not merely because they question the value of cultures other than the 'Euro-centric' one, but because they indicate a fundamental misunderstanding of what constitutes music education. Not only is a multicultural curriculum necessary to provide equal access for all pupils, it can also be of great significance in enhancing the music education of all children. The intention of this chapter is to show ways in which the curriculum can be planned to give full and effective value to our culturally diverse society whilst promoting learning for all, including the musically very able, of all ethnic groups.

As with all the foundation subjects, the National Curriculum working group for music was required to recommend Attainment Targets and Programmes of Study, appropriate for assessing a pupil's performance at each key stage and for preparing for the pupil's development. The act has subsequently been amended so that art and music will not be foundation subjects in Key Stage 4. There are now two Attainment Targets AT1, 'performing and composing', and AT2, 'listening and appraising'. The Secretary of State wishes that the proposed Attainment Targets should be weighted 2 to 1 in favour of the first target. AT1, 'performing and composing', requires the development of the ability to perform and compose music with understanding. AT2, 'listening and appraising', requires the development of the ability to listen to and appraise music, including the knowledge of musical history. When the NCC Music Working Group was set up in 1990, the Secretary of State required that, for music, Attainment Targets and Programmes of Study be in less detail than for other subjects so that each school might develop its own schemes of work. However, the Secretary of State has subsequently accepted the NCC's view that there should be a clearer emphasis than in the original proposals, on the acquisition of knowledge about the history of music and on the western musical tradition (DES, 1992a). This fails to understand the original document which states:

> The main aim of music education in schools is to foster pupils' sens-
> itivity to, and their understanding and enjoyment of, music, through
> an active involvement in listening, composing and performing.
> (NCC, 1991b, p. 7)

but which also argues that a full acquisition of these skills would not be possible without developing knowledge and understanding of a range of facts
about music, its concepts, its notations, its structures, and its context, historical, geographical, and social. If the principles behind the National Curriculum document *Music for ages 5 to 14* (NCC, 1991b) are understood, this flexibility could lead to imaginative and rewarding musical experiences for our
children, allowing them to encounter and understand the music of many
traditions. By adhering to the general requirements for Programmes of Study
2 (DES, 1992a) 'Pupils should perform and listen to music in a variety of
genres and styles, from different periods and cultures.' It is still possible to
follow these principles.

The purpose of music education in schools has changed markedly over
the years. The status of school music had become so low that in 1963 the
Newsom report noted that more than half the schools in the survey had no
kind of music (Paynter, 1982). Fortunately, a deeper understanding of the arts
and how they affect all people has changed the emphasis in schools to a music
curriculum which enables the pupil to enjoy a much more participatory role.
The success of this can be seen in the increasing numbers opting for GCSE
music. The working party has clearly understood the place of music
education and the part it can and should play in the development of young
people.

Music teachers in secondary schools require a wide range of skills, as
classroom enablers and managers and as directors of musical activities.
Traditionally their expected knowledge of music has been wide and their
musical skills extremely varied. Many have acquired the majority of their
musical skills outside the classroom, proceeded to *conservatoires* or universities where they have continued to study their instrument in the Euro-
classical tradition. They have then completed their training in training
colleges with little experience of music outside this tradition and then
progressed straight into schools where they have been expected to continue
this tradition. Frequently they have had no support in the teaching of world
music, of which they have little knowledge. Their pupils may have had very
varied experiences by the time they leave primary schools. Some have
considerable skills on playing an instrument, some have none. Many are very
knowledgeable about popular music. Some may have experience of Euro-
classical music. They will have brought to school varying attitudes received
at home and from the media with regard to music, its status in their
education and the place of world musics within that. They may have come to
expect that only pupils with instrumental skills will be able to benefit from
any form of musical education. Occasionally the music lesson is still looked

upon by pupils and other school staff as a relaxation period, for fun but not of lasting value.

As stated by HM Inspectorate in their document *Aspects of Primary Education, The Teaching and Learning of Music*:

> Overall, policies for teaching music and planning work received less attention than most other subjects in the primary schools visited. (DES, 1991, p. 11)

Similar criticism can be levelled at some secondary schools. The emphasis in the curriculum will vary according to the ethos of the school. The concerns of governors and teachers in church schools, inner-city schools, rural schools or schools where children may have between them more than fifty mother tongues, will be different. It is perfectly possible for all these pupils to have equal access to a valuable music education using the principles outlined by the NCC report.

Challenges

The main challenge in implementing the National Curriculum report in the manner in which it is intended, that is equal access for all pupils, is to demonstrate that this curriculum is academically and pedagogically sound. It is not sufficient to talk of the necessity for a multicultural curriculum. It is also necessary to demonstrate how educational progression and development will be positively enhanced by broadening the content to include music from as wide a range of cultures as is practicable. This should give opportunities for developing range, width, depth and rigour. One joy of the cultural diversity of our society is the way in which it can enrich our work. Such diversity should not be seen as something which brings to the teaching profession yet another problem but as presenting new opportunities. To exploit these opportunities teachers need to be shown how they can structure their teaching and planning for this, using the skills they already have. As the document states, in order to open up opportunities for all, three points need to be borne in mind:

- pupils may need positive steering towards experiences and activities in which they can succeed;
- the tasks towards which pupils are steered may need to be adapted to enable them to respond positively; [and]
- additional resources may be needed if we are to ensure equal opportunities for all pupils. (NCC, 1991b, p. 51)

For pupils to learn, it is necessary for them to be involved in the learning process. This is as true for music education as it is for any other subject in the National Curriculum. It is not sufficient to say that a music curriculum must be delivered in a certain way, it will only work if certain factors are taken into account. To ensure equal access to the opportunities as outlined in the document, provision must be made for the differing experiences which individual pupils bring to the classroom. If it is accepted that (Swanwick, 1988, p. 141) 'Music teaching can be effective only when the nature of music itself is understood and the development of students respected', then music educators must be concerned with both the very essence of this art form and with the way pupils perceive the organization of sounds that we refer to as music. Pupils talk of the music which they choose to listen to, as something which they enjoy, which makes them 'feel something'. When involved in music the participator may have an affective experience, uncluttered by conventional language or symbols. Music communicates 'feelings' to which the listener responds. To be worth responding to it must 'say something' to the listener. There is ample documentary evidence to show that much school music has failed to fulfil this need (Paynter, 1982).

If the development of students should be respected and if the nature of music is indeed an aesthetic experience created by an agreed organization of sound, it should be recognized that agreed organization may well be culturally dependent. Music consists of various elements, which can be separated out and thus recognized, but it is the relationship between these elements that create music's particular expressive qualities. Pupils respond to the expressive qualities that they perceive in music, and it is the nature of the pupils' response that will determine how well they learn.

To illustrate this, two diagrams are included (Figures 10.1 and 10.2), which show an adaptation of Bruner's spiral of learning, and the links between the differing concepts which are essential to the understanding of music (London Borough of Harrow, 1988). Each element may be looked at separately when teaching, but it is the relationship between them which creates the particular expressive quality to which the listener responds. The diagrams have been further altered to include the words which the interim report uses to indicate progression, 'recognize, identify, distinguish and discriminate'. Also added is the word so often missed in music teaching, but so vital to the development of musical understanding, and that is 'response'. Pupils may be able to analyse and discuss various features within a composition, but if they have not developed a facility to respond to the expressive qualities, it is facts that are being absorbed, not music.

The National Curriculum music document makes it clear that response can only be nurtured by direct involvement with the music itself. This has been defined as participating in performing, composing, and appraising. Although the Attainment Targets are divided in this way, the working party wishes there to be a holistic approach to music teaching. The study of music should be, and should remain, one which integrates all aspects of musical experience.

The interim report maintained that:

[Music] is an important mode of communication and understanding, which has its own conventions and rules, and may thus be described as a non-verbal language. (NCC, 1991a, p. 3)

Figure 10.1: The Spiral Curriculum: An Elevation Showing the Progression of Musical Development

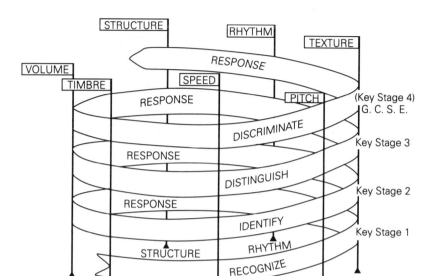

Note: The spiral represents the path of growing understanding and musical awareness, as musical concepts are visited and revisited. It is the relationship between these concepts which creates the particular expressive qualities to which the listener responds.

This has a direct bearing on the introduction of world music in the classroom. Each musical culture has its own particular concerns. Each creates an affective experience for the participator by selecting from the same palette of musical elements as other musical cultures, but blended in its own way. This does not mean that music is an international language in which, if one dialect is understood, it will automatically be possible to communicate and become involved in any other. To respond to the music of a culture, other than that with which the pupil is familiar, requires that the pupil must be introduced not only to the ingredients of the music (the concepts of melody, rhythm etc.) but also to the way these ingredients affect each other. It is the interaction of vocabulary, grammar and syntax which creates the aesthetic experience.

Reimer reflects this view when writes:

> Trying to respond musically to sounds in an unknown style is like watching a game being played in which none of the rules or regulations or purposes are known to the person watching. (Reimer, 1970, p. 101)

Figure 10.2: *Links between Concepts Essential to the Understanding of Music*

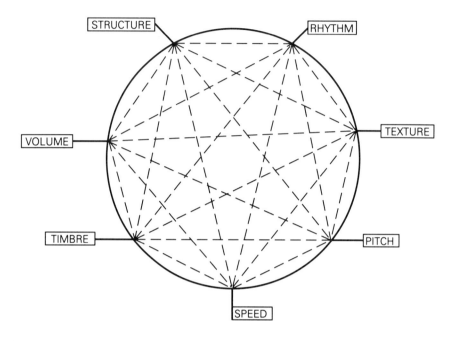

Note: The significance of the relationships between these concepts will vary between different cultures. To understand and value the resultant musical languages, the listener needs to be sensitive to these differences.

To respond constructively, the pupils must have had some behavioural experience upon which that response can be founded. Therefore it is necessary to start from the pupils' experience, what ever that might be. Further, to ensure equal access to the curriculum, it is essential that the teacher structures the pupils' Programmes of Study in such a way as to utilize the pupils' experience. Too often the curriculum is seen as something imposed from on high, rather than a recognition of the possibilities for learning that arise, in part, from the environment in which it is to be applied. Pupils themselves are a resource and come with many experiences, through their primary school experience, their various tuitions, their links with the community, their own listening experiences through the media etc. and their need to express through emotions and feelings, their own development.

The intrinsic qualities of various world musics also need to be valued. The inclination to dismiss other musical cultures as 'primitive' may come from lack of familiarity and understanding.

> When western musicians speak of 'primitive music' they are generally discussing music which is interested in other matters than those with which our music is concerned. (Small, 1980, p. 49)

To give proper value to the varying musics of our diverse society, it is necessary to help teachers and pupils to recognize these different concerns. It is necessary to show that breadth of learning will not dilute the intensity that musicians find valuable but rather will strengthen it. One danger which must be avoided is that of tokenism which is superficial and patronizing. This was a charge levelled at some GCSE, music examination boards. Further, misunderstandings of the nature of Euro-classical music must be tackled.

> Artists have always been 'magpies', appropriating aspects of styles and traditions other than their own. Thus, the history of European artistic adoption of foreign influences is not at odds with an educational policy that advocates the study of a wide range of musical styles and traditions. (AEMS, 1989, p. 5)

Professor Scruton (1991) recommended, as the basis of a suitable music curriculum, the classical music tradition 'not only the highest achievement of European culture, but also a universal language of the human spirit.' It is appropriate to remember that this classical music tradition is rich with the influences of Gregorian chant, acknowledged to be adaptations of early Jewish synagogal patterns, the music of the troubadours, who worked alongside the gypsies from India. The music of Mozart exhibits Turkish-Janizary influences (Sadie, 1980). The music of Debussy and countless respected composers of the late nineteenth and twentieth century have openly acknowledged the debt they owe to other musical cultures (Griffiths, 1987). By studying other musical cultures we are not watering down what already exists, we are complementing it. The integrity of a culture's music can enrich others and help pupils develop an understanding of their own.

> Musical skills and understanding are enhanced by drawing on specific examples from different cultures and styles. Pupils can be introduced to music from other cultures through a recognition of their common elements as well as their differences. (NCC, 1991b, p. 51)

Responses

Shown below are possible aspects of a scheme of work for Year 9, preparing for Key Stage 3. They are designed to enable pupils of all abilities and experiences to attain their highest possible potential, and ensure that they experience a properly balanced multicultural music curriculum.

In the draft statutory orders for music (27 January 1992) the AT1, performing and composing, includes the following:

- perform in a range of styles, interpreting signs, symbols and musical instructions; and

- compose, arrange and improvise music, developing ideas within musical structures.

AT2, listening and appraising, includes the following:

- discriminate between, and respond to, harmonic, rhythmic and melodic structures, and
- understand the principal features of the history of music and appreciate a variety of musical traditions.

A working example leading to these Attainment Targets is offered in Table 10.1. As has been stated before, music is comprised of various elements which, although they are heard in conjunction with each other, may be studied individually. The music of all cultures is concerned with repetition and contrast, tension and resolution and this unit is concerned with the pupils' recognition of the repetition of short phrases in music (a phrase in music may be thought of as similar to a short sentence in a speech). The ability to recognize characteristics (in this instance, repetition) in differing musical cultures helps not only to remove the 'strangeness' of that culture but also facilitates the recognition of that characteristic in the listeners' own music. Each of the repeat features chosen is interlinked with other parts within the music. The listener must therefore be able to 'filter' out the relevant feature. This provides opportunities for the development of a high degree of aural discrimination. Extensive vocabulary may be learned. In music, these repeating patterns have acquired different names according to the source or style of music from which they come. The material may be used as a listening activity, as a stimulus for composition and improvization, and as performance material. Discussions about the music could influence pupils' performance of other music. Differentiation, i.e., taking into account the very wide range of attainment to be expected by pupils in music, is built into this plan. For example, the very able will perform music requiring advanced skills. In composition, the more experienced pupil could compose intricate patterns around a repeating bass pattern; a less experienced pupil could be responsible for composing that suitable repeating pattern.

The aim in this example is that the pupils should recognize the structure of repeated patterns and the expressive character thus created in music, by the study of their use in different musical cultures.

Teachers should first take into account the experiences of their pupils and start with material which is accessible to them. Other material should then be chosen which will develop their learning. By so broadening their musical experience they should be able to apply these skills to a range of music. Teachers will readily envisage and develop a variety of similar models and strategies. These should help their pupils to develop their understanding of, and response to, a range of musical conventions, traditions, and styles from across the musical spectrum and come to value such music and the communities from whence it stems.

Table 10.1: Varieties of Music and their Attributes

Content	Repeat Feature	Vocabulary	Context and Considerations
Bangra music	rhythm	tabla and tala	Asian influence, mixture of traditional and electronic instruments
'Hill St Blues' by Post.	melody	melodic motive	composing for TV
Trinidad 'Panama' '88	melody	calypso	carnival and steel-pan arrangement of calypso
Shalom Chavarin	bass	modal canon	Israeli song of peace
Guantanamera	bass and harmony	harmonic ostinato	music of Brazil and its various influences
Javanese Gamelan	all parts	scale names slendro and pelog	influence on Debussy
Musicians of Rajasthan	melody	raga	music in the villages
Qawwali	rhythm in tabla	tala	music in Pakistan
Barundi drums	specific instruments	rhythmic ostinato	community activity
Nkosi sikele'i Afrika	vocal	call and response	Bantu national anthem
Pachelbel Canon	bass line	canon	use of classics for adverts, comparison with Bach Air with little repetition
Ravel Bolero	side drum, melody	bolero	composition for dance
Holst 'Planets'	rhythm	rhythmic ostinato	comparison of musical effect of ostinato in Mars and Jupiter

Note: Jazz, rock, folk and popular music also provide interesting examples which can offer similar opportunities arising from a variety of cultural traditions.

Until recently there was a great shortage of useful material for the teaching of world music in schools. Now, most good music-education suppliers have a relevant section in their catalogues. Local record shops can often supply recordings valued by pupils, and popular in many different communities. The music working party of the 'Arts Education for a Multicultural Society' (AEMS) project, chaired by Professor Blacking and David Peacock, produced a report on music education, *Breaking the Sound Barrier* (AEMS, 1989). This document reviews aspects of music and multicultural education including rationale, strategies for curriculum development, teacher training, sources and resources, assessment and recommendations. It also has a valuable list of classroom resources and books and is available from AEMS, 105 Piccadilly, London W1V OAU.

In addition the following may be found useful.

- *Music File*, Mary Glasgow Publications Ltd, publishes resource material, which is added to each term. In addition to providing practical suggestions for teachers as to how they may use music as a stimulus for performing, composing, and listening, it has had several sections which have concentrated on the use of various world musics.
- *Silver Burdett and Ginn Music* (Simon and Schuster International), a music course in four parts covering the ages 4–14 years, is based upon sound multicultural and cross-curricular principles, providing a comprehensive range of materials for use in performing, composing, and listening.
- Books such as Jean Gilbert's *Festivals*, June Tillman's *Oxford Assembly Book* (both OUP) and *Light the Candles* (June Tillman, CUP) have material chosen for primary-age children. However, these can be a valuable resource for teachers of older pupils, providing material suitable for performing and composing, supported by useful background information.
- The latest edition of Groves' *Dictionary of Music and Musicians*, contains comprehensive details of different world music traditions.
- The resource which should not be overlooked, is that which may be provided by the pupils themselves and their families. In addition to their personal skills as performers many have contacts with other musicians in the community and possess or have access to a wide range of recorded material.

This chapter has been concerned with the aims of music education in schools to develop aesthetic sensitivity and creative ability in *all* pupils (NCC, 1991b, p. 7). There has not been the opportunity to detail the recommendations of the working party with respect to the exploring of cross-curricular principles, the instrumental services, extended curricular activities and links with the music profession, business and industry. These important areas are fully and sensitively covered by the working party in both the interim and the final reports. The Final Order for music was laid before Parliament on 10 March 1992 and sent to schools later, in the summer (DES and WO, 1992b). Non-statutory guidance was also provided (NCC, 1992).

References

AEMS (Arts Education for a Multicultural Society) (1989) *Breaking the Sound Barrier*, London, AEMS.

DEPARTMENT OF EDUCATION AND SCIENCE (1991a) *Aspects of Primary Education, The Teaching and Learning of Music'*, London, HMSO.

DEPARTMENT OF EDUCATION AND SCIENCE (1992a) *Music in the National Curriculum: Draft statutory Order*, London, DES.

DEPARTMENT OF EDUCATION AND SCIENCE (1992b) *Music in the National Curriculum* (England), London, DES.

GRIFFITH, P. (1987) *A Concise History of Modern Music*, London, Thames and Hudson.

LONDON BOROUGH OF HARROW (1988) *Music in Harrow Schools and Colleges*, LBH, Education Department.

MARLAND, M. (1992) 'New world for the arts?', *Education Guardian*, 21 January.

MORRISON, R. (1991) 'A generation drummed out', *The Times*, 13 February.

NATIONAL CURRICULUM COUNCIL (1991a) *Interim Report*, London, DES.

NATIONAL CURRICULUM (1991b) *Music for ages 5 to 14*, London, DES.

NATIONAL CURRICULUM COUNCIL (1992) *Art: Non-statutory Guidance*, York, NCC.

O'HEAR, A. (1991) 'Out of sync with Bach, the emphasis on pop, rock and heavy metal in the national curriculum threatens our musical tradition', *Times Educational Supplement*, 22 February.

PASCALL, D. (1992) *Teaching Today*, London, NAS/UWT.

PAYNTER, J. (1992) *Music in the Secondary School Curriculum*, Cambridge, Cambridge University Press.

REIMER, B. (1970) *A Philosophy of Music Education*, New Jersey, Prentice-Hall.

SADIE, S. (Ed) (1980) *Groves' Dictionary of Music and Musicians*, London, Macmillan Press.

SCRUTON, R. (1991) 'Rock around the classroom: contempt for traditional values now extends to the teaching of music.', *Sunday Telegraph*, 10 February.

SMALL, C. (1980) *Music — Society — Education*, London, John Calder.

STEVENSON, D.A. (1991) 'Music curriculum has low expectations', *Daily Telegraph*, 23 February (letters column).

SWANWICK, K. (1988) *Music, Mind and Education*, London, Routledge.

Chapter 11

Geography

Dawn Gill

Context

The idea that to provide education for cultural pluralism is an important creative response to the National Curriculum is one which needs to be seriously questioned. It carries the implicit suggestion that ignorance about culture is what divides people, and that if we all learn about each other's cultures then the end result will be more harmonious relationships between different groups. A focus on cultural pluralism may divert attention from issues of economic inequality and power.

This paper argues that education for cultural pluralism as currently conceived is likely to help preserve an inequitable status quo. It suggests that the ideologies of racism, sexism, nationalism and the class structure should become the focus of attention in curriculum design. The approach to the National Curriculum in geography suggested here would provide a framework within which to expose and challenge inequalities based on racism, sexism and social class. In addition it would aim to carry students towards a recognition of the global economic forces which affect their lives. The introduction of this book suggests that its two main purposes are to describe and discuss cultural diversity and the whole curriculum from various perspectives and to consider how the legitimate educational concerns of minority ethnic groups, and those of large groups can be addressed within the framework of the National Curriculum.

First, the perspective of this chapter is on education for cultural diversity and, in outlining this, attention is given to geographical issues and a range of economic issues — local, national and global — which provide the contexts for, and also the legitimate content of, geographical education. Education for cultural diversity deals centrally with prejudice, a prejudgment of 'other' cultures as inferior to, or even just 'different' from, one which is assumed to be British, although this in itself may be a fiction based on mythology and stereotype (Solomos, 1991). Multicultural education fails to address the racism which operates at an interpersonal level, in the institutions of British society, and in the functioning of the global economy (ACD, 1989; Levidow, 1988; King and Israel, 1989; Wright, 1990). Discourse about racism is part of a broader political analysis, which takes as its subject a whole economic system and its historical roots, and the way that economic, ideological and cultural systems interrelate. The formal education system is of relevance to this discourse; multicultural education, although also relevant, is only one part of the area of debate which focuses on education.

In the past decade or so 'ethnic minorities' have become the focus of attention in schooling. However, multicultural education has impinged minimally on the mainstream curriculum. Instead, this has been concerned with the perceived needs of pupils from (some) ethnic-minority backgrounds. In some enlightened schools there is mother-tongue maintenance; school assemblies may celebrate the festivals of religions other than Christianity; and home-economics classes experiment with curries. The more sensitive teachers label classroom displays and work trays in a variety of languages, and ensure that a variety of reading material is available to reflect a range of cultures and in a range of languages. There may be lessons about 'other' people and 'their' cultures for the white British pupils. Usually these lessons form part of social or religious education, until recently, marginalized curriculum areas with no examination status. Stereotyped versions of 'other' cultures are presented in terms of the clothing, art, food, religious practices, and music which are considered 'typical'.

Within this scenario, however, several cultural groups inevitably receive more attention than others. In addition the cultural stereotyping and 'positive-image' approach deny the reality of many of the ethnic-minority children in our classrooms, every bit as much as it is denied by resources, which assume all children to be white and middle-class. In addition, wider political issues are ignored.

Those pupils whose historical roots are in Jamaica, for example, are beginning to learn in school alongside their white and black friends that what is important about Jamaica is Rastafarianism and the steel band. They do not learn how vast profits from bauxite mined in Jamaica end up in Europe or the USA, nor why the United Fruit Company and Del Monte dominate agribusiness, or that tourist hotels are owned, in the main, by multinational companies, are managed largely by foreigners, and that local people tend to be employed only at lower levels in the management hierarchies. They do not learn of the history of colonialism and the effects of neo-colonialism on the Jamaican economy, or of the reasons for poverty and unemployment in Jamaica. In fact, to mention poverty and unemployment in connection with Jamaica is somehow not quite decent. Multicultural education requires, first and foremost, that schools should foster a 'positive image' of all groups of people. The economic reasons for migration to Britain tend to be glossed over in favour of personal accounts of migration — stories about what it feels like to be in a strange new country.

The argument here is not that schools should devalue the importance of building the confidence of black and ethnic-minority students in any way possible. Clearly, to value the culture of *all* students is important. But schooling which focuses on a small part of what its decision-makers or the educational publishers see as culture, to the exclusion of political and economic analysis, is divisive, diversionary and reactionary. It is likely to serve the same purpose as the rest of schooling by socializing pupils into acceptance of the dominant ideology and the status quo. Multicultural approaches do not explain why there is such a high level of unemployment in Britain as manufacturing industry is being moved to Korea and the Philippines. The scapegoating of black people as the cause of unemployment and homelessness is another area which multiculturalism fails to address. Neither has it anything to say about the ways in which racism permeates the laws and institutions in Britain and leads to discrimination in housing, employment, and other areas of life.

To promote cultural pluralism in education may well be divisive because it is based on ethnocentric multiculturalism. The way that it operates is less blatant than overt racism because it depends less on presumptions of physical and biological differences, and more on ideas about cultural disparities. Ethnocentric multiculturalism promotes the stereotyping of individuals and leads to mythologizing of certain groups, which are presented as culturally static; it helps to prevent the sharing of common experiences and the realization of unity. Multiculturalism can also directly reinforce patriarchy and the oppression of women (Chapakis and Enloe, 1983). In pedagogic terms it is purely descriptive. Cultures are not analysed critically, they are merely described – and falsely, since what counts as culture is generally determined by an élite, which happens to be male-dominated in some cultures.

To make ethnicity or culture the centre of an educational debate and a focus of the curriculum has been, in the past, to divert attention from inequality and its determinants. Whether this will continue to be the case needs to be demonstrated. The National Curriculum has dominated debate in education since 1986, and education for a multicultural society has received comparatively little attention. The arguments made in the early 1980s need to be re-examined as critics of the National Curriculum begin to marshall a response (ILEA, 1986). The point to be made here is that in terms of challenging racism and inequality through education, the cultural pluralists may be off course. Multiculturalism had little to offer as a challenge to racism in the 1980s, and in the 1990s; repackaged as cultural pluralism, it may be equally impotent.

Racism, sexism and ethnocentrism are ideologies which facilitate oppression. Black people in Britain are over represented in work which has low pay and low status; this is more acutely the case for black women than for black men (Mama, 1992). White women also tend to occupy lower status and income positions than white men (Skellington, 1992). Analysis of employment statistics locally and nationally is a legitimate part of the geography curriculum. Oppressions based on myths of physical, intellectual or cultural superiority and inferiority (or just inherent 'difference') have been used throughout history by governments and employers to ensure that some groups of people are made available for low-paid and hazardous work; this needs to be demonstrated alongside any statistical analysis of employment figures.

Economic oppression operates across national boundaries: It is a subtly racist and sexist rationale which allows so many British and companies based in the USA to close down textile factories in Britain and the USA, for example, and open up new factories in Asia where, in particular, female-labour costs are lower. Asian women are supposedly (traditionally, culturally, naturally, inherently) willing to work for low wages and to endure tedious, repetitive, unhealthy work and harsh discipline. Women in the Philippines, Hong Kong and Sri Lanka, because of their 'Asia-ness', are supposedly prone to accept exploitative work and conditions. The idea that factories in south-east Asia will be more profitable than those in Europe represents a form of institutionalized racism and sexism, which operates at a global scale to promote the interests of capitalism (Chapakis and Enloe, 1983). The assumption that Third-World workers, in particular women, will accept low wages and poor working conditions reflects not their desire to be thus exploited, but the economic conditions which dominate their lives. The ethnocentric, racist and sexist 'justification' for relocation of textiles factories serves to divide people in many ways: men and women are placed in competition with each other; Asian women are classified as 'cheap labour', and are pitted against working-class people in Britain and the USA whose jobs are threatened. This may well be useful for the companies, because competition between people in the same country, and between people in different countries, tends to work against international trades-union solidarity. It is likely to depress wages and increase profits.

The operation of capitalism across international boundaries is made comparatively easy if racist and sexist ideologies permeate the consciousness of an international workforce. In the global economy Asian women seem to be taking 'British' jobs and industry because 'they are prepared to work for low pay'. In Britain 'black people are taking our jobs'. Immigration is held to blame for unemployment, not the economic system which brought black people to Britain as 'cheap labour'. It is the same economic system which now exploits 'cheap labour' in the Philippines and in the tea and coffee plantations of India, Africa and South America (Sivanandan, 1982; *New Internationalist*, 1990; Braham, Rattansi and Skellington, 1992). It may be interesting to examine the ways in which ideologies of racism and sexism intertwine with nationalism and xenophobia to buttress oppression and inequality.

A critical approach to National Curriculum delivery in a range of subjects can take young people some way along this road. The concern of this chapter is with geography which could, if carefully interpreted, help students towards analysing inequalities at a range of scales, from the local to the global. Such an analysis can be undertaken more easily if geography and history departments work together to coordinate a response to the National Curriculum.

Challenges

An antiracist interpretation of the National Curriculum in geography would not necessarily take cultural diversity as its starting point; instead, it would focus on some of the other issues outlined above. Geographical education, even that 'delivered' through the National Curriculum, could usefully examine some facets of important economic questions such as these. The geography curriculum has clearly not been designed to answer such questions, however, therefore a careful choice of optional sections would be necessary, and the content of geography would need to be linked with the content of the National Curriculum in history.

It is in the interpretation of geography that there lies potential for challenging racism on local, national and global scales. Geography is, essentially, the study of spatial patterns and the processes which have produced them. Geographers study spatial patterns at a range of scales from the local to the global. If we are studying patterns in the physical world, we may be interested in matters such as the global distribution of precipitation (water, which reaches the earth from the atmosphere in whatever form), or the global distribution of mountain ranges. In either case a geographer would be concerned to map the distribution patterns, and examine the physical processes which have produced, continue to reproduce or have modified these. So it is with human geography. Distribution patterns are mapped, and attempts are made to explain them.

A variety of maps in the annually published World-Bank report (World Bank, 1990) show the distribution of wealth on a global scale. Maps at a local scale may show the distribution of black and white populations in cities such as Cape Town, New York or Detroit. A detailed population-distribution map of London, for example, may show concentrations of people with African or Caribbean roots in Brixton and Hackney, and people whose family roots are in the Indian subcontinent concentrated in Tower Hamlets. Clearly, an understanding of racism and the part it plays in local, national and international economies is pertinent in explaining a distribution of population which reflects skin colour in British cities. Also relevant is an understanding of the roots of racism, in colonialism and imperialism. The slogan 'we are here because you were there' expresses not only a resistance to racism, but also a whole history and geography. It is impossible to explain contemporary, human, spatial patterns without reference to the past.

The challenge for geographical education is to analyse inequalities based on racism, sexism, and class at a range of scales, from the local to the global, and to explore the extent to which these are reflected in spatial patterns. In describing and explaining patterns of inequality at a range of scales, students will need a knowledge of colonialism and imperialism, which can be provided through history, although it must be acknowledged that the construction of the National Curriculum in history seems to be designed to frustrate such an understanding (Hackney, 1990). Careful syllabus construction will be necessary, in which history and geography are linked. Education must also demonstrate that divisions between people are not insurmountable. An alternative notion of positive image will need to be promoted, which celebrates struggle against oppression. Geographical education can, and should, provide the context within which such analysis and celebration are possible.

Responses

During the first year of National Curriculum implementation heads of department in Hackney secondary schools have met to discuss how to provide a Key-Stage-3 curriculum which has a clear rationale and as much coherence as possible within the imposed constraints. We have debated several possible 'best routes' through both history and geography with a view to maximizing the potential to challenge inequalities, and promoting economic and industrial understanding, as well as delivering other cross-curricular themes.

For two compelling practical reasons most of the secondary schools in the borough aim to work together in delivering the National Curriculum in history and geography. A shared route through the content would ensure continuity and progression for students who move from one school to another, as many do in the borough. The most obvious reason, however, is that the burden of detailed syllabus construction and preparation of materials can be shared. A complete change of curriculum content leaves schools poorly resourced, and having to start almost from scratch in preparing to teach.

Before the imposition of a National Curriculum, much of the published material available for history and geography was inappropriate for some of our students for a variety of reasons. For example, the language was too complex in many texts, and the layout confusing. In addition, teachers were critical of many history and geography textbooks because the intellectual responses they required of students were limited and the tasks tended to be based mainly on comprehension-type activities. Teachers, in humanities departments, working alongside Section 11 teachers, and others with 'special-needs' expertise, had attempted to resource courses appropriately for classes with a wide range of needs. The National Curriculum removed at a stroke the usefulness of work done by teachers in the past, by making irrelevant for future use the content of school-produced resources. The main reason for our decision to work collaboratively was to do with sharing the work involved in starting again to provide materials for students with a variety of language and learning needs.

How to make sense of the geography curriculum in its own terms has not been immediately obvious. There are five Attainment Targets: geographical skills; knowledge and understanding of places; physical geography; human geography; and environmental geography. Each of these is subdivided, so that there are effectively seventeen separate lists of Attainment Targets, all to be studied at ten levels (NCC, 1991). At Key Stage 3 there are 103 separate Statements of Attainment. The National Curriculum in geography is seen by many teachers as incoherent, lacking in overall rationale, and virtually incomprehensible in its present form, not least because levels of attainment are linked to specific content. Apparently it is more difficult to learn about the USA, which is level 7, than it is to learn about the local area, which is a level-2 attainment (NCC, 1991).

For a variety of reasons, some of which have been outlined above, heads of department in Hackney secondary schools decided to introduce an 'adopt a study unit' project. Each school would 'adopt' one history topic and one geography topic, and take the lead coordinating role in producing resources for these. Ideas, strategies and resources would be shared. In practice, schools have worked more collaboratively than anticipated, so that the topics so far resourced are a result of a sharing across the borough. Schools have been equipped with desktop-publishing facilities. This means that attractively produced materials can be edited with ease after trialling. The success of the project so far has relied partly on the involvement of learning-support departments and special-needs staff, who have put much effort into making school-produced resources accessible to all.

The possible route outlined here (see Table 11.1) is our first response to the National Curriculum, and it will be refined in the coming years. The suggested programme would allow for a range of styles of delivery, through separate subjects taught by separate departments or through a humanities core, in which students spend all of their history and geography time allocation with one teacher. It has not been feasible to create an integrated humanities course from the two National-Curriculum foundation subjects, but it may be that as teachers develop new materials, full integration would be possible for some terms. In schools where there is a functioning humanities department, in which both history and geography are taught by the same teacher, the content could, perhaps, be delivered in a succession of half-termly units.

Then and Now

In constructing a modular humanities course we have chosen history as an organizing framework, and have decided to teach it chronologically. The optional units selected for history offer an opportunity to examine the roots

Table 11.1:   A Suggested Modular Humanities Programme for Key Stage 3

Term	History	Geography
1 Core	The Roman Empire	Study of the local area
2 Core	Medieval realms	The home region
3 Core	The Crusades (or French Revolution or India)	Physical geography
4 Core	The making of the UK 1500–1750	Europe (focus on Germany: patterns of migration)
*5 Option	Black peoples of the Americas	USA, USSR, Japan: focus on USA
*6 Core	Expansion, trade and industry 1750–1900	Focus on India
*7 Option	The British Empire	Environmental geography
*8 Core	) The era of World War II)	International trade: economic/industrial understanding
9	))	

* 'Then and now' studies

of racism while promoting an understanding of the current-world economic order. A study of such content is likely to make human and economic geography more comprehensible, and facilitate economic and industrial understanding. 'Then and now' is the general principle on which we have based links between the two subject areas, wherever possible.

Hackney teachers, like teachers in other areas, are waiting for the National Curriculum in geography to be rationalized. This has happened for science and mathematics recently, as it became increasingly obvious that they would be unmanageable in their original form. The problem of content over-load in geography will also need to be addressed. In the meantime, and as far as possible, we have made criteria related to equality our first priority in selecting content. We shall attempt to link the five Attainment Targets, as the curriculum spirals through particular content foci. These are the local area and home region; a country in Europe; a 'developed' economic superpower; and a 'developing' country.

The National Curriculum places strict limits on the 'places' which may be studied. The acceptable areas and countries are clearly specified in the Programme of Study (NCC, 1990, p. 43). For the purposes of NC geography the European Community consists of France, Italy, Germany and Spain. We have chosen Germany for reasons which are explained below. The USA, Japan and the USSR are the choices available as examples of an economic superpower. In view of recent events, the USSR would present difficulties: we have chosen the USA.

The National Curriculum document (NCC, 1990, p. 43) specifies which 'economically developing' countries children are permitted to study in schools. These are Bangladesh; China; Egypt; Ghana; India; Kenya; Mexico; Nigeria; Pakistan; Peru and Venezuela. The term 'development' is euphemistic in relation to most of these. Most are caught up in a process of active underdevelopment as primary products are syphoned off to the superpowers, along with much of the profit from their embryonic manufacturing industries, many of which are merely subsidiaries of western-owned transnational corporations. Our choice is India. In addition we have chosen physical, human and environmental geography, and a study of international trade and the global economy as topics through which other content can be covered. There are effectively only eight terms at Key Stage 3. We therefore suggest that human geography could best be taught in connection with other content areas, being covered through both history and geography.

The Suggested Course

In term 1, a study of the Roman Empire would need to be evidence-based, and a study of the local area would need to be enquiry-based. Common pedagogies, rather than common content link history and geography here. Students would be offered the opportunity to develop further the skills of historians and geographers as they move from primary to secondary school.

An understanding of imperialism as practised by the Romans may help students to make sense of later periods in history where there are similarities. A study of Roman imperialism may also illuminate the reasons for colonization in general. The need for minerals and agricultural products was as much a reason for the Roman invasion of Britain as the British invasions of Africa and India in later centuries. And later still, when direct rule became no longer necessary, the need for minerals and agricultural products continues to determine the relationship between ex-colonizer and ex-colonies. Clearly, the content of history can do much to support an understanding of geography. A study of the local area would inevitably cover migration in recent years. For many communities, this has been a direct result of British imperialism, and any explanation of this in geography would be supported by reference to Roman Britain.

Hackney has large communities from many parts of the world, some of which are ex-colonies and some of which are not. Global patterns of wealth and poverty lead to migration. Students would need to study the clothing industry in Hackney as part of the local environment. This would prepare the ground for a study of Europe, later in the course. There are obvious parallels between a local economy which relies on Turkish workers as 'cheap labour'' nd Germany a more distant European economy which has similar features.

The first two terms would incorporate human geography, and would complement the work in history successfully. Settlement patterns are usually covered in connection with the Middle Ages, for example. Mapping contemporary settlement patterns in geography would inevitably raise questions of equality and quality of life, as students link studies of housing and employment. A focus on racism is essential in explaining housing patterns in the borough, as a recent report from the Commission for Racial Equality demonstrates so clearly (CRE, 1989).

Through a study of Medieval realms in term 2, a focus on feudalism could provide the basis of an understanding of people's relations with the land, property ownership, the links between the economic and class systems, and the ways in which the State and the Church are interrelated. The geography module in term 2 would include a study of variations in economic prosperity in 'the home region'. Maps of the South-East could provide the focus for an analysis of spatial patterns and the social processes, including racism, which have produced and continue to reproduce them.

A 'developing world' focus — Brazil, perhaps — may also be worth considering alongside Medieval realms. This would allow students to consider the links between land ownership and wealth distribution alongside class, and focus on the influence of religion. One of the last terms of the primary school is likely to have dealt with these issues, however (see Volume 3 in this series, which outline the Hackney humanities programme at primary level).

In term 3 a study of the Crusades in history has no obvious parallel in geography, nevertheless, in studying the Crusades, students would need to focus on travel and transport, mapping and weather. Thus history departments would be able to compensate for remarkable deficiencies in the geography curriculum. The 'official' world map (NCC, 1991, p. 67) excludes Mecca. Hackney has a large Muslim community; Muslim students and their families may be perplexed by this omission. There are excellent resources on the Crusades, which allow a consideration of both Christian and Muslim perspectives. Students could also examine the creation of myths and 'images of the other'. Humanities' teachers could usefully work with colleagues in English and religious education here, as in other areas of the suggested curriculum. Heads of department in some schools have decided to cover the French Revolution, instead of the Crusades. They see this as an important event in world history, and stress its importance to black resistance in the Caribbean.

The geography focus for term 3, the summer term, could be physical geography. In term 4 a history of 'the making of the UK' would build on earlier content in helping students to understand the links between class and culture, and religion and culture. A consideration of political unification would inevitably involve geographical work on the British Isles, and would need to be linked with a study of Anglo-Irish relations today, for example. Again, the literature offered in English, and the religious-education curriculum would be a matter for negotiation with other departments. The history module could cover geography Attainment Targets in schools which currently have integrated humanities courses, and in which students will continue to be taught both history and geography by the same teacher.

If a pattern of local to global studies is considered appropriate, term 4 is as good a place as any to study European geography. A focus on patterns of migration is suggested here. The use of Turkish 'guest workers' is an integral part of the German economy. Europe makes use of 'cheap' foreign labour, especially in work which is monotonous, dirty and poorly paid. Turkey is Germany's Bantustan, although increasingly the former East Germany is likely to take this role in the economy. An understanding of the economies of migration could give an insight into racism outside the UK, and would disconnect the 'black people equals racism' link, suggesting instead a possible 'economic imperatives equals racism' link.

Coherence

Terms 5, 6, 7 and 8/9 provide the suggested programme with a coherence impossible to achieve in the first four terms. History and geography can be linked through a 'then and now' approach. Thus, in history, the topic 'Black peoples of the Americas' is presented alongside a geographical study of the USA today. An analysis of patterns of poverty and wealth, population distribution, the location of industry, and an examination of agribusiness in the USA can all be usefully informed by an understanding of slavery and plantation agriculture. Resistance to oppression, then and now, could be covered as a legitimate part of both geography and history. There are many examples of women, as well as men, who have been involved in the struggles against slavery and racism, and further examples of black and white people uniting against oppression. Such examples are important in demonstrating first of all that resistance is possible, and can lead to change, and also in redefining the notion of 'positive image'.

In term 6 'Expansion, trade and industry 1750–1900' is a study of the rise of Britain to prominence as an industrial power. The participation of the colonies in this process will necessarily be covered in history. In most schools India is to be used as a case-study here. This would provide a context in which students could be helped to understand India's poverty and efforts to industrialize today. This they could cover in geography. In some schools teachers have begun to negotiate with religious-education departments so that Sikhism and Hinduism are covered at about this time, and with English departments to ask whether it would be possible for students to read literature which would give them an insight into events in India today and in the past.

Term 7 could further extend students' understanding of the links between Britain and its colonies. The global pattern of agriculture and mineral resource exploitation established at the time of the British Empire is still evident today, and could be studied through the unit on environmental geography. Deforestation, soil erosion, pollution of the lakes, rivers and air can all be better understood in the context of an analysis of the economic imperatives which took root in an earlier historical period. Terms 8 and 9 have been combined because assessments for other subjects are likely to occupy much of the students' time and demand a lot of emotional energy.

The course structure suggested above is intended to facilitate particular emphases on equality. The understanding of racism, sexism, social class, and imperialism can be pursued throughout the programme, as can an analysis of the economic systems within which these inequalities thrive. The suggested course would also offer specific opportunities to examine resistance to oppression by particular individuals, groups, organizations, and movements. The structure suggested here also offers a coherent framework within which the cross-curricular themes can be integrated.

References

ALL LONDON TEACHERS AGAINST RACISM and FASCISM (1983) *Race in the Classroom*, London, ALTARF.

ASSOCIATION FOR CURRICULUM DEVELOPMENT (1989) *Anti-racist Strategies: a course for teachers*, London, ACD.

BRAHAM, P., RATTANSI, A. and SKELLINGTON, R. (1992) *Racism and Anti-Racism*, Milton Keynes, Open University/Sage.

CAMPAIGN AGAINST RACISM AND FACISM (1990) 'Why Beggars should be choosers', *Searchlight*, 177.

CAMPAIGN AGAINST RACISM AND FACISM (1990) 'We're not racist but . . .', *Searchlight*, 178.

CHAPAKIS, W. and ENLOE, C. (1983) *Of Common Cloth: Women in the Global Textile Industry*, Amsterdam, Transnational Institute.

COLE, M. (1988) *Bowles and Gintis revisited*, Basingstoke, The Falmer Press.

COMMISSION FOR RACIAL EQUALITY (1989) *Racial discrimination in property developments*, Report of the formal investigation into Oaklawn Developments Ltd, Leicestershire, London, CRE.

HACKNEY METROPOLITAN BOROUGH (1990) 'The proposed National Curriculum in History: a report on consultation with teachers', Unpublished, but available from the Education Directorate.

INNER LONDON EDUCATION AUTHORITY (1986) *Report of the ILEA Centre for Education*, London, ILEA.

INSTITUTE FOR RACE RELATIONS (1990) 'Police Media Research Project', *Bulletin*, 58, 1.

GILL, D. and SINGH, E. (1989) *No racism here: we treat them all the same*, London, Association for Curriculum Development.

KING, M. and ISRAEL, M. (1989) 'The pursuit of Excellence, or how Solicitors Maintain Racial Inequality, *New Community*, 16, 1.

LEVIDOW, L. (1988) 'Racism in scientific Innovation', in GILL, D. and LEVIDOW, L. *Anti-racist Science Teaching*, London, Free Association Books.

MAMA, A. (1992) 'Black Women, the Economic Crisis and the British State', in BRAHAM, P., RATTANSI, A. and SKELLINGTON, R. (Eds) *Racism and Anti-racism Racism*, Milton Keynes, Open University/Sage.

NATIONAL CURRICULUM COUNCIL (1990) *Geography in the National Curriculum*, York, NCC.

NATIONAL CURRICULUM COUNCIL (1991) *Geography in the National Curriculum: Non Statutory Guidelines*, York, NCC.

NEW INTERNATIONALIST (1990) The Philippines, 205.

ROGERS, A. (1989) 'Young Black People and the Juvenile Justice System, *New Community*, 16.

SIVANANDAN, A. (1982) 'Race, Class and the State', in *A Different Hunger: Writings on Black Resistance*, London, Pluto Press.

SKELLINGTON, R. (1992) *Racism, Education and Society*, Open University Course ED362 Statistical Supplement, Milton Keynes, OUP.

SOLOMOS, J. (1991) 'Contemporary Forms of Racial Ideology in British Society', *SAGE Race Relations Abstracts*, 16, 1.

WARD, D. (1988) 'Financial Famine', in *Children First: the magazine of UNICEF UK*, Summer.

WRIGHT, J. (1990) 'Out of School', *New Statesman New Society*, 3, 89.

WORLD BANK (1990) *World Bank Atlas*, New York, World Bank.

Chapter 12

The Arts in the Climate of the ERA: A Focus on Art and Design

Horace Lashley

Context

The Education Reform Act (ERA) has set dilemmas in continuing the progress of much of the curriculum innovation that was taking place in the 1980s. This was no more evident than in the arts where a series of reports, curriculum projects and other self-interest groups were pressing for changes. The Gulbenkian report (1982) is important as a benchmark which opened the debate for drastic change. The study concluded: 'We maintain that a positive concern with the enrichment of our public life through the practice and appreciation of the arts would confer immeasurable benefits in our society'. The report also identified six areas in which the arts can make a positive contribution to the curriculum (Gulbenkian Report, 1982, p. 141). These included:

- developing the full variety of human intelligence;
- developing the capacity for creative thought and action;
- contributing to the education of feeling and sensibility;
- developing physical and perceptual skills;
- contributing to the exploration of values; and
- understanding the changing social culture.

It therefore highlighted specific aspects of arts education that could benefit each child. In many ways it reinforced the argument set out by Rees-Mogg (1984) in *The Glory of the Garden* where he argued 'The arts — human, creative, inspiring, individual, warm, alive — provide a natural healing to this sense of depersonalisation, and the appreciation of beauty can transcend the moon-like chill of an electronic world. For those of religious faith the human creativity of the arts can be a way of sensing the beauty of God's creation. Perhaps we demean the arts more than earlier generations; perhaps we need the arts more than earlier generations'.

The Gulbenkian study was followed up by a much more in-depth one set up by the School Curriculum Development Committee (SCDC) in 1985 entitled the 'Arts in School Project' (1990). This project concluded in 1989 under the National Curriculum Council's guidance with the publication one year later of *The Arts 5–16: Practice and Innovation*. A central argument of this report is that an effective and coherent programme of art education is an essential part of cultural education, that is, one which:

- helps young people to recognize and analyse their own cultural values and assumptions;
- brings them into contact with the attitudes, values and institutions of other cultures;
- enables them to relate contemporary values to the historical forces that moulded them; and
- alerts them to the evolutionary nature of culture and the potential for change.

The context identified as central in this area was much more concerned with the affective than the cognitive domain of the curriculum, and encompassed the wider cultural aspects of our lives. It also alluded to a natural multiculturalization of these areas of feeling since the arts are influenced by a variety of cultural inputs that naturally cross any single cultural specificity. In this respect the arts have always been seen as multicultural inputs in what may sometimes be cultural-specific situations. They have not always been seen as transcending deeper aspects of the socio-economic relationship across groups of different ethnic and racial origins.

Challenges

The presence of substantial ethnic-minority communities in Britain since the 1950s increasingly impressed itself on the wider cultural life of the society in a variety of arts media. This was probably most evident in the area of music and dance, although identifiable in other art forms as well. Khan (1978) highlighted the extent to which this occurred, the lack of 'official recognition' paid, and the possible effect this could have on the survival of the arts of some of the ethnic-minority groups. She concluded: 'The arts have always been humanising factors, offering an understanding of people. They are specifically a potent counterweight to the common stereotyping of different races.' Central to the argument of her book was the view that the arts can 'add variety and colour to the texture of life'; afford the chance of not only seeing fresh cultural forms but also learning of them; [and can help in] 'stretching knowledge and understanding'.

The central thesis of her work was that the arts can add to good race relations:

- the host community will have greater understanding of minorities as they become more familiar with the arts of these new communities;
- minorities will have a higher value of themselves by being able to maintain their own art forms; and
- development within the education system needs to be followed through and related to opportunities for young people to continue the artistic interests they develop after they leave school.

Khan's *The Arts Britain Ignore* was both a milestone and a crossroad. It marked a turning point for the arts of minorities and the part they had to play in British society. It also raised the profile of minority artists and put firmly on the agenda issues concerned with minorities being both consumers and producers of art forms at the highest level. It ensured public recognition of the art forms and artistic needs of ethnic minorities subsequently and, for a short time thereafter, placed it amongst the priorities of the work of the Commission for Racial Equality (CRE).

A part of the high profile given to arts education by the CRE in the very early years of its existence, derived from a series of national conferences held in Glasgow, Birmingham, Manchester, Cardiff and London during 1979 and 1980. The series concentrated on the use of practitioners' case-studies and as a consequence unearthed a wealth of good practice that was taking place at the time across the country. The CRE subsequently followed up with an in-depth study of funding and the status accorded to the art forms of ethnic minorities (Baker, 1985). Baker did not focus on education in the study since that aspect of concern was otherwise dealt with. He concentrated on the development of, and relationships between, the arts of minorities in the wider society, as well as looking at the status of those arts and the response of arts-funding agencies to them. He examined the issue of identity and the arts for young people of ethnic-minority backgrounds. His conclusions were pertinent to the development of a multicultural facet to the arts in the new National Curriculum. However, it may very well be that the National Curriculum is not aiming at this since in the very term there seems to be a notion of 'oneness' and 'unity' in thought. Baker sees minority young people as having 'multiple' identifications . . . with a wider range of artistic options. He therefore suggests:

In establishing an ethnic identity, different from parents and from the majority white society, the new generation of ethnic minority British are using the arts in a unique and constructive way. Ethnic arts are expressing the experience of a new generation. The arts are a useful and necessary medium for this expression and may be the only legitimate way in which they can make themselves heard. They are often all too young to vote, and remote from the political processes which drive the system. (Baker, 1985, p. 56)

This paper highlights the particular kinds of restrictions, perceived and actual, that seem to have brought about a change of direction from the progressive innovations that were being called for, before putting the case into the relevant contemporary setting of the ERA. The reports and projects that have been referred to so far ought not to be seen as the totality of innovation but merely a sample of a much longer list. In the process of developing the arguments in this paper, others will be referred to as necessary.

The Art and Design in a Multicultural Society (AIMS) project is the first of two further studies which is examined here. This project (1981–5) was undertaken by the Centre for Post-graduate Studies in Education at Leicester Polytechnic, with an interim report which was finally completed in 1986. The study was undertaken based on two major dimensions: an international one, and a local one centred on the Leicester experience. The study ran simultaneously with one of the most thorough investigations into education related to multicultural concerns, namely that of the Committee of Inquiry into the Education of Children from Ethnic-minority Groups (1981, 1985). The AIMS study concluded that:

> From the international, national and local surveys it would seem that the extent of discussion surrounding the need to meet the needs of a multicultural society through curricular changes has not been matched by the extent of change actually occurring in the curriculum and educational practice. (Allison, Denscombe and Tehe, 1985)

Put briefly, the study found that there was a lot more talk than action in the area of the arts. However, the AIMS project, like many other studies, revealed numerous examples of excellent practice and innovation. Much of it seemed to be 'grass-roots' and locally-based movements, 'prompted and activated by individuals' commitment rather than the product of an articulated educational framework produced at national, regional or local authority level'. This conclusion related the arts more generally to the wider curriculum since there seemed to be a far greater awareness of curricular needs and development in subjects other than art and design where such innovation and development were relatively sparse (Lashley, 1986). The AIMS report, as a consequence, pointed out: 'There is also some indication that art and design teachers recognize from within the subject area itself the need to incorporate material from non-western culture.' Lashley (1986a) therefore argued that, 'to a large extent we have not moved on significantly. The hindrance to any meaningful advancement has been due much more to the lack of "know-how" and expertise than an awareness that something has to be done.' This point was borne out by the data of the AIMS study which indicated that only 10 per cent of the art and design teacher sample had attended courses principally concerned with multicultural education, while a mere 20 per cent of the sample classified as 'teachers in multicultural schools' attended any such courses. With this point in mind, the report finally suggests:

'There is an evident need to foster multicultural approaches to art and design education through the development of a curriculum framework which':

1   meets the following facets of multicultural education: (a) fosters a global or internationalist perspective, (b) fosters and perpetuates respect of the traditions of minority cultures, and (c) fosters an anti-racist perspective in schools;
2   is applicable across the range of ethnic composition context in contemporary Britain;
3   draws on the 'cultural' context and content of art and design; and
4   can be adopted as policy at a range of levels including national, regional and local, exclusive of specific ethnic composition.

The other major study was undertaken by the Oxfam Education Department and was based in South London. The project was run in two separate phases beginning in 1982 and finally reporting in 1991 with a National Curriculum workshop at the Commonwealth Institute in London. The first phase was centred around a part-time course for teachers entitled 'Using Third-World art forms for creative activities'. This was based at Lambeth Teachers' Centre (LEA) and focused on social and arts-related issues in Guatemala, Ghana, India and Indonesia. Six workpacks or project boxes were consequently produced from the course, drawing on concepts of development education and the production and distribution of art-and-craft objects. The second phase of the project concentrated on school-based work around the same conceptual themes and entitled 'art and development education 5–16' project. The purpose of the overall study was to 'Explore how art and development education could be linked within the art-teaching syllabus and wider curriculum'. The second phase was given a wider purpose, building on that of phase one. It was intended to look at 'practical ways [in which] any art-development education link might be made within the 5–16 age range — both in terms of content [materials used] and process [classroom methods adopted]'.

The central curriculum concept of the project was its cross-curricular focus. One of the provisional educational objectives set out in the project proposal was 'To contrast how we have come to learn art in this society with the experience of other societies through critical analysis of the cultural (historical, social, political, economic and aesthetic) factors which have relevance to our study'. This objective was underpinned by a view of development education that 'aims to bring about a climate in which participation can occur and naturally therefore stands in opposition to education which takes the receipt of cultural information as its prime end' (McKenzie, 1983). McKenzie, in a further development of the neo-Marxian development-education critical-analysis approach, argued that art was depicted in the curriculum 'as something of an educational "back water", barely modified by the internationalist undercurrents that have started to pervade other disciplines'. She further argues that this is due 'to the devaluation of art as a subject'. It is, as a consequence, not seen as 'academic' and is therefore not 'taxed with contemporary educational consideration' (Lashley, 1980; McKenzie, 1983). The Oxfam project viewed art as a form of social action, and art education as a process of empowerment in all transactions that occurred in the production and utilization of such products.

The two projects outlined above are examples of a large number of initiatives that have specifically addressed the issues of art and the multi-cultural society. They provide two very important extremes or poles that can be related to the contemporary educational climate we now find ourselves in as a result of the Education Reform Act (ERA). They point out the wider issues of curriculum debate relevant to a multiracial, multicultural Britain. The extremes represented provided, at one pole, a 'cultural-survey' approach and at the other a 'destructuralist', antiracist approach. McKenzie argues that the 'cultural-survey' approach will do little to counter the way situations appear to be and may succeed in reinforcing the very racist, sexist, class-bound and eurocentric stereotypes it presumably wishes to dispel. It may do this through presenting 'passive' or at best 'responsive' cultural images requiring its audience to be recipient, rather that participant, and thus absorb information which confirms, as opposed to questioning, dominant social biases. In contrast, a more 'hard-nosed' antiracist approach suffers the draw-back of the current climate of curriculum 'non-innovation' where a required essence of vocationalization hinders a socially proactive innovative climate. This is particularly so where issues of equal opportunities and antiracism are concerned. Shah (1990) therefore suggests that 'the National Curriculum is a miserable failure in regard to the desire for equality by black people'. She however concedes that in the National Curriculum, 'some lip service has been paid to equal opportunities, but all children are unlikely to receive the type of education that could counteract, for example, the rising racist incidents in this country' (see Chapter 1). Can art in the National Curriculum provide a positive educational direction to help counter such events?

Responses

Turning specifically to art and design, as a precursor to the Education Reform Act, the DES produced a series of documents on curriculum matters and teacher education through the HMI. The series included a document on *Craft, Design and Technology from 5–16* (1987). The document suggested that one of the aims and objectives of CDT is 'to encourage respect for the ways in which people of different cultural backgrounds, past and present, have shown their ability to enrich their environment.'

At an earlier point than art and design, the preparation of the new curriculum statement concentrated on design and technology (see Chapter 8). Steers (1990) responded to this focus by stating that 'the establishment of the Design and Technology Working Group before that for Art inevitably gives rise to concern that the high ground, so far as design and IT are concerned, will have been captured before the art is even discussed'. He further suggested that 'while the Government does seem to recognise that art makes a major contribution to the curriculum as well as to design and technology education, art and design teachers cannot be complacent'. The analysis was in a wider context that encompassed the relevance of the report to 'multicultural and gender issues in order to ensure that the proposals provide genuinely equal opportunities for all pupils'. Steers felt that not enough consideration had been given to these issues or is the detail of their applications. There seemed to be a naive jubilance that 'every school is required to make appropriate provision for art as a foundation subject in its own right'. It is not the intention here to pursue the conflicts of interests which seem to have emerged between art and design and design and technology as competing curricular interest areas. However, it cannot be denied that the areas have been accorded somewhat different values in recent years as education has seen a greater drive to make the product and outcomes of education more pertinent to the world of work and our industrial economy. The Interim report of the National Curriculum Art Working Group thus argues: 'The success of our business, industrial and professional enterprises depends increasingly on the way products and services combine functional and aesthetic requirements to satisfy the needs of the international community.'

This commercial function of the subject area is further emphasized by the report suggesting that 'if companies are to continue to be run by managers with financial training, it will be increasingly important for them to learn the aesthetic and functional requirements of design from an early age'. This obviously fits in with the wider political context in which the National Curriculum is being framed.

Steers (1990) in his trenchant criticism of the inadequacy of the National Curriculum Design and Technology Working Party's consideration of equal opportunities issues and multicultural education presented a challenge, which he obviously thought the art subject-area working party would have to address more extensively. And it has done so in both its interim report published in 1990 and the final report published in 1991 (DES and WO, 1990, 1991).

A number of very different important facts emerged from the reports which need to be highlighted in order to show the importance and scope of the subject in the curriculum of British schools, at the secondary level, and therefore the significant impact it is likely to have on the wider education of our citizens. It was pointed out that it is normal practice to include art in the curriculum in the first three years of secondary schooling, years 7–9 (age 11–14). Beyond 14 almost 40 per cent continue to study it and at years 12–13 (age 16–18) almost 15 per cent study art for Advanced GCE. It was also pointed out that in 1990 approximately 240,000 16-year-olds were entered for public examinations in art, design and history of art and design. Also of interest was the scope of the subject area outlined and based on HMI surveys in the 11–14 age band. 'In most schools, the activities and aspects of art and design covered consist largely of drawing and painting, with some ceramics, print making and working in textiles.' Additionally, the report identified a diversity of current practice which includes, in addition to those already stated, modelling, sculpture, graphic and product design, jewellery, weaving, photography, film and video, theatre and interior design, and the historical and critical study of the work of artists, designers and craftworkers. It was further emphasized that this was in addition to the use of computers and other new technologies which is increasing rapidly in arts areas. It was also shown that a mere 1.5 per cent of schools did not have art as a formal provision on the curriculum.

Another major barrier that needs to be considered at this point is that of teacher preparation to deal with issues of multicultural education in art and design, as well as other areas of the curriculum. It has been previously found that, in relation to the arts, teacher education has not been adequately responding to the needs of teachers preparing for the multicultural and multi-racial society that Britain has become over the last four decades (Lashley, 1985). Subsequently it was pointed out that the lack of teacher knowledge and expertise had been supplemented by the use of a system of teacher-managed outside expertise provided by visiting artists. This obviously was only appropriate as a stop-gap measure. It was expected that the arts departments of teacher-education institutions would give consideration to the issues and make adequate provision. There does not seem to have been any substantial improvements made in mainstream initial teacher-training courses, despite the requirements of the Council for the Accreditation of Teacher Education (CATE). The indications seem to point to a demise of the main resources which had supplemented Initial Training (IT) as well as in-service (INSET) inputs into teachers' continuing professional development. The inadequacy could have a major impact on whatever opportunities the new curriculum will provide for multicultural and possible antiracist work in art and design and other areas of the arts. An indication of any real commitment to these issues will need to highlight the importance of adequate teacher education if pupils are to attain the objectives set out in the Attainment Targets and Programme of Study, which specifically relate to multicultural education.

The art working group for the National Curriculum was set up in July 1990. It published an interim report at the very beginning of 1991 with the end of June 1991 as the anticipated submission of the final report to the DES. The period of preparation of this chapter took in the final report entitled *Art for Ages 5 to 14*. The title indicates that Key Stage 4 is excluded. This was confirmed by the decision of the Secretary of State who held the view 'that pupils aged 14–16 should not be required to take art and music foundation subjects of the National Curriculum although they should be offered an opportunity to take these subjects if they wish' (DES and the Welsh Office,

1991). The interim report of the working party contained curricular aspects which are strongly multicultural and provide the scope and opportunities for the art education to develop multicultural work. It was suggested that 'all pupils should be given the opportunity to study art in the context of our culturally diverse society' [and] be made aware of the historical and traditional roots of the many art forms available . . . and how artistic conventions are shaped by cultural influences'. It is hoped as a consequence that pupils will be able to view other cultures in a positive and non-stereotypical way.

The final report which is presented under the auspicies of the 'Proposals of the Secretary of State for Education and Science and the Secretary of State for Wales' reaffirms the multicultural context within which the proposals are submitted:

> It is essential that the art curriculum is interpreted in ways which are sensitive to the particular needs of individual pupils of cultural and linguistic background and to the cultural diversity of British society. (DES and WO, 1991, par., 11.5, p. 59).

The report also reaffirms the view that art can provide a focus within which a better understanding of 'issues such as racial stereotyping can be achieved through the study of the work of artists, craftworkers and designers from other cultural traditions'.

For some time now, art and design education has been in the process of change and re-evaluation in a variety of respects. Not least amongst these has been issues of equality of opportunity. Collins and Sandell (1984) examined the subject in relation to general needs, while Allison (1972), Khan (1978) and Lashley and Rose (1980) were among those who initially raised the issues with regards to race and multicultural education. It therefore is a most fitting contribution to see equality of opportunity issues well enshrined in both reports by recent working parties' acknowledgment in the Attainment Targets and Programme of Study outlined. The Attainment Targets (AT) were initially suggested in three objective categories across the four Key Stages: AT1, understanding and evaluating art; AT2, making; and AT3, observation, research, and developing ideas. These have since been simplified in the final report to AT1, understanding; AT2, making; and AT3, investigating. (A further reduction to 2 ATs occurred in the Final Order.)

The multicultural aspects of the key-stage statements and Programme of Study can be classified into three categories: explicit, implicit, and interpretational. These categories are defined as follows:

- Explicit — where it is clearly spelt out within an example of, or by reference to, multiculturalism.
- Implicit — where the wider context alludes to difference or diversity but without the use of specific examples or references.
- Interpretive — where the general context is such that it is adaptable to a variety of different interpretations and where multicultural examples could rationally be one of these interpretations.

Of the three areas, AT1 had a clearer multicultural targeting than the other two ATs. Here many of the examples of Attainment Targets are quite explicit, covering the four key stages and ten levels. There are also pointers to implicit examples at this Attainment-Target area as well. The other Attainment-Target areas seem to be much less well-developed in terms of explicit and implicit examples of multiculturalism, but have the scope for a great deal of interpretation bearing on multicultural art development at the secondary-school stage.

For the faint-hearted there may be a reluctance to tease out the less obvious interpretive developments. There may be some hesitance to fulfil the more obvious explicit and implicit directives. This issue needs to be given very serious consideration if the multiculturalism professed by the document is to be realized: 'We believe the approach should be a positive one, finding ways in which pupils of all cultures can be given access to a rich art education' (DES and WO, 1991 p. 59). Some of these concerns have been examined in some depth earlier in the text and have been related to specific areas such as teacher preparation, INSET and examinations. It is not the intention of this paper to repeat the debate but to highlight the obstructive nature of some of the issues if they are not fully considered.

Examples of art activities are suggested with each of the Attainment-Target objectives across the Programmes of Study and Statements of Attainment. The vast majority of examples of work pertinent to the areas of multicultural and antiracist education are related to multicultural education i.e., issues focusing primarily on culture and cultural differences. There is no adequate attention to social structures and the ways in which these perpetuate discrimination, inequality, and racism which antiracist education does. There was one exception which was a clearly antiracist example and appeared at Key Stage 2, AT1 of the interim report. It was suggested that pupils should:

> Look at racial stereotypes and how different races are depicted in the visual arts and mass media; compare these with positive images in contemporary painting and illustrated books as in the work of Sonia Boyce and Maud Sutter. (DES and WO, 1990, p. 28)

Reading what is considered to be a most important exampled suggestion is somewhat disappointing in that it was aimed at Key-Stage-2 pupils and not at Stages 3 and 4. At the secondary level, pupils can better understand the use of such methods to investigate the effect of stereotyping as a major element in the development and exercise of racism. The earlier part of this chapter points out some of the ways in which racism affects us and the need to provide a curriculum experience at the secondary stage which is antiracist and can clearly address the task of reducing racism and its debilitating effects on the equality of opportunity of black, and other minority, young people. In this endeavour the arts can play a central role.

The final report did not provide any such explicitly antiracist work examples, although it does talk about racial stereotyping in a less threatening sense within what is ostensibly a strong multicultural arts context.

The identification of appropriate resources has been a longstanding and major concern of educationists involved with multicultural education and the arts (Allison, 1972; Lashley and Rose, 1980). Some of the early multicultural art projects concentrated on building resource banks and identifying pools of experts in a wide range of arts. Despite these developments there still seemed to be an excuse for proposing curricular development, which more often than not, was unrelated to resources. The working-party reports seem to have made a desperate attempt to deal with this issue by collating some very useful details on resources, applications and organization in carrying out the recommended new art and design curriculum (e.g., DES and WO, 1991, Chapter 13).

The report recommends the use of galleries and museums as a 'valuable educational resource for the development of art education in schools'. It also suggests that 'multicultural issues might form the basis of a visit to an ethnographic museum. Racial and gender stereotypes might be explored in exhibitions of painting and photographs'. The fact is that a great deal of the activities recommended in the Programme of Study and Attainment Targets are related to pupils developing art through first-hand experience of artefacts in both historical and contemporary contexts: 'Any worthwhile art education involves more than simply making. It is also about observation and the appreciation of the impact of the work of others.' The report also talks about outreach projects set up by museums and galleries which provide loan collections and outreach workers who run workshops directly in schools. These projects ought to provide invaluable help in the development of the multicultural aspects of the new curriculum in art and design (e.g., Commonwealth Institute, Chapter 3).

The use of artists in residence has always provided a novel experience for pupils. It represents a collaboration in which there seems to be a realism to the activity which is almost 'not really like school'. Another strength of the scheme is that, in areas like multicultural art, it provides an opportunity to make available expert practitioners. This is particularly appropriate since, as the report points out, 'many teachers have commented upon how their own skills and understanding have developed as a result of their participation in such schemes'. Even more importantly, the report points out that, in relation to teacher-training needs, 'some of our advice will entail departures from common practice and will challenge some assumptions'.

The 'artists-into-schools' movement poses the questions: Do we need artists when there are teachers in schools?; How expensive are such artists?; How can we contact artists? Help with the third question has been provided by the publication of a directory of 120 artists or artistic groups with experience of working in schools. Published by the Arts Education for a Multicultural Society (AEMS), the publication provides valuable information concerning each artist or group. Thus cultural origins, languages spoken, their field(s) of artistic expertise, the type of contribution they could make, their geographical location and mobility, and referees who can be approached (Arts Education for a Multicultural Society, 1992).

The school, as part of its local environment will always find community relationships potentially creative. How well schools use this community potential is a measure of their willingness to be involved with their communities. This 'natural' and inexpensive resource is sometimes ignored by schools to their own disadvantage and to the disadvantage of pupils who could otherwise benefit. In relation to the arts in schools, and multicultural education in particular, the usefulness of the local community as a resource is strongly recommended. The report also addresses the issue of continuity as an aspect of art in the wider environment focusing on two major ideas: a structured environmental awareness, and collaboration with local institutions. Much valuable multicultural work will fall in the second category. The observational recording aspect of AT3 at all the Key Stages provides an opportunity for interpretive, multicultural community-orientated projects. Earlier, at Key Stage 1, explicit multicultural work should ensue from the given example: 'Make drawings of people wearing traditional costumes at special events or festivals.' The inherent dangers of stereotyping and oversimplification in such approaches must be avoided.

Most of the major cities in England with substantial populations of an Afro-Carribean background hold an annual West Indian carnival. The 1991 festival is claimed to have attracted over a million visitors and revellers to Notting Hill while the Birmingham one drew nearly half a million to Handsworth. Other areas, such as Manchester and Leeds, also have large carnivals. The opportunity exists in these areas for substantial collaborative work by schools in the area of art and design. There are also many other festivals as well as other activities that take place in the ethnic-minority communities that represent a focus of good art-and-design work. It is hoped that the new art curriculum will stimulate such activities.

Black young people are yet to select in substantial numbers art and design as a career-oriented field. Some years ago, Jackson (1979) highlighted the negativity of the visual literacy to which minority children were subjected and the effect it seemed to have on their self-perceptions. He pointed out that of the 996 images of human faces seen in the classroom and corridors over the child's first term 'only one represented a brown face; there was no representation of a black face or "any other variety"; and one was unclassifiable'. He therefore concluded in his research that 99.8 per cent of the human visual imagery that the black children were subjected to was representative of white faces. It was not surprising therefore to see, in Jackson's further experiment, that the black children's iconographic representation of their parents and family was white faces and pink eyes while in the case of the white children there was no perceptual confusion. The adverse effect of this was such that white children had a negative imagery of black people as well. The size of the 'non-white' population in Britain has increased significantly since 1979 (see Chapter 3). Have pupils' educational experiences and perceptions changed? The arts provide opportunities in which individuals can profitably engage, irrespective of ethnic or cultural allegiances. This is not to deny that art forms define, in part, the nature of a culture.

The art-and-design curriculum recommended by the NC working party has provided a very important opportunity to examine and deal with essential issues of culture and cultural differences. Some of these differences have proved a major stumbling block in the past to providing a non-racist and at times an antiracist challenge in education. The proper use of this opportunity can only bring benefits to a multicultural Britain. Cross-curricular work will inevitably lead into a host of other subjects of the new secondary school curriculum that will necessitate multicultural exploitation. History will provide a major facet to explore the history of art and the way in which it was intertwined with the wider aspects of history, such as European imperialism, colonial conquest, and the evolution of modern European 'schools' of art, design, music, and dance. The report argues the importance of crosscurricular work based on the fact that 'pupils' work in other subjects often has a beneficial effect on their work in art'. Reciprocally, one would wish to add, from the subject working-party publications to date, that the work in art and design would positively assist multicultural education in all other subjects of the National Curriculum. What effects has the controversy concerning the number and native of the ATs in the Final Order had on this point?

The Final Order for art was laid before Parliament on 10 March 1992. It was to be distributed to schools by the end of the Summer term. The statutory requirements came into effect in the first years of Key Stages 1 and 3 as from August 1992. Art will not be compulsory at Key Stage 4. The NCC will be issuing free non-statutory guidance soon after the subject orders have been distributed (Schools Update, 1992).

The controversy concerning whether there should be two or three Attainment Targets has been resolved by a compromise. The new AT1 'Investigating and Making' carries twice the weight of AT2 'Knowledge and Understanding'. The Secretary of State for Education makes clear his belief that art must be seen as essentially a practical subject having a major emphasis on 'our national and European heritage'. In AT1, creativity has apparently been subjugated to collection, observation and discussion. AT2 also presents considerable problems. Its Statements of Attainments are illustrated by examples of activities that have been described as both non-practical and more concerned with cognitive processes ill-matched to the Key Stages, rather than affective ones (DES and WO, 1992).

What many will find depressing about the Final Orders is the way that an opportunity to make art, at least in part, into a vehicle for multicultural studies in schools has been so firmly suppressed. Now, what remains of art from other cultures are the icons of an imperial past, so that the Chinese have kites, the Greeks have urns and frescos and the Africans have carved masks whereas we, whosoever we are, can study the "distinctive contributions" of Gainsborough and Turner' (Sweetman, 1992).

How valid is this interpretation? Does it represent undue pessimism concerning the contibution that NC art can make to education in a culturally diverse community? Fortunately, by their very natures, art and design are not cultural straightjackets, unless teachers and pupils allow them so to become. The discussions and deliberations preceeding the publication of the Final Order contain a wealth of constructive ideas concerning resources waiting to be utilized and pedagogies capable of development. These can be used in capitalizing on the potential of art and design to facilitate aesthetic communication, appreciation, understanding and creativity by culturally diverse groups. The imaginative development of NC art and design curricula by teachers can contribute towards more cohesive and tolerant schools, communities and society.

References

ALLISON, B. (1972) *Art Education and Teaching about the Art of Asia, Africa and Latin America*, VCOAD Education Unit, London.

ALLISON, B., DENSCOMBE, M. and TOYE, C. (1985) *The Art and Design in a Multicultural Society*, A Survey of Policy and Practice, Leicester Polytechnic, Leicester.

ARTS IN SCHOOLS PROJECT (1990) *The Arts 5–16: Practice and Innovation*, London, Oliver and Boyd.

ARTS EDUCATION FOR A MULTICULTURAL SOCIETY (1992) *Artists for Education Directory*, London, AEMS.

BAKER, W.J. (1985) *The Arts of Ethnic Minorities: Status and Funding*, London, Commission for Racial Equality.

COLLINS, G. and SANDELL, R. (1984) *Women, Art and Education*, London, National Art Education Association.

COMMITTEE OF INQUIRY INTO THE EDUCATION OF CHILDREN FROM MINORITY ETHNIC GROUPS (1981) *West Indian Children in our Schools: Interim Report*, (Rampton Report) Cmnd., 8273, London, HMSO.

COMMITTEE OF INQUIRY INTO THE EDUCATION OF CHILDREN FROM MINORITY ETHNIC GROUPS (1985) *Education for All* (Swann Report), Cmnd., 9453, London, HMSO.

DEPARTMENT OF EDUCATION AND SCIENCE AND THE WELSH OFFICE (1990) *National Curriculum Art Working Group: Interim Report*, London, DES and WO.

DEPARTMENT OF EDUCATION AND SCIENCE AND THE WELSH OFFICE (1991) *Art for ages 5 to 14*, London, DES and WO.

DEPARTMENT OF EDUCATION AND SCIENCE AND THE WELSH OFFICE (1992) *Art in the National Curriculum*, London, HMSO.

GULBENKIAN REPORT (1982) *The Arts in Schools: Principles, Practice and Provision*, London, Calouste Gulbenkian Foundation.

HER MAJESTY'S INSPECTORATE (1987) *Craft, Design and Technology from 5–16: Curriculum Matters 9*, DES, London, HMSO.

JACKSON, B. (1979) *Starting School*, London, Croom Helm.

KHAN, N. (1978) *The Arts Britain Ignore*, London, Commission for Racial Equality.

LASHLEY, H. (1980) 'Arts Education, The Curriculum and the Multicultural Society' in Ross M. (Ed) *The Arts and Personal Growth*, London, Pergamon Press.

LASHLEY, H. and ROSE, T. (1980) *Cultural Pluralism: Implications for teaching arts in schools*, CRE Internal Paper.

LASHLEY, H. (1985) 'The Editorial' *Education Journal* (Commission for Racial Equality), 6, 3.

LASHLEY, H. (1986a) 'Arts Education as an element of Multicultural Education', in ARORA, R. and DUNCAN, C. (Eds) *Multicultural Education: Towards Good Practice*, London, Routledge and Kegan Paul.

LASHLEY, H. (1986) 'Prospects and Problems of Afro-Caribbean in the British Education System', in BROCK, C. (Ed) *The Caribbean in Europe*, London, Frank Cass.

McKENZIE, A. (1983) 'The Visual Arts; A Response from development education', *World Studies Journal*, 5, 1.

NATIONAL CURRICULUM COUNCIL (1992) *Art N-SG*, NCC, York.

REES-MOGG, W. (1984) (Preface) *The Glory of the Garden*, London, Arts Council for Great Britain.

SCHOOLS UPDATE (1992) 'National Curriculum at, music and physical education', *Schools Update for Teachers and Governors. News from the DFE, NCC and SEAC*, Summer, London, DFE.

SHAH, S. (1990) 'Equal Opportunity issues in the Context of the National Curriculum: a black perspective', *Gender and Education*, 2, 3.

STEERS, J. (1990) 'Design and Technology in the National Curriculum', *Journal for Art and Design*, 9, 1.

SWEETMAN, J. (1992) 'Icons of an imperial past', *Education Guardian*, 25 May.

Chapter 13

Physical Education: Challenges and Responses to Cultural Diversity

Robert Carroll

Context

Although the challenge of cultural diversity is a challenge for all schools in our society regardless of their ethnic composition, it is not a challenge which affects all schools in the same way (Committee of Inquiry, 1985). This is because some schools have a large and varied ethnic-group population, others have small numbers and others still have practically none at all. Some schools have a large number of Asians and others Afro-Caribbeans. British pupils with many other minority ethnic-group allegiances also attend schools. Although it may be convenient to categorize ethnic-group populations into groups such as Asian etc., it is often a mistake to do so in this way. The Asian communities include Bangladeshi, Pakistani, Indian and other groups. These have their own distinct cultural patterns, religious affiliations and local customs, which can significantly affect their beliefs and behaviour. Likewise the Afro-Caribbean groups comprise a multiracial, multilingual, multicultural collection of peoples. The ethnic composition of our secondary schools is increasingly heterogeneous, especially in urban areas. In a given school this is true for all subjects not just physical education, but physical education has a distinctive role and sets a qualitatively distinct curricular context in schools. Its central core is movement and physical activity and it therefore presents different challenges and requires different responses to other National Curriculum subjects.

Schools have attempted to meet the challenges of cultural diversity through policies which have ranged from assimilation, integration, multicultural and antiracist and which have reflected changes in thinking (Troyna and Williams, 1986; Pumfrey and Verma, 1990). However, it is one thing to create policies: it is another to effect change. The policies are often general or vague enough to cover all subjects and contexts and often not specific enough to guide the teachers in the working situation. The practical issues of dealing with large groups of children composed of different ethnic origins has had to be faced in their daily work by teachers, but has not been addressed fully by the policy makers. This has often been the case for physical-education teachers. This situation has led, in a few instances, to a call for more urgent action and specific guidelines by some authorities, for example, Rotherham, which has a large Muslim-Asian population in its schools (Rotherham MBC, 1986). But in spite of the warnings of the Swann report (Committee of Inquiry, 1985) that particular conflicts can occur in physical education because of religious belief (referring in particular to Muslims), the developments such as those by Rotherham, have been exceptional and rare rather than common. Furthermore, the initial training of physical-education teachers, and development of in-service training work have lagged behind the development of policies. The result has been that physical-education teachers have been faced with what they see as 'problems' of ethnic groups on a growing scale. Their attempts at dealing with issues that have arisen have met with accusations of racism and racist practices (Bayliss, 1989), whilst the children have suffered racist abuse (Fleming, 1989), and severe conflicts (Carroll and Hollinshead, 1990). The teachers' attempts to operate policies of equality of opportunity have often failed because teachers do not fully understand minority ethnic-group cultural norms and values. The effect of professional practices pose problems. These have been documented in the case of Caribbean youngsters (Carrington and Wood, 1982; Cashmore, 1982) and of Asian pupils (Carrington and Williams, 1988; Carroll and Hollinshead, 1990). Such issues point to training needs which will be returned to later.

Challenges

The particular challenge at the present time is the introduction of the National Curriculum. Physical education is a foundation subject in the National Curriculum, but it is not to be introduced until Autumn 1992. It is surprising and disappointing that there is no reference to ethnic groups or equality of opportunity in some important government documents on the National Curriculum, for example, the *National Curriculum: from Policy to Practice* (DES, 1989). In this document it is stated that the authors are talking about an education and entitlement for all pupils, so obviously, this includes all the different minority ethnic groups in our society. However, it is surprising and disappointing, because of the large amount of literature in recent years which has indicated that racism is endemic in British society and schools, that there is concern over the educational attainment of ethnic minorities and the apparent failure of integrationist and multicultural policies (Committee of Inquiry, 1985; Troyna and Williams, 1986; Modgil *et al.*, 1986; Verma and Pumfrey, 1988; Pumfrey and Verma, 1990).

From Policy to Practice is concerned that the National Curriculum is not merely accessible to all pupils, but that it must be taken up by all pupils. This principle needs to be applied to the education of all ethnic groups but, in view of the issues identified in the literature and in practice, it is not enough to assume that this will be done. It must be stated categorically that there must be no barriers to an adequate PE curriculum because of race, culture, or gender. Indeed, each National Curriculum subject must produce antiracist and multicultural policies within their Programmes of Study where appropriate. A positive lead of this nature would assist subject working parties and encourage whole school policies. These are essential if an attack is to be made on racism and inequality of opportunity in PE and other subjects. The research of Carrington and Williams (1988), Carroll and Hollinshead (1990) and Fleming (1989) points to the need for such a lead in the context of physical education.

The working group on the National Curriculum was only formed in 1990, and at the time of writing, has just produced its interim report (DES 1991). Along with art and music, the terms of reference for PE were different to other subjects. The group was asked to produce 'attainment targets in terms of what is to be expected of pupils at the end of the key stages' which then 'form part of the statutory order for the subject'. In addition the group 'should make recommendations for non-statutory Statements of Attainment calculated into ten levels'. The interim report contained these proposals but not the Programmes of Study which would be produced in the final report due at the end of June 1991. The terms suggest a lower status than that accorded to other subjects. This is to be deplored by all who consider PE essential.

The interim report is clearly influenced by the earlier BCPE working-party report (BCPE, 1989). The British Council of Physical Education is a body representing all the physical education organizations. It set up a working party to consider the National Curriculum in PE in advance of the government's working party. The structure and content of the current DES report and its proposals and recommendations clearly follow the model and thinking of the previous BCPE report. However, in respect of equal opportunities and minority ethnic groups, the interim report is a big improvement in the BCPE's proposals. Unlike the document the *National Curriculum: From Policy to Practice*, the interim report does have a section on equal opportunities in PE. Within this section it recommends that all children regardless of their cultural or ethnic background should have access to all the skills and activities for a physically well-educated person. It is good to see that the report points out that 'mere *access* cannot be equated with real *opportunity*. The distinction between access and opportunity is crucial'. As the report says, this is a central point which is often missed by PE teachers. They are often happy at providing the access to PE and leave it at that, but do not fully understand many of the other factors which prevent access becoming opportunity. Such factors affecting practice lie in the organizational culture of the school. They include issues such as pupil groupings, interactions between ethnic groups, and the cultural expectations and values of various ethnic groups. Teachers and departments have not always given enough thought to the groupings, teacher–pupil interrelations, and to the way opportunities are presented. The research work of Carrington and Williams (1988) and Carroll and Hollinshead (1990) is particularly pertinent here. Carrington and Wood (1982) show that whilst opening opportunities in one direction, for West Indian children that may be in sport, they are perceived to be closing them in another, for example, the academic. In doing so, teachers are both limiting opportunities for success that matters in society, and stereotyping pupils. The other two studies show that equal opportunity for Muslim children cannot really be said to be offered without taking into full consideration their cultural and religious beliefs and values. These beliefs and values not only place physical activity and sport low in cultural value, but actually prevent children taking part in specific conditions or contexts, for example, in activities involving exposing their bodies, during Ramadan and extra-curricular activities. The details of precisely how these affect participation are available in the studies quoted.

As most teachers know, it is not enough merely to have a specific approach or model to secure the desired outcomes. It is the way practice is carried out in the teacher–pupil interaction that really decides the value of outcomes. Thus the challenges of cultural diversity, the carrying out of antiracist policies, the change in teacher–pupil relations and attitudes must be dealt with at this level. Informal sensitivity to what actually goes on in these interaction sequences is essential. Current attitudes and practices are not always easily changed or even tackled as Evans (1986) and Sparkes (1987) have shown in other spheres. Traditional beliefs and hierarchies are not easily challenged. This clearly points to the need for practical guidelines in the Programmes of Study and for in-service training to accompany them.

A recently completed national study of the participation in sports and recreational activities by ethnic minorities has described, in vivid terms, their differential involvements. The factors contributing to low or non-participation by minority ethnic groups are identified. These represent challenges to education in general and PE specialists in particular. The findings are highly relevant to the development of constructive responses. Thus a summary of the study is presented in the next section on responses (Verma *et al.*, 1991). The NC working party has proposed three Profile Components:

- performing;
- planning and composition; and
- appraisal and evaluation.

Each is divided into ten Attainment Targets to coincide with the levels of attainment required by the National Curriculum. The working party has not produced Programmes of Study to go with the statements, nor has it tackled the crucial question of how the targets are to be assessed. It has not stipulated the context of the activities at this stage, and this is clearly left for the Programmes of Study. They have deliberately not focused on activities or content, but on the processes of learning. The emphasis is neither solely on the achievement of performance, nor solely in the practical performance *per se*. It includes these plus planning, understanding, being in the roles of organizer, leader, official, and being able to analyse and evaluate performance. These involve the pupil in both observation and making considered judgments. The model is also developmental. It clearly shows progression from fundamental movement skills and general motor control at Key Stage 1, through laying the foundation skills of more discrete activities, to a higher level in a selected activity. It is a sound progressive model based on a rationale located in experience of good practice.

This type of model challenges physical education's traditional role in the development of practical performance *per se*, the traditional role of the pupil solely as a performer, the traditional teacher–pupil relationship and teaching styles. This is not entirely new. PE has been moving steadily away from a longstanding traditional role of practical performance and recreational activity to one which has a more theoretical and educational base through its examination work (Carroll, 1982, 1990), and through the health-related fitness movement (Armstrong, 1990). PE has therefore already incorporated an increasing emphasis on knowledge and understanding, an extension of its knowledge base, and changes in its assessment procedures without sacrificing its essential practical nature. However, the report does place more emphasis on planning, composing, analysis and evaluation, and on resulting different roles for the pupil than the examinations (Carroll, 1990). The proposals will set new challenges to PE staff. They will allow the pupils to show what they can do in spheres related to practical performance but not necessarily on the performance itself. Thus, the evaluating dimension may give pupils a better understanding of techniques, skills, tactics or prepare better for the role of coach or spectator. This may suit many children regardless of ethnic origin.

The report recommends making available a wide variety of activities. These include: athletics, games, dance, swimming, outdoor pursuits and health education. These should be followed by all pupils at least to the end of Key Stage 3. Many schools have already increased the range of activities in their PE curriculum in recent years. This has been helped by the increased provision of local-authority sports halls, which have been made available to schools, have been dual-use centres or community education provision. This wider PE curriculum has been based on the rationale that the pupils would find an activity of interest which they could continue in their leisure time. Although, perhaps, assisting ethnic groups and different cultures, it has often created an illusion of a successful multicultural policy. Schools often provide policies which give opportunities for culturally valued activities. However, the questions which are often not explicitly addressed are: Whose culture?; Whose values? In essence, it usually has meant the dominant white English culture. The ethnic groups new to the community are expected to take part in whatever is provided. It has been, in reality, an integrationist policy, sometimes offered with benevolence, sometimes patronizing, and nearly always without real choice though with well-meaning intentions

(Cashmore, 1982). The National Curriculum gives an opportunity to allow minority ethnic groups to select acceptable activities. The major problem is that, in the practical situation, teachers have to work within the available facilities and staff expertise. Another problem is that teachers must not fall into the trap of only providing activities valued by one group's culture, otherwise the education is limited and it will not be a multicultural education in the sense demanded by modern society and the ERA 1988. The advantage of being able to select activities which are culturally valued is that the pupils are likely to be able to reach a higher standard, with the obvious implication for the pupils. The issue of competition against oneself rather than competition against the standards of others in any given activity becomes a central concern. Not all cultural groups value the competitive team games that have held a key position in PE in this country.

One can readily see that minority ethnic groups are sometimes at a disadvantage with certain activities because they have not had prior opportunity to take part in them. For example, if they have recently come from abroad, they may not have taken part to any extent in soccer, rugby, netball or hockey. Nor do they necessarily take part in these activities regularly in their own time once they are in this country. This can be because such activities are not valued, or because of numerous other reasons. This leads to lower performance levels than their white-pupil counterparts who take part regularly outside school in these activities. The lower level of attainment in certain activities have been noted by teachers in Carroll and Hollinshead's study. On the other hand, high levels of attainment and participation have been noted in other ethnic groups in other studies, for example, the Afro-Caribbean group (Carrington and Wood, 1982). What one must guard against is that this does not lead to stereotyping particular ethnic groups, as has been noted in many schools (Bayliss, 1989). This has led to many erroneous beliefs and encouraged incipient racism.

It has been suggested that lower attainment in physical education does not matter to the same extent as in many other subjects. After all, there was no formal assessment, and school reports on PE were often vague and not valued highly. In the future, with the advent of Records of Achievement (RoA) examinations in PE and the National Curriculum in PE, lower attainments will matter much more. The assessment of PE is now formally recorded for RoA and examinations and forms part of the National Curriculum requirements. In the National Curriculum the assessment at the end of the Key Stages is part of the statutory order and will have to be incorporated into a RoA. In order to show both progression and what the child can do, records will have to be kept of the pupils' performance in more specific Attainment Targets in terms of the levels reached (Carroll, 1991). Assessment is central to the National Curriculum and therefore to the new PE programmes. Attainment level is going to become more important to all pupils. The disadvantages in PE of minority ethnic-group pupils will need to be looked at more closely. In one respect, this should help all pupils, because the formative assessment process in the National Curriculum should help pupils and teachers to become aware of individual difficulties and/or deficiencies. The procedures will point to where improvements are needed.

Responses

Many physical-education teachers often find it hard to accept that not all pupils are interested in physical activity or sport. Pupils have often been alienated by the way PE has been taught in schools, particularly its heavy emphasis on competitive team sports (Hendry, 1978; White and Coakley, 1986). The image of sport and of femininity in society have often not been compatible (Scraton, 1986). These factors would have worked to the disadvantage of certain ethnic groups who do not value the highly competitive or sporting image and whose views of the role of females differ from that of the dominant culture. Some groups do not place an active life style or sport as central in their leisure activities as many other cultural groups may do, e.g., the Asian-Muslim community (Carroll and Hollinshead, 1990; Carrington *et al.*, 1989; Fleming, 1989). PE teachers often come up against cultural and religious barriers which are not easy to overcome and cause conflicts for the pupils. They may well be heightened by statements in the interim report.

The report contains a number of references to extra-curricular activities. These make a clear link between participation both inside and outside the allocated curriculum time and both inside the school and in the community. For example, for AT1: 'we regard extra curricular activities as a valuable extension of the normal curriculum . . . pupils should be encouraged to join clubs, teams, expeditions and outings . . . such opportunities provided by the local community on by organisations . . . be able to set up a programme linking school and community.'

In view of what has already been said, these statements raise a number of issues. First, the expectation of time spent out of school on what is a National Curriculum subject during inside school time. This will inevitably disadvantage those not interested in taking part in PE activities outside school. These include working-class groups who do not have the support of the parents or the means to participate in activities which cost money and time (e.g., travel by accompanying parents), and ethnic groups who do not value these types of leisure activities. Particularly disadvantaged will be females, Muslims, broken families, and low-income groups. Paradoxically, Caribbean groups may also not get their family and community support as it has been shown that some believe that such involvement may depress their children's academic achievements and may do a disservice to the Caribbean community as a whole (Cashmore, 1982). The working group's proposals aim for equality of opportunity, but their reference to extra-curricular activities and community links fails to take into consideration that equality of opportunity is not realistic without taking cognizance of religious and cultural beliefs (Carrington *et al.*, 1989; Carroll and Hollinshead, 1990). It is not suggested that these aims should be abandoned. They are worthy and should lead to a more active and varied lifestyle of all pupils from all cultural groups. However, the subject and the pupils will have to be taught carefully and not dogmatically.

Links with the community might very well provide opportunities for the school and community to come together in relation to PE in a way that they have failed to do so far. This may then overcome the problems and conflicts which Carroll and Hollinshead have identified as faced by many Asian pupils, and the effects of the channelling of Afro-Caribbean talents which Carrington and Wood (1982) and Cashmore (1982) have discussed. Such issues will have to be handled very sensitively indeed if a constructive resolution is to materialize. Ethnic group, cultural and religious beliefs are not only strong but central and salient to the lives of pupils and their families. It is these aspects which have been underestimated in the past by schools and education policy makers in relation to PE. The equally valid interests of many other minority ethnic-group pupils must also be taken into account.

The areas and activities which have caused the most difficulties with Muslim Bangladeshi and Pakistani children have been the wearing of PE kit, showers, Ramadan, and swimming (Carroll and Hollinshead, 1990). The issues of wearing PE kit and of showers are connected with the Muslim rejection of exposing the body to other people. A sensitive and flexible approach may overcome these difficulties. A mixed-gender approach to the activities in the National Curriculum, which may be prompted by policies of equal opportunity, will be out of the question for devout Muslims. The fasting required at Ramadan can cause hardships to youngsters who have to take part in strenuous physical activities. A careful look at the activities on offer at this particular time, and ways in which physical demands can be lessened, is required. Blocking PE activities or modularizing the programme to take account of Ramadan could be considered. During this time it may be that more of the planning, evaluating or theoretical aspects of the PE programme can be carried out and is one way of meeting these particular cultural demands. Developing policies and Programmes of Study to cope with these particular cultural requirements will be steps in accepting the challenges of cultural diversity and multicultural educational principles rather than adopting the integrationist policies which had usually been the case in PE to date.

At the present time the Secretary of State for Education has indicated that he would like to see some changes in the formal report (DES, 1991). He would prefer only one Attainment Target, that related to performance. Possibly he lacks a full understanding of the proposed structure of PE. However, a compromise is possible on this issue involving the inclusion of some elements of planning and evaluation through Statements of Attainment. The Secretary of State has also asked for more general statements at the end of Key Stages. These will not be satisfactory from the assessment point of view. However, if Statements of Attainment are more specific but allow flexibility of context, then the problems may be overcome. The range of activities proposed up to Key Stage 3 is also of concern to the Secretary. He suggests these need not be compulsory, and his obvious reluctance to approve anything which will entail extra resources may mean that economic and political factors take precedence over educational ones.

A period of consultation during the Spring term 1992 involved a series of conferences at which key topics were discussed. These included implementation, planning schemes of work, progression, differentiation, special educational needs, cross-curricular matters, partnerships, non-statutory guidance, in-service training, assessment and examinations. According to the NCC, the report of the working group for physical education provided a sound basis for the subject within the National Curriculum (NCC, 1992a). The final order for physical education was laid before Parliament on 10 March 1992 and distributed to schools (DES, 1992).

The final order for physical education is, as anticipated, based on a single Attainment Target. This incorporates planning, performing and evaluating, with the major emphasis on active performances by pupils. In Key Stage 3, pupils are required to cover at least four out of five of the following areas of activity: athletic activities, dance, games, gymnastic activities, outdoor and adventurous activities. Games are compulsory in *each* year. Swimming is excluded at the secondary-school stage, but is a requirement at Key Stages 1 and 2. At Key Stage 4 the breadth of the curriculum is reduced. Pupils are required to cover the Programmes of Study for at least two activities. These may derive from the same, or different, areas of physical activity.

The NCC's non-statutory guidance was sent to all school at the end of June 1992 (NCC, 1992b). In addition to a consideration of the aims of physical education and an explanation of the Attainment Targets, Programmes of Study and attainments at the end of Key Stages, it includes guidance on the wide range of topics addressed during the spring-term conferences.

A two-year study has recently been concluded by researchers in the Centre for Ethnic Studies in Education and the Centre for Physical Education for the Sports Council (Verma, MacDonald, Darby and Carroll, 1991). The central objective of the research was to explore the relationships between ethnicity, culture and gender on the one hand and participation in sport and recreation on the other. The results showed that sport was the most popular leisure activity for males in six out of the eight ethnic groups studied. For two groups (African and white British) it came a narrow second. For females it fell to third place behind passive entertainment (such as watching TV or listening to music) and socializing. Nearly half of all Bangladeshi, African, and Pakistani and over a third of all Indian females reported that they took no part at all in sport or any other form of physical recreation. Whilst there were minor variations between ethnic groups in their choices of games played, they were insignificant. There were, however, significant differences between the ethnic groups in the numbers of those who took part in no activities and these were heightened by gender difference. It was found that much of the difference could be accounted for by the greater influence of parents, religious beliefs, and the opinions of the community over the lives of women.

One of the most significant findings — particularly in the light of current financial restrictions on local authorities and the effects of legislation, such as the Local Government Act (2) 1988 and the Education Reform Act 1988 — was the importance of local-authority provision to all ethnic groups. Respondents reported that half of all their activities were dependent on them. All ethnic groups, males and females, said there were activities they would like to take part in but could not.

What are the immediate courses of action which the research work mentioned indicates should be taken and especially in the light of the demands of the National Curriculum? The following are suggested as being constructive responses to the current situation.

1 **Initial training of teachers**
   There is a need to capitalize on the CATE requirements for multi-cultural and antiracist policy modules on all courses for teachers. At present the extent to which this is done is not known. Particular issues for teachers when taking PE lessons need to be introduced into all primary courses and those with specialist options in secondary courses. Teachers need to understand the different cultural patterns of various minority ethnic groups. The importance of various aspects of religion in the Muslim community that bear on PE for boys and girls is a particularly sensitive area.

2 **In-service education for teachers**
   A rolling programme of in-service training for all teachers involved in physical education, primary and secondary is required. At present there appears to have been very little INSET work related to PE. Teachers will need to understand the issues raised by the researchers mentioned in the above chapter and how to address them in the school curriculum.

3 **Links with the community**
   Closer links with local communities, and discussions between local communities and teachers, are required so that both teachers and the community can understand and appreciate each other's points of view. Schools have generally not been good at such liaisons. PE and sport will be one topic in the discussions that take place.

4 **More teachers from ethnic groups**
   There is an urgent need for teachers from different ethnic groups to be recruited. It is perhaps surprising that although there have been many black children who have excelled in school sport and many black sportsmen who have excelled in their chosen activities and provided role models in sport, there are few who join the ranks of the teaching profession. There are still fewer Muslim PE teachers, which is perhaps not so surprising.

5 National Curriculum

Antiracist and multicultural statements should be included in the Programmes of Study, but not at a general level. Explicit statements are required at a level which teachers can follow in practical terms. These should be based on good practice. This can be identified from successful programmes now taking place.

References

ARMSTRONG, N. (1990) *New Directions in Physical Education*, Human Kinetics.

BAYLISS, T. (1989) 'PE and Racism: Making Changes', *Multicultural Teaching*, 7, 2, pp. 19–22.

BCPE (1989), 'Physical Education in the National Curriculum', *Report by the Interim Working Group*, London, BCPE.

CARRINGTON, B. and WILLIAMS, T. (1989) 'Patriarchy and ethnicity: the link between school physical education and community leisure activities', in EVANS, J. (Ed) *Teachers, Teaching and Control in PE*, Basingstoke, The Falmer Press.

CARRINGTON, B. and WOOD, E. (1982) 'Body talk: Images of sport in a Multi-racial school', *Multi Racial Education*, 11, 2.

CARROLL, R. (1982) 'Examinations and Curriculum changes in Physical Education', *Physical Education Review*, 5, 2.

CARROLL, R. (1990) 'The Twain Shall Meet: GCSE and the National Curriculum', *British Journal of Physical Education*, 21, 2.

CARROLL, R. and HOLLINSHEAD, G. (1990) 'Ethnicity and Conflict in Physical Education', Unpublished research report, Manchester University.

CARROLL, R. (1991) 'Assessment and the National Curriculum. What the teacher has to do?; *British Journal of Physical Education*, 22, 2.

CASHMORE, E. (1982) *Black Sportsmen*, London, Routledge and Kegan Paul.

COMMITTEE OF INQUIRY (1985) *Education for All*, The Report of the Committee of Inquiry into the Education of Children from Ethnic Minority Groups, London, HMSO.

DEPARTMENT OF EDUCATION AND SCIENCE (1989) *National Curriculum: From Policy to Practice*, London, DES.

DEPARTMENT OF EDUCATION AND SCIENCE (1991) 'National Curriculum in Physical Education', *Interim report of the Working Group in PE*, London, DES.

DEPARTMENT OF EDUCATION AND SCIENCE (1992) *Physical Education in the National Curriculum*, London, HMSO.

EVANS, J. (1986) *Physical Education, Sport and Schooling*, Basingstoke, The Falmer Press.

FLEMING, S. (1989) 'Sport and Asian Youth Culture', Paper presented at BSA Workshop, Sport and Ethnicity, Warwick, University of Warwick.

HENDRY, L.B. (1978) *School, Sport and Leisure*, London, Lepus Books.

MODGIL, S., VERMA, G.K., MALLICK, K. and MODGIL, C. (1986) *Multicultural Education: The Interminable Debate*, Basingstoke, The Falmer Press.

NATIONAL CURRICULUM COUNCIL (1992a) 'Art, music and PE', *Schools Update*, York, NCC, Summer.

NATIONAL CURRICULUM COUNCIL (1992b) *Physical Education in the National Curriculum Non-statutory Guidance*, York, NCC.

Pumfrey, P.D. and Verma, G.K. (1990) (Eds) *Race Relations and Urban Education*, Basingstoke, The Falmer Press.

Rotherham MBC (1986) 'Physical Education in a Multicultural Society', Guidelines and General Information leaflet, Rotherham MBC.

Scraton, S. (1986) 'Images of Feminity and the Teaching of Girls' Physical Education', in Evans, J. (Ed) *Physical Education, Sport and Schooling*, Basingstoke, The Falmer Press.

Sparkes, S. (1987) 'Focusing on the Subjective Meaning of Change in the Process of Innovation', *Physical Education Review*, 10, 1.

Troyna, B. and Williams, J. (1986) *Racism, Education and the State*, London, Croom Helm.

Verma, G. and Pumfrey, P. (1988) (Eds) *Educational Attainments: Issues and Outcomes in Multicultural Education*, Basingstoke, The Falmer Press.

Verma, G., Macdonald, A., Darby, D. and Carroll, R. (1991) *Sport and Recreation with Special Reference to Ethnic Minorities*, Research report, Centre for Ethnic Studies in Education, University of Manchester.

White, A. and Coakley, J. (1986) *Making Decisions*, London, Sports Council.

Chapter 14

Modern Foreign Languages: The Paradoxical Situation of Ethnic Languages

Anthony R. Neasham

Context

This chapter deals with an area of the National Curriculum that is still evolving and one which, currently, only affects Key Stage 3 directly.[1] Since September 1992, all pupils in Year 7 (i.e., 11-year-olds) have been required to undertake the study of a modern foreign language as a foundation subject. Even though it is an area that is still developing, the full requirements will only affect those pupils aged 11 and older. There is no difference between what is being asked of ethnic-minority children and children from majority groups. All pupils will have the same opportunity and requirement to study a modern foreign language. On the surface, therefore, it might seem that little more needs to be said, however . . .!

The situation is not as clearcut as would first seem. This is not because of the National Curriculum requirements themselves but because of the conjunction of other factors. Very often, one of the differences between ethnic-minority youngsters and their peers in the majority group is language. Many ethnic-minority pupils come to school, exposed to a language in the home that is distant from that used in school. This increases the culture shock experienced by youngsters as they begin the adjustment to school life and the inexorable route through the series of 'quality-control' tests that punctuate the National Curriculum. These require competence in English as a language and as a transmitter of English-led cultural assumptions of the world to which they are adjusting. In contrast, children living in Wales and attending Welsh-medium schools have the benefits of a bilingual education — in Welsh and in English. The National Curriculum requirements in terms of the study of a modern foreign language as a foundation subject only relate to pupils in the later phases of compulsory schooling. It would therefore be inappropriate here to dwell on the home-to-school transfer process.

In the last two decades or so, the teaching of home languages (or ones relating to the language of the home) had become a feature in the classroom of pupils of secondary age, in those areas where concentrations of particular ethnic groups have led to demands for the introduction of a particular ethnic language. One of the principal means of supporting such innovations has been through support given to LEAs through funding from central government under Section 11 of the 1966 Local Governmemt Act (see Appendix 3).

Section 11 funding was originally set up to provide additional financial support to local authorities with high levels of ethnic-minority settlement. It provides 75 per cent of costs for any support project approved by the Home Office. Initially the scope of such projects was limited to assisting ethnic-minority settlers to develop the necessary skills, especially the acquisition of English, to enable them to be assimilated into the host community. One of the results of the steadily widening of the range of ethnic-minority projects approved for support has been the introduction into the curriculum of 'Community Languages', as ethnic languages are typically, albeit somewhat ambiguously, called.

In this chapter it will be argued that, as far as ethnic languages are concerned, there is a strong element of paradox in the National Curriculum modern foreign languages requirements. That paradox is partly inherent within the National Curriculum itself. This lies firstly in the fact that an ethnic language for the vast majority of those currently studying one could not be said to be a modern foreign language and secondly in the National Curriculum's response to ethnic languages. Largely though, the paradox lies in the conjunction between the onset of the National Curriculum, the 1988 Education Reform Act and, more significantly, the reassessment of criteria for projects eligible for Section 11 funding.

The past twenty years or so have seen the steady growth in some British secondary schools of the study of ethnic languages, notably Urdu and Panjabi. That provision has come in response to demands from ethnic-minority parents and communities for their cultural experience and roots to be reflected more greatly in the curriculum of their children. Equally importantly perhaps there was the feeling that, without formal assistance in instructing their children in the language, there was the risk of their cultural heritage being shut off from their children, quite apart from its role in fostering contacts with relatives in their families' country of origin. The teaching of 'ethnic' languages was not a new phenomenon in Britain, there having been a tradition of self-help within immigrant and settled communities, often in 'Saturday schools', going back to the early part of this century.

The recent growth of provision in the maintained sector of British education marked a difference from previous practice. That growth has been assisted by changes in attitudes and policy to immigrant ethnic-minority settlement in Britain. Parallel changes have also been seen in Europe and in other areas of the world, for example, the USA, Canada and Australia.

It would be wrong to assume that provision made within the maintained sector of education in the different countries was identical in scale or response. It would, however, be fair to say that much of the response arose out of an increasing awareness of ethnic consciousness that began to emerge during the 1960s and 1970s.

Ethnic-languages provision in Britain's maintained-sector schools owes a great deal not merely to a more generous response by central government and LEAs to ethnic-minority settlement. A crucial factor was the 1966 Local Government Act which included provision for Section 11 funding. As noted earlier, this was to assist local authorities with relatively high concentrations of ethnic-minority settlers in making special provision for ethnic-minority needs. Initially much of that provision concentrated on enabling ethnic-minority settlers to acquire English. Over succeeding years the interpretation of its terms of reference widened and resulted in the award of grants for ethnic-minority related projects that went beyond the acquisition of English. Therewith began the growth of ethnic-languages provision in the maintained sector, quite apart from some support being given to community-led initiatives often in the mosque or other religious centre. Some of these developments sprang out of the multicultural wave of the 1970s and 1980s when responses to the growing numbers of ethnic-minority pupils in relatively few schools in some local education authorities extended to the introduction into the secondary-school curriculum of Asian studies and Caribbean studies. Many of those initiatives soon died a death, as they were dismissed as 'tokenist gestures' and a distraction from the real issues underpinning the education and educational achievement of ethnic-minority children (Stone, 1981).

Ethnic languages came through that phase gaining in strength in face of community demands and EEC policy on provision for immigrant populations. In respect of the latter, the most interesting element was the 1976 EEC directive on mother-tongue teaching, which called on member countries to make provision in their schools to support the teaching of home languages to children of 'immigrants'. The extent to which the British government supported that directive is problematic, quite apart from the irony of the perceptions behind the directive; this seemed to be aimed primarily at ensuring that the children of immigrants would be able to return to the country of their family's origins 'if they so wished' and not be deterred by being unable to speak the language there. The tone and intent of the directive seemed to refer more to the situation of children in other European countries where immigration was a more fluid affair, given the practice of 'guest workers' and where the level of settlement was less clearcut than that in Britain (Singh, 1988).

A further boost was given to ethnic languages by the Swann report which recommended that ethnic-minority languages should be part of the secondary school curriculum as part of a culturally pluralist response to the ealities of modern Britain. This recommendation was viewed as a mixed blessing. Yet it confirmed the place of ethnic languages in the secondary school curriculum and gave recognition to the cultural validity of the languages of ethnic minorities in the British setting. What was viewed as unsatisfactory by some in the ethnic minority communities was that the Swann report did not recommend the provision of bilingual education for ethnic minority children especially in the initial stages of their schooling. This argument was rejected by the committee in favour of concentrating on the promotion of English among ethnic-minority children in order to maximize the opportunity for them to master English. Without that mastery children would have their access to the mainstream curriculum restricted with consequent detrimental effects on their life chances.

Challenges

The National Curriculum requires the study of a 'modern foreign language' as a foundation subject (DES/WO, 1990, p. 3). It requires pupils to study one language from an approved list for a period of five years from Year 7 to Year 11 inclusive. It provides for four Attainment Targets to cover the four basic linguistic skills of listening, speaking, reading, and writing, defining ten levels of performance in each. Pupil progress is to be assessed on an on-going basis and at the end of Key Stages 3 and 4.

The National Curriculum breaks new ground in its requirement that all pupils shall study a language through to the age of 16. Previously, as many as two-thirds of pupils did not study a language beyond the age of 14, usually the point at which pupils selected their 'options' in anticipation of preparation for public examinations (Neasham, 1986). By the time the Modern Foreign Languages Working Group reported (MFLWG, 1990), official figures put the rate of drop-out at to only 50 per cent of the age group. At that point, some pupils began an *ab initio* course in another language, either as an additional language or as a replacement one.

The National Curriculum also seeks to break the stranglehold of French as the foreign language more or less exclusively taught and declares itself in favour of linguistic diversification:

> There is a national need for more people with the ability to use and understand a more diverse range of foreign languages effectively. This need is widely acknowledged and specifically addressed by the Government's commitment to the diversification of language teaching in schools. (DES/WO, 1990, p. 83)

(It should also be pointed out that the National Curriculum makes provision for studying, and encourages pupils to study, more than one modern foreign language. Since such study would occur in non-core and foundation time, it is not intended to explore that aspect, beyond acknowledging its existence and particularly with regard to its potential for contributing to diversification.)

Predictably, the two main rationales behind the National Curriculum requirements are that:

- particularly with the onset of the single market within the EC, it is of crucial importance in 'a rapidly changing and increasingly competitive world' that the UK develops its foreign-language competence (DES/WO, 1990, p. 4); and
- the enforced study of a foreign language will increase awareness of pupils' own language (DES/WO, 1990, p. 4).

The requirements will demand two further things. Firstly, there is the expectation, consistent with modern and continental practice, that the language studied shall be essentially taught in the 'target language'. Thus, it expects that French, for example, should be taught through the medium of French. This, it is considered, is not only consistent with the current philosophy of education but also increases the practicality and realism:

Learning to use a foreign language means learning to communicate with speakers of that language. Communication ... is a vital and interactive process. In communicating, people interact with each other, negotiating meanings together, thus affecting the way they each speak, think and act. Communicating in a foreign language must thus involve both teachers and pupils using the target language as the normal means of communication. (MFLWG, 1990, p. 6)

Secondly, there is the assumption that there will be sufficient teachers suitably qualified and trained to deliver the programme. At the DES's own estimate, some 1750 further language teachers will be needed to meet the full programme, although the working group's own estimates put the figure at 3000 (DES/WO, 1990, p. 89). It should also be noted that no separate figures and estimates are provided for ethnic-language teaching, beyond the recognition that:

There are no detailed national statistics about the extent of bilingualism in schools. But the information available from those LEAs which do have a monitoring system reveals a picture that is both more diverse and more extensive than might initially be predicted. There are now several LEAs whose bilingual pupils make up between 10 per cent and 50 per cent of the total school population. (DES/WO, 1990, p. 83)

Explaining its use of the term bilingual, the working group observes:

The term bilingual is used as a shorthand to describe pupils who come from homes or communities where languages other than English are spoken, and who in consequence have developed some competence in those languages. The term does not necessarily imply a high level of proficiency in two languages. It describes pupils with a variety of language profiles. (DES/WO, 1990, p. 83)

Quite apart from clarifying the working group's use of the term, the observation serves as a timely reminder of the dangers in assuming that bilingualism necessarily implies mastery of two languages. Indeed, as Tosi (1984) reported, when discussing the nature of bilingualism in his study on Bedford's Italian community, research on isolated rural Finnish-speaking minorities in Sweden had rated some youngsters as 'semi-lingual'. By force of circumstance they were exposed to limited or incomplete models of both Finnish and Swedish in their daily interactions. In consequence they were severely limited in their capacity to express themselves in either language at an important stage in their cognitive development. While that condition may not be reflected to the same extent among Britain's young bilinguals, it does remind one of the potential dangers of the failure to make adequate provision for such children in the early days of their formal schooling.

The document setting out the National Curriculum requirements in respect of modern foreign languages is produced by the Department of Education and Science and the Welsh Office (DES/WO, 1991). It also outlines how provision will differ in Wales from that in England in terms of the overall National Curriculum framework. In 'Welsh-medium' schools in Wales, Welsh will be studied as a core or foundation subject from Year 1. As far as Key Stages 3 and 4 are concerned, Welsh schools will be subject to the same modern foreign language requirements as their counterparts in England.

Under the original proposals from the Secretaries of State for Education and Wales, nineteen languages were drawn up as 'approved for study'. These were set out in two schedules. Schedule 1 contained eight EC working languages: Danish, Dutch, French, German, modern Greek, Italian, Portuguese and Spanish, while Schedule 2 contained 'eleven other languages of commercial and cultural importance': Arabic, Bengali, Chinese (Cantonese or Mandarin), Gujerati, modern Hebrew, Hindi, Japanese, Punjabi, Russian, Turkish and Urdu (DES/WO, 1990a, p. 144). Under the terms of the Education Reform Act (1988) schools were to be required to offer at least one of the languages listed for study under Schedule 1 to pupils as a foundation subject, before a language listed under Schedule 2 could be studied as the modern foreign language requirement language.

Part of the remit of the Modern Foreign Languages Working Group set up under the chairmanship of Martin Harris, then vice-chancellor of Essex University, was to offer advice on the appropriateness of the languages approved for study. In its interim report (DES/WO, 1990a) the working group confirmed the nineteen languages put forward but recommended that the 'two-schedule' element be removed. This was accepted by the Secretaries of State for Education and Science and for Wales. The stricture remained that each school must be able to offer all its pupils one of the eight EC working languages before any of the other eleven languages could be studied for foundation-subject purposes.

The elements considered above constitute the National Curriculum element of the challenges facing ethnic languages. As was pointed out in the introduction to this chapter, there is a strong element of paradox that transcends the National Curriculum itself. Beyond the National Curriculum itself there is also the broader framework of the 1988 Education Reform Act (ERA) and the changes that have been made in arrangements for Section 11 funding.

The 1988 ERA required local education authorities to take steps towards the delegation to individual schools of responsibility for the management of their own budgets. Under this requirement LEAs are restricted as to the proportion of their total educational budget that can be retained for central purposes. Thus, the initiative for the financial management of the curriculum rests increasingly with the schools themselves. The control, role and influence of the LEA is much reduced. Many might welcome this change, since it leaves the individual school to plan the best use of the available resources according to its perceptions of its needs, rather than decisions being driven by overriding policy aims of the LEA, which might not be entirely congruent with those of the individual school. One of the potential consequences is that schools may be forced to make decisions which weigh heavily on the basic needs of the school, rather than take full account of specialist needs. Thus in schools where the teaching of ethnic languages was still developing, there might not yet be classes viable in number and size to provide 'economic' justification for the continuation of ethnic-language provision. It should also be pointed out that it is typical for ethnic-language teaching to be arranged on a team basis. Under this, although ethnic-language teachers may do all of their teaching in one school rather than be 'shared' between two or more schools, they remain at present part of a central team. At the time this chapter is being written, it is far from clear how LEAs intend to respond to the changes required by the ERA and by the dramatic changes taking place in Section 11 funding (see Appendix 3).

It would be unfair to lay the blame entirely at the door of LEAs, since ethnic-language teachers, as far as the writer has been able to ascertain, typically hold what are called Section 11 posts. As was mentioned earlier, 75 per cent of costs of approved Section 11 posts are met from central government funds with the remaining 25 per cent of the costs being met by the local authority. Changes have been made in the criteria under which Section 11 funding can be granted. These took effect from 1 April 1992.

In essence, the old system has been scrapped in favour of a system of specific projects for which local authorities are required to make bids for funding. Under the old arrangements, local-authority bids for Section 11 funding were more or less automatically renewed annually. Now local authorities haves been required to present bids for support for specific projects of five years duration, which are consistent with the original remit of Section 11 support. That means that the nature of bids has to be shown to be aimed at assisting the integration of ethnic-community members, not at projects that would support cultural maintenance. Local authorities were required to make bids by 30 April 1991, and it was expected that the government would announce its decisions in September 1991, in order to allow local authorities time to make the necessary arrangements for the 1992–3 financial year. The decisions were still awaited in December 1991.

Responses

It is extremely difficult in the space available to consider the issue of responses to the National Curriculum, given the paradox in the situation of ethnic languages which extends beyond the requirements of modern foreign language foundation subjects. Such responses relate or would relate to 'technical' matters. There is no doubt that the modern foreign language NC component will present very real challenges to schools, language teachers and ultimately, the pupils. Constructive ideas are being advocated (NUT, 1992).

In terms of arrangements for the introduction of the modern foreign language element of the National Curriculum, a working group was set up to respond to the proposals of the Secretaries of State for Education and Wales. Evidence of its work is reflected in the discussion earlier in this chapter. The working group under the chairmanship of Martin Harris, formerly vice-chancellor of Essex University, had teachers of ethnic languages among its consultation groups and indeed, on publication of its interim report, invited and received comments from interested parties on its responses to the government's proposals.

Broadly speaking, however, those challenges will be much the same for all of the nineteen languages approved for study. It will require significant changes in the structure of present syllabuses and teaching methods and the gathering and sequencing of suitable teaching materials in order to meet the defined levels of performance in each of the four skills. If there is a difference between languages, it lies within the demands that writing skills will place on pupils. Languages with scripts that differ considerably from the Roman script used in English as well as the eight EC languages will pose additional demands. This was an area of particular concern to organizations such as the National Council for Punjabi Teachers, who made representations to the Modern Foreign Languages Working Group and to the Secretary of State for Education and Science. No concessions were made over the requirements for Punjabi or Urdu, but special arrangements were made for Cantonese and Mandarin Chinese and Japanese given the complex structure of their written symbols. (These are detailed in the documentation provided to schools on 'Modern Foreign Languages in the National Curriculum' (DES/WO, 1991, p. 18) and in the DES Circular 15/91, p. 7). The complementary publications by the National Curriculum Council also merit attention (NCC, 1990, 1991).

The National Curriculum requirements in respect of modern foreign languages represent a welcome impetus to the teaching of languages whether European or non-European. The inclusion of languages used within the cultural framework of Britain's ethnic communities in the list of languages approved for study is also welcome because their inclusion increases the recognition given to their importance to the communities and to the growth in the teaching of those languages in Britain. The quality of the syllabuses for the study of those languages has been greatly improved in the wake of the Swann report and the advent of the GCSE Examinations.

Influenced by the experience of teaching those languages in a British context alongside the more traditional languages of the secondary curriculum (especially through the development of CSE, Mode 3, examination syllabuses), examinations in ethnic languages have moved on from the sterile and academic approach that characterized the old O level languages examinations. That approach has been replaced by one that is modern and practical in its orientation. This is reflected in the current GCSE syllabuses for modern languages, which are built on nationally agreed criteria for all languages. The inclusion of ethnic languages on the approved list is all the more welcome in the context of the government's commitment to diversify the range of languages to be taught.

It is also welcome that the Secretary of State for Education has been 'minded' to respond to calls from various quarters, most notably the Modern Foreign Languages Working Group, to avoid the ill-considered 'two-language schedules for approved languages for study', whereby the ethnic languages central to the discussion in this chapter were apparently 'relegated' by their being listed under Schedule 2. Some might feel aggrieved that there is still the stipulation that an ethnic language cannot count as the foundation language unless an EC language is available in the school. However, this would seem a severe and somewhat naive stance to take. Britain is committed to membership of the European Community and, in light of the development of closer union between member countries, it becomes ever more important that *all* pupils, regardless of ethnicity, have every opportunity to equip themselves for life in the new Europe. To give separate status to ethnic languages could restrict the educational horizons of ethnic pupils. It is also encouraging in face of the eurocentric, even anglocentric orientation of the National Curriculum, that the National Curriculum has given recognition to ethnic languages.

On the negative side, it must be said that the National Curriculum, as it presently exists, has not grasped the nettle of bilingualism among ethnic pupils. The National Curriculum requirements in respect of ethnic languages confine themselves to cultural maintenance rather than bilingual development. In this respect, the Welsh language could be said to have received more favourable treatment. However, it has to be pointed out that provision for Welsh is within a more discrete area, i.e., Wales itself, and thus easier to systematize. It does not, it should be noted, apply to children of Welsh-speaking families living elsewhere in the United Kingdom. And moreover, as the DES/WO (1990, p. 83) points out: 'Welsh cannot in legal terms be defined as a modern foreign language'.

In essence, cultural maintenance in the context of bilingual education involves the teaching of a language so that the learner can gain easier access to a particular culture associated with it. Bilingual development, on the other hand, would mean the teaching of two languages in parallel, so that the learner's cognitive development could continue unimpeded, with each language supporting the other and the learner. Bilingual education has long been the subject of study. Although the findings generated have been mixed, more recent studies have tended to view bilingual education as being beneficial rather than detrimental (Neasham, 1986).

Thus, it was interesting to note that children in Welsh-speaking primary schools, 'according to this year's National-Curriculum tests for 7-year-olds . . . achieve[d] better results than their English counterparts' and that '11-year-olds from English-speaking homes . . . educated in Welsh-speaking schools. . . . score[d] as highly in English reading and spelling tests as those educated in England' (*The Times*, 1991, 30 December). It will also be interesting to see whether the continued monitoring of performances against National Curriculum criteria will come to provide irresistible evidence for extending the scope of bilingual education to ethnic-minority children.

The Modern Foreign Languages Working Group reported that languages were being taught in some maintained sector schools to pupils below the age of 11 and that it would have welcomed exposure to another language being a requirement for all pupils before that age. However, it recognized that, in the present situation, this was impractical. At least a further 3000 specialist language teachers would be required to meet the present level of National Curriculum requirements. The working group did express the hope that an earlier start to language learning would later become the norm in British schools.

Very few concrete data are available as regards the supply available of ethnic-language teachers. On the strength of an earlier study, the present writer found that there was little institutional provision for the training of ethnic-language teachers, that the existing teaching force did not meet the current demand and that it relied heavily on teachers nearing retirement age (Neasham, 1986). A recent study by Singh (1991) showed nothing that would contradict those findings.

Even when adequate provision is available, these are possible pitfalls. To assume that pupils from ethnic-minority groups will necessarily elect to study for examination purposes a language that is spoken at home, could be mistaken. On the other hand, there can be little doubt that many would choose so to do, given the opportunity. When a school offers a language such as Gujarati or Urdu, it must be open to all pupils and also given equal status through the school's timetabling arrangements.

Students should learn about the ways in which different forms of a language are spoken by groups in various parts of the world. One of the linguistic legacies of the period of European colonization is that, for example, English, French, Spanish, Portuguese and Dutch are second languages in many now autonomous countries. There is a potent argument that a form of linguistic imperialism has followed from colonization. Such arguments must be addressed in the study of modern languages. Bilingualism and multilingualism are the norm in many countries. The considerable benefits of such skills in modern languages should be presented. The assumption that one modern language is sufficient must be challenged. This presents difficulties when many teachers in this country remain monolingual. Travel to foreign countries is now a common experience to many secondary-school pupils and their families. Are these opportunities capitalized upon? Are pupils from minority ethnic groups under-represented in such activities for reasons that are largely economic?

To learn a language requires that the culture of the country is also studied. Its literature is an essential component. Only when the richness of a culture is appreciated, albeit partially as is inevitably the case when a language is being learned, can the richness of a foreign language be increasingly appreciated. In providing opportunities for systematic study of such concerns, modern languages represent a path along which mutual understandings between language communities, on which multicultural and antiracist education is predicated, can be furthered.

Offering ethnic-minority languages to GCSE and A level is one means of publicly acknowledging their important status. The provision within a school of instruction in community languages is another constructive strategy that has the added advantage of building links between school and community.

Finally, as has already been observed, the situation as regards ethnic languages and the National Curriculum is very much one of paradox. The National Curriculum offers a useful boost to the recognition of ethnic languages in Britain, but does so at a time of shrinking support from central government for ethnic-minority interests. It is too early to judge as yet the effect that the changes to the rules affecting Section 11 funding will have on ethnic-language teaching posts, particularly when schools are wrestling with the management of their own budgets for the first time.

It will be tragic if the advent of the National Curriculum proves to be the kiss of death to the considerable progress that has been made in the development of ethnic-language teaching in the maintained sector. More tragic still will be any resultant reduction in competence among ethnic groups in languages that access their cultural heritage.

Note

1   The writer would like to acknowledge the invaluable contribution of Gurbachan Singh in the collection of information and documents used in the preparation of this chapter.

References

DEPARTMENT OF EDUCATION AND SCIENCE (1985) *Education for All*, Report of the Committee of Inquiry into the Education of Children from Ethnic Minority Groups, (The Swann Report), London, HMSO, Cmnd. 9453.

DEPARTMENT OF EDUCATION AND SCIENCE AND THE WELSH OFFICE (1990) *Modern Foreign Languages for ages 11 to 16*, Proposals of the Secretary of State for Education and Science and the Secretary of State for Wales, London, DES/WO.

DEPARTMENT OF EDUCATION AND SCIENCE AND THE WELSH OFFICE (1990a) 'Initial Advice of the National Curriculum Modern Foreign Languages Group', Interim report of the MFLWG submitted to the DES/WO, Feb 1990, (Mimeograph, circulated to secondary schools through the DES).

DEPARTMENT OF EDUCATION AND SCIENCE AND THE WELSH OFFICE (1991) *Modern Foreign Languages in the National Curriculum*, London, HMSO, November.

EUROPEAN ECONOMIC COMMUNITY (1977) *Directive on Mother-Tongue Teaching*, Brussels, EEC.

NATIONAL CURRICULUM COUNCIL (1990) *Modern Foreign Languages*, York, NCC.

NATIONAL CURRICULUM COUNCIL (1991) *Linguistic Diversity and the National Curriculum*, York, NCC.

NATIONAL UNION OF TEACHERS (1992) *Anti-Racist Curriculum Guidelines*, London, NUT.

NEASHAM, A.R. (1986) 'Language, Culture and Education: a Study of Cultural, Social and Educational Issues relating to Community Language provision in British-maintained secondary schools', Unpublished PhD thesis, University of Bradford.

SINGH, G. (1988) *Language, Race and Education*, Birmingham, Jaysons and Company.

SINGH, G. (1992) 'The Development of Pluralism in British Education with particular reference to the role of the LEA', Unpublished PhD thesis, University of Manchester.

STONE, M. (1981) *The Education of the Black Child in Britain: The Myth of Multiracial Education*, Glasgow, Fontana.

THE TIMES (1991) 30 December.

TOSI, A. (1984) *Immigration and Bilingual Education*, Oxford, Pergamon Press.

Implications of Race-Relations Legislation

Prabodh Merchant

Earlier chapters have provided ethnic and cultural contexts which should be taken into account if the educational needs and aspirations of all students are to be properly fulfilled. In an increasingly competitive environment with an ever present scarcity of resources it is particularly important that those with the primary responsibility of education are also aware of the legal context in relation to race and culture within which they carry out their work. It will be helpful therefore to look briefly at the development of race-relations law in this country over the past twenty to thirty years, resulting from the changing racial, cultural and religious composition of the population.

Background to the Laws

While it is true to say that the UK has always has migrants who have been assimilated into the social and economic life of the country, these have been, up to the mid 1950s, generally of white-European origins. For these migrants, difficulties in the main were those resulting from differences in language, religion and those flowing from newness: i.e., lack of contacts, availability of, and access to, goods and services. It was assumed that most, if not all, of the problems likely to be encountered by these migrants would resolve themselves without any special intervention by the State in a matter of a generation or two at most. The differences such as those relating to religion, custom and practice could be accommodated within the existing legal framework. Problems of race discrimination were thought to be virtually non-existent and could similarly be left to be dealt with by the common-sense application of existing public order legislation supported by the innate sense of fair play on the part of the majority of the British people.

Post-war reconstruction of shattered cities and economies and the scarcity of labour in all the European countries necessitated a wider search for suitable labour. Thus, throughout the 1950s, various European countries actively encouraged recruitment of labour from their colonies or from countries newly given their independence. For the United Kingdom the most fruitful sources of labour were the islands of the Caribbean, and the newly independent countries of the Indian subcontinent. People from these countries were already familiar to the British and, as members of the Commonwealth, were free to enter the mother country without any restrictions. Throughout the 1950s people came to work and mostly returned to the countries of origin to visit the families whom they supported. As their prime concern was to obtain work, they were attracted to towns and cities offering opportunities for unskilled and semi-skilled work. Again, with the responsibility of supporting their families in their country of origin, it was important that living expenses in this country were kept to a minimum. This typically meant living in Victorian terraced housing shared with friends and relatives in the cheapest areas of town, close to mills, factories and transport depots where they worked. Inevitably, differences in priorities, culture, language, religion, and so forth caused friction between these newcomers and the white working-class residents.

Towards the end of the 1950s, in response to public clamour, the government made known its intention to introduce restrictions on the entry of Commonwealth citizens. This intention was translated in 1962 into the Commonwealth Immigrants Act. Commonwealth citizens entering the UK for work after the passing of the Act in mid-1962 needed vouchers. Dependents of those already in the UK were, however, allowed to come without vouchers. This had a significant impact on the nature of immigration and the pattern of their settlement in the UK. Initially there was a rush to beat the deadline of unrestricted entry. This was followed by a need for entrants of both the pre and post-period of the 1962 Act to take up permanent settlement and make arrangements for their families to join them here in the United Kingdom. Thus, by introducing an element of sponsorship, the voucher system reinforced bonds of friendship and kinship and provided a further incentive for the new entrants to settle among existing communities and into similar work areas. This change in the composition and pattern of migration had, in its turn, implications for the various services including the education service. The arrival of families with school-age young people into areas which were already the poorest in terms of housing, education, and social and environmental amenities created further tensions and friction.

The 1962 Act was followed in 1965 by the first of the three Race Relations Acts. The 1965 Race Relations Act created a race-relations board with powers to take up individual cases of overt discrimination in a very limited sphere of public life. The emphasis of the Act was on conciliation, with the reserve power to take those few who behaved in an illegal way to court. As yet there was no official acceptance of racial discrimination as a significant factor in the continuing disadvantage and harassment suffered by those who were now being euphemistically referred to as 'New-Commonwealth immigrants'.

The task of helping the newcomers to adjust to British society was largely left to the newcomers and voluntary groups such as the Joint Council for the Welfare of Immigrants, the National Committee for Commonwealth Immigrants and concerned individuals. However, the extra burden on local authorities with substantial populations of migrants from the New Commonwealth was recognized. Section 11 of the Local Government Act 1966 therefore provides that the Secretary of State may pay grants towards expenditure on additional staff to those 'local authorities who in his opinion are required to make special provision in the exercise of any of their functions in consequence of the presence within their areas of substantial numbers of immigrants from the Commonwealth whose language or customs differ from those of the community'. Up to 75 per cent of salary costs of approved posts was payable. By far the largest proportion of this grant was used to fund posts in education. Thus, in 1986–7, of the estimated £100m Section 11 expenditure, 79.5 per cent went towards funding posts in education mainly as generalist teachers, English as a Second Language (ESL), school-based peripatetic teachers and classroom assistants.

The next substantial piece of legislation covering race relations was the second Race Relations Act in 1968. This act extended the powers of the Race Relations Board to cover employment, housing, education, and the provision of goods, facilities and services and the publication or display of discriminatory advertisements and notices. The Board was also given the power to investigate suspected unlawful discrimination where there was no individual complainant. Due to inadequate resources and the absence of any provision to tackle indirect discrimination, in practice the Board's investigations were largely confined to individual complaints. The 1968 Act also established the Community Relations Commission (CRC) and charged it with the responsibility for creating better understanding and harmonious relations between peoples of different races and cultures. The CRC in turn provided funds to local voluntary committees to employ officers to undertake work in pursuance of these objectives. Both the Race Relations Board and the Community Relations Commission did some very valuable work in tackling the difficulties experienced by New-Commonwealth migrants.

However, by the early 1970s, it was apparent that the law needed widening to include indirect discrimination and strengthening to allow a proactive rather than a merely reactive approach to be taken to counter the continuing high levels of direct and indirect discrimination based largely on colour. It was also recognized that equality of opportunity and treatment could not be made conditional upon the total abandonment of cultural and ethnic identity by racial minorities, increasing proportions of whose members were either born here or had been substantially brought up in the United Kingdom.

The Current Law

With these considerations and the experience and lessons learned from the 1965 and 1968 Race Relations Acts, a new Race Relations Act was enacted in

1976. The Act merged the Race Relations Board and the Community Relations Commission to form a new body, the Commission for Racial Equality, with new and stronger powers for the creation of a society based on equality of opportunity for all racial groups. The Commission has a duty of:

- working towards the elimination of discrimination;
- promoting equality of opportunity and good relations between persons of different racial groups generally; and
- keeping under review the workings of the Act and, when required by the Secretary of State, or when it otherwise thinks it necessary, drawing up and submitting to the Secretary of State proposals for amending it.

The 1976 Act gave a wider definition of unlawful discrimination to include traditional practices and procedures which, although they may not be intended to discriminate or disadvantage, nevertheless had that effect on ethnic minorities. A requirement or condition which although applied equally, or would be applied equally, to all racial groups constitutes unlawful indirect discrimination if:

- a considerably smaller proportion of persons of a racial group can comply with it as compared with the proportion of persons of another racial group;
- which cannot be shown to be justifiable irrespective of colour, race, nationality or ethnic or national origins of the person or persons to whom it is applied; and
- which is to the detriment of the person who cannot comply with it.

Thus unnecessarily demanding educational qualifications for jobs which do not require such high qualifications could be indirectly discriminatory. Similarly, unjustifiable dress or language requirements could constitute unlawful indirect discrimination. The 1976 Act also enables measures to be taken to meet the special needs of particular racial groups in regard to their education, training or welfare, or any other ancillary benefits. Additionally, the Act allows provision to be made for training and encouragement to apply for work in which particular racial groups are underrepresented. Actual selection for a job must, of course, be on merit.

The two basic objectives of the Race Relations Act 1976 can therefore be stated as follows: firstly to regulate behaviour by laying down minimum acceptable standards which should govern relations between groups and individuals in any civilized society. The second objective is to encourage behaviour and actions necessary to overcome the effects of discrimination and disadvantage and thereby help to create a society in which groups and individuals enjoy genuine equality of opportunity. As both objectives aim to bring about a qualitative change in society, their importance to educationalists cannot be overstated.

This then, is the broad legal context in terms of race relations, within which the education service has to operate. Detailed guidance on the implementation of the Race Relations Act with specific reference to every section is, of course, available from a variety of sources. Thus, for example, the Commission for Racial Equality's code of practice for the elimination of racial discrimination in education sets out the implications of every relevant section of the 1976 Act to help those involved with education to provide it without discrimination made unlawful by the Act. Other publications provide detailed guidance on important issues relating to the encouragement of awareness and initiatives necessary for the creation of an education service which is capable of meeting the needs and aspirations of a multiracial, multicultural and multifaith society. However, it may perhaps be useful to consider, albeit very briefly, one or two important avenues for making progress towards achieving these objectives within the framework of the Race Relations Act.

Multicultural Education

Clearly this has been, and continues to be, important in disseminating information relating to the culture, traditions, and beliefs of various groups within society. However, the need is to build on the understanding and tolerance which will, hopefully, result from greater awareness of other ways of living by ensuring that the more positive aspects of different systems and values are identified and respected.

Antiracist Education

A careful and sympathetic review of teaching materials and methods is necessary to ensure that they are as free as possible of cultural and racial bias based on negative and/or stereotypical images and assumptions. Their replacement by appropriately based materials and methods will be helpful in promoting self-development and mutual respect amongst students and teachers. Encouragement can also be given to underrepresented groups to apply for work in the Education Service, especially in teaching posts. This would not only provide much needed role models, but could also be an additional cultural resource.

The National Curriculum

Implementing some of the initiatives discussed above within the constraints of the National Curriculum is inevitably going to pose challenges to both resources and commitment. As far as may be practicable, attempts should be made to ensure that teaching materials and methods in various subjects within the National Curriculum are such as to enable the various minority groups to understand and value their particular ethnic identities.

Finally, there are also other Acts which impose various duties and obligations on those involved in providing education. For example, the 1988 Education Reform Act with its provision for the Local Management of Schools (LMS), opting out, the National Curriculum and the character of religious worship. All of these issues have racial as well as cultural and religious dimensions. Similarly, the right of parents to a school of their choice for their children poses challenges, which sometimes may be in conflict with obligations under other legislation. Consider, for example, the recent test cases in Dewsbury and Cleveland. In both, the High Court upheld the right of parental choice under the 1988 Education Reform Act, even though such judgments appeared to undermine the 1976 Race Relations Act. Under the terms of the latter, LEAs are not allowed to act in any way that would constitute racial discrimination. The parents won the right to have their children transferred to other schools from the ones to which they had been originally allocated. The parents were white and the schools had a high proportion of Asian pupils (see Chapter 2 in this volume about parental choice).

Section 18 (I) of the Race Relations Act 1976 as originally enacted made it unlawful for a local education authority (LEA) to discriminate racially in carrying out those functions under the Education Acts 1944 to 1975 which do not fall under Section 17 of the 1976 Act. The Education Acts of 1980 and 1981 updated Section 18 so that it covers functions under those Education Acts also. There is no similar reference in the 1986 or 1988 Education Acts. There is a suggestion that the words in Section 235 (7) of the 1988 Act that it 'shall be construed as one with the 1944 Act' are intended to deal with this point. But the position is not clear.

It should be mentioned that what we have learned as a result of twenty years' experience is that the law is a necessary but not a sufficient condition of solving the problems of race relations. The aims of legislation have to be translated into practice by various institutions in our society (e.g., courts, industries, universities, schools, politicians, employers, and all citizens).

As with all laws, race-relations legislation must be kept under review to ensure that it addresses contemporary concerns adequately. The Commission for Racial Equality (CRE) undertook a review of the Race Relations Act 1976 in 1985, and made recommendations to which the government made no formal response. In the light of subsequent events, the CRE undertook a second review and published a consultation document in 1991 entitled *Second Review of the Race Relations Act 1976: A Consultative Document* (CRE, 1991). The review is in two sections. In the first of these, the CRE sets out proposals for changes in the legislation which it considers will improve the effectiveness of the law-enforcement process. The second part of the consultation document reflects on issues closely related to race relations and on ways in which society might better manage the many and varied tensions that occur across the boundaries of race, religion and sex, bearing in mind the implications of the move towards a more integrated Europe.

Lists of Recent ERA-Related Publications (secondary-schools orientation): National Curriculum Council (NCC); School Examinations and Assessment Council (SEAC); Department of Education and Science (DES)*; and Her Majesty's Inspectorate (HMI)

P. D. Pumfrey and G.K. Verma

Section A: National Curriculum Council

Key: (CR) = Consultation Reports
      (CG) = Curriculum Guidance
      (N-S G) = Non-Statutory Guidance
      (NOP OPs) = National Oracy Project, Occasional Papers
      (INSET) = In-Service Education for Teachers

General Publications

NCC (1989) *An Introduction to the National Curriculum* (INSET).
NCC (1989) *Developing INSET Activities* (INSET).
NCC (1989) *The National Curriculum: A Guide for Employers.*
NCC (1989) *NCC Annual Report 1988–89, December.*
NCC (1989) *A Curriculum for All — Special Educational Needs in the National Curriculum* (CG).
NCC (1989) *National Curriculum: Developing INSET Activities, Video* (37 mins) (INSET).

---

* The Department of Education and Science (DES) became the Department for Education (DFE) on 1 July, 1992

NCC (1989) *Circular 8: Technology 5–16 in the National Curriculum: A digest.*
NCC (1989) *Circular 9: English 5–16 in the National Curriculum: A digest.*
NCC (1990) *Circular 10: The National Curriculum at Key Stage 4.*
NCC (1990) *Incorporating Programmes of Study into Schemes of Work.*
NCC (1990) *Corporate Plan 1990–91.*
NCC (1990) *The Whole Curriculum,* March (CG).
NCC (1990) *The National Curriculum: A Guide for Parents of Secondary Pupils,* May (also published in Greek, Turkish, Chinese, Bengali, Gujerati, Hindi, Punjabi and Urdu).
NCC (1991) *NCC Annual Report 1990–1991,* December.
NCC (1991) *Circular 11: Linguistic Diversity and the National Curriculum.*
NCC (1992) *NCC Annual Report 1991–1992,* December.
NCC (1992) *The National Curriculum and Pupils with Severe Learning Difficulties* (CG).
NCC (1992) *The National Curriculum and Pupils with Severe Learning Difficulties* (INSET).

National Curriculum Council: Religious Education and the Foundation Subjects

Religious Education
NCC (1991) *Religious Education — A Local Curriculum Framework.*
NCC (1992) *Analysis of SACRE Reports.*

English
NCC (1989) *English,* November (CG).
NCC (1989) *English for Ages 5–11.*
NCC (1989) *English for Ages 5–16.*
NCC (1990) *English* (N-S G).
NCC (1990) *Conclusion* Information Sheet (N-S G).
NCC (1991) *English Key Stages* 2–4 (N-S G).
NCC (1991) *Aspects of English: English in the National Curriculum: Key Stages 1 to 4* (INSET).
NCC (1991) *Teaching, Talking and Learning in Key Stage 3.*

Mathematics
NCC (1988) *Mathematics for Ages* 5–16.
NCC (1989) *Mathematics* (N-S G).
NCC (1991) *Mathematics,* September (CR).
NCC (1991) *Mathematics Programmes of Study: INSET for Key Stages 3 and 4* (INSET).

Science
NCC (1989) *Science* (N-S G).
NCC (1991) *Science Explorations* (INSET).

NCC (1991) *Science* (CR).

NCC (1991) *History and Geography at Key Stage 4; Science at Key Stage 4; Whole classes taking examinations for GCSE or equivalent qualifications in National Curriculum subjects early* (CR).

NCC (1992) *Teaching Science to Pupils with Special Educational Needs* (CG).

Technology

NCC (1989) *Technology in the National Curriculum.*

NCC (1989) *Technology*, November (CR).

NCC (1989) *Design and Technology for Ages 5–16.*

NCC (1990) *Technology — Design and Technology Capability* (N-S G); *Technology — Information Technology Capability* (N-S G).

NCC (1990) *Incorporating Programmes of Study into Schemes of Work* (N-S G).

NCC (1991) *Implementing Design and Technology at Key Stage 3* (INSET).

History

NCC (1990) *History.*

NCC (1991) *Implementing National Curriculum History: Key Stages 1 to 3* November (INSET).

NCC (1991) *History* (N-S G).

NCC (1991) *History Non-Statutory Guidance England.*

NCC (1991) *History Non-Statutory Guidance England; Supplementary Study Units: Key Stages 3 and 4.*

NCC (1991) *Geography and History at Key Stage 4.*

NCC (1991) *History and Geography at Key Stage 4; Science at Key Stage 4; Whole Classes Taking Examinations for GCSE or Equivalent Qualifications in National Curriculum Subjects Early* (CR).

Geography

NCC (1990) *Geography.*

NCC (1991) *Geography* (N-S G).

NCC (1991) *Geography and History at Key Stage 4.*

NCC (1991) *History and Geography at Key Stage 4; Science at Key Stage 4; Whole Classes Taking Examinations for GCSE or Equivalent Qualifications in National Curriculum Subjects Early* (CR).

Music and Art

NCC (1991) *Art and Music at Key Stage 4* (CR).

NCC (1991) *Art for ages 5–14* (CR).

NCC (1991) *Music for ages 5–14* (CR).

NCC (1992) *Art* (CR).

NCC (1992) *Music* (CR).

NCC (1992) *Art* (N-S G).

NCC (1992) *Music* (N-S G).

Physical Education
NCC (1991) *PE for ages 5–16* (CR).
NCC (1992) *Physical Education* (N-S G).

Foreign Languages
NCC (1991) *Modern Foreign Languages* (CR).
NCC (1991) *Linguistic Diversity and the National Curriculum*.
NCC (1992) *Modern Foreign Languages* (N-S G).

Section B: School Examinations and Assessment Council

Key: (AAS)   A/AS Levels
     (ASSM)   Assessment Matters
     EMU   EMU
     GCSE   GCSE
     KS3   Key Stage 3
     KS4   Key Stage 4

General Publications

SEAC (1989) *The Recorder* (Autumn).
SEAC (1989) *Teacher Assessment in the Classroom*, Pack A.
SEAC (1989) *Teacher Assessment in the School*, Pack B.
SEAC (1989) *A Source Book for Teachers*, Pack C.
SEAC (1990) *Examining GCSE: First General Scrutiny Report* (GCSE).
SEAC (1990) *GCSE AS level Chief Examiners' Conference Report* (AAS).
SEAC (1990) *Your Questions Answered* (ASSM).
SEAC (1990) *A sourcebook for Teacher Assessment* (ASSM).
SEAC (1990) *The Recorder* (Spring).
SEAC (1990) *The Recorder* (Summer).
SEAC (1990) *The Recorder* (Autumn).
SEAC (1991) *National Curriculum Assessment; Responsibility of LEAs in 1991– 92*.
SEAC (1991) *Decision Analytic Aids to Examining — The DAATE Report* (EMU).
SEAC (1991) *Examining GCSE: Second General Scrutiny Report* (GCSE).
SEAC (1991) *A and AS Examinations 1989: General Scrutiny Report* (AAS).
SEAC (1991) *Coursework: Learning from GCSE Experience — An Account of the Proceedings of a SEAC Conference* (GCSE).
SEAC (1991) *A and AS Level Results 1990* (AAS).
SEAC (1991) *Key Stage 4 Assessment: Quality Assured* (KS4).
SEAC (1991) *Teacher Assessment at Key Stage 3 1992* (KS3).
SEAC (1991) *National Pilot for Mathematics and Science KS3: End of Key Stage Assessment Arrangements 1992* (KS3).

SEAC (1991) *NCA Arrangements — National Pilot Leaflets for LEAs* (KS3).
SEAC (1991) *Chief Examiners' Conferences 1991 Evaluation Report* (EMU).
SEAC (1991) *National Curriculum Assessment at Key Stage 3: A Review of the 1991 Pilots with Implications for 1992* (EMU).
SEAC (1991) *The Recorder* (Spring).
SEAC (1991) *The Recorder* (Summer).
SEAC (1991) *The Recorder* (Autumn).
SEAC (1991) *Timetable for Assessment Cycle 1991–92* (ASSM).
SEAC (1991) *Information and guidance for LEAs and Governing Bodies of Non-LEA Maintained Schools*, Autumn (KS3).
SEAC (1991) *The Parents' Charter*.
SEAC (1991) *Teacher Assessment in Practice 1992* (KS3).
SEAC (1992) *Briefing Note 2: Tests for 14-year-olds* (KS3).
SEAC (1992) *A and AS Level Results 1991* (AAS).
SEAC (1992) *GCSE Criteria: Welsh First Language*.
SEAC (1992) *GCSE Criteria: Welsh Literature and Welsh Second Language*.
SEAC (1992) *GCSE Criteria: English, English Literature, Mathematics, Science (Biology, Chemistry, Physics)*.
SEAC (1992) *GCSE/KS4: Standards for Assessment and Certification*.
SEAC (1992) *Principles for GCE Advanced and Advanced Supplementary Examinations*.

Schools Examination and Assessment Council

English
SEAC (1991) *Language for Learning* (ASSM).
SEAC (1991) *Teacher Assessment at Key Stage 3 — Mathematics*.
SEAC (1992) *GCSE Criteria: English, English Literature, Mathematics, Science (Biology, Chemistry, Physics)*.

Mathematics
SEAC (1990) *APU Mathematics Monitoring 84–88 (Phase 2)* (ASSM).
SEAC (1991) *Teacher Assessment at Key Stage 3 — Mathematics*.
SEAC (1991) *Teacher Assessment at Key Stage 3: An In-service Resource for Mathematics*.
SEAC (1992) *School Assessment Folder: Mathematics* (KS3).
SEAC (1992) *Pupils' Work Assessed: Mathematics* (KS3).
SEAC (1992) *GCSE Criteria: English, English Literature, Mathematics, Science (Biology, Chemistry, Physics)*.

Science
SEAC (1990) *Measurement in School: Science* (ASSM).
SEAC (1990) *Graphwork in Schools: Science* (ASSM).
SEAC (1991) *Teacher Assessment at Key Stage 3 — Science*.
SEAC (1991) *Profiles and Progression in Science Exploration* (ASSM).

SEAC (1991) *Planning and Carrying-out Investigations* (ASSM).

SEAC (1991) *Patterns and Relationships in School: Science* (ASSM).

SEAC (1991) *Observation in School: Science* (ASSM).

SEAC (1992) *School Assessment Folder: Science* (KS3).

SEAC (1992) *Pupils' Work Assessed: Science* (KS3).

SEAC (1992) *GCSE Criteria: English, English Literature, Mathematics, Science (Biology, Chemistry, Physics).*

Technology

SEAC (1990) *Learning through Design and Technology: The APU Model* (EMU).

SEAC (1991) *Negotiating Tasks in Design and Technology* (EMU).

SEAC (1991) *Structuring Activities in Design and Technology* (EMU).

SEAC (1992) *Technology Pupils' Work Assessed* (KS3).

Modern Foreign Languages

SEAC (1992) *Modern Foreign Languages Teacher Assessment Leaflet.*

Section C: Department of Education and Science (DFE after 1 July 1992)

Key: (NCSO) National Curriculum Statutory Orders
     (SI) Statutory Instruments
     (SO) Statutory Orders
     (C) Circulars
     (TGATR) Task Group on Assessment and Testing Reports

General Publications

DES (1985) *Better Schools.*

DES (1986) *Children at School and Problems Related to AIDS.*

DES (1987) *Task Group on Assessment and Testing: A Report.*

DES (1988) *Education at Work — A Guide for Schools.*

DES (1988) *Education at Work — A Guide for Employers.*

DES (1988) *National Curriculum Task Group on Assessment and Testing* (TGATR).

DES (1989) *Report of the Task Group on Assessment and Testing* (TGATR).

DES (1989) *National Curriculum: From Policy to Practice, February.*

DES (1989) *Further Education.*

DES (1989) *Higher Education — the Next 25 Years.*

DES (1989) *School Governors — How to Become a Grant-Maintained School, 2nd edition.*

DES (1989) *National Curriculum: A Guide for Parents.*

DES (1989) *Education (National Curriculum) (Temporary Exceptions for Individual Pupils Regulations* (SI).

DES (1989) *Education (School Curriculum and Related Information) Regulations* (SI).

DES (1989) *Education (School Curriculum and Related Information) (Amendment) Regulations* (SI).

DES (1989) *Education (School Records) Regulations* (SI).

DES (1989) *Planning for School Development 1.*

DES (1990) *Good Behaviour and Discipline in Schools, revised.*

DES (1990) *HMI Short Courses: 1990.*

DES (1990) *National Curriculum for 14–16-year-olds.*

DES (1990) *National Curriculum and Assessment.*

DES (1990) *Records of Achievement* (C).

DES (1990) *The Education Reform Act 1988: The Education (National Curriculum) (Assessment Arrangements for English, Mathematics and Science) Order 1990,* July (C).

DES (1990) *Education (Individual Pupil's Achievements) (Information) Regulations* (SI).

DES (1990) *Education (Special Educational Needs) (Amendment) Regulations* (SI).

DES (1990) *Education (School Curriculum and Related Information) (Amendment) Regulations* (SI).

DES (1990) *Education (National Curriculum) (Assessment Arrangements for English, Mathematics and Science) Order* (SI).

DES (1991) *Development Planning — A Practical Guide.*

DES (1991) *Education Statistics for the UK 1990 Edition.*

DES (1991) *School Governors — The School Curriculum.*

DES (1991) *Your Child and the National Curriculum: A Parent's Guide to What Is Taught in Schools.*

DES (1992) *Children with Special Needs.*

DFE (1992) *Education Statistics for the UK 1991 Edition.*

DFE (1992) *Education Europe.*

Department of Education and Science

Religious Education

DES (1989) *Agreed Syllabuses and Religious Education: The Influence of the Agreed Syllabus on Teaching and Learning in Religious Education in Three Local Authorities.*

English

DES (1988) *Report of the Committee of Inquiry into the Teaching of the English Language.*

DES (1989) *English in the National Curriculum.*

DES (1990) *English in the National Curriculum, No. 2.*
DES (1991) *English* (SO).
DES (1991) *GCSE — Poor Spelling, Grammar and Punctuation.*

Mathematics
DES (1989) *Mathematics in the National Curriculum.*
DES (1989) *Mathematics* (SO).
DES (1991) *Mathematics in the National Curriculum: (revised) Order and Circular.*

Science
DES (1989) *Science Policy — The Way Ahead.*
DES (1989) *Science in the National Curriculum.*
DES (1989) *Science* (SO).
DES (1991) *Science in the National Curriculum: (revised) Order and Circular.*
Technology
DES (1990) *Technology in the National Curriculum.*
DES (1990) *Technology* (SO).

History
DES (1990) *History for Ages 5–16*, July, NCC Working Group Report for DES.
DES (1991) *History* (SO).
DES (1991) *History in the National Curriculum.*

Geography
DES (1991) *Geography* (SO).
DES (1991) *Geography in the National Curriculum.*
DES (1991) *Geography in the National Curriculum: Supplementary Order and Circular for Short Course at KS4.*

Music
DES (1992) *Music* (SO).

Art
DES (1992) *Art* (SO).

Physical Education
DES (1992) *Physical Education* (SO).

Foreign Languages
DES (1988) *Modern Languages in the School Curriculum: A Statement of Policy.*
DES (1989) *Education (National Curriculum) (Modern Foreign Languages) Order* (NCSO).

DES (1990) *Modern Foreign Languages 11 to 16*.

DES (1991) *The Education (National Curriculum) (Modern Foreign Languages) Order*.

DES (1991) *Modern Foreign Languages in the National Curriculum*.

Section D: Her Majesty's Inspectorate

Key: (CMS) = Curriculum Matters Series

Each year, several hundred HMI inspection and survey reports are published by the Department of Education and Science. These contain evidence and evaluative comment relevant to schools' preparedness for, and implementation of, National Curriculum requirements.

General Publications

HMI (1985) *Quality in Schools — Education and Appraisal*.

HMI (1986) *The Curriculum from 5–16* (CMS).

HMI (1987) *Teaching Poetry in the Secondary School: An HMI View*.

HMI (1987) *The New Teacher in School*.

HMI (1988) *Secondary Schools: An Appraisal by HMI*.

HMI (1989) *Education Observed 10: Curriculum at 11-plus*.

HMI (1989) *Education Observed 12: The Lower Attaining Pupils' Programme 1982–88*.

HMI (1989) *The Curriculum from 5–16 (2nd Ed)* (CMS).

HMI (1990) *Education Observed 14: Girls Learning Mathematics*.

HMI (1990) *Standards in Education 1989–90: The Annual Report of the Chief Inspector of Schools*.

HMI (1990) *Special Needs Issues*.

HMI (1991) *Standards in Education 1990–91: The Annual Report of the Chief Inspector of Schools*.

HMI (1991) *Assessment, Recording, and Reporting*.

HMI (1991) *National Curriculum and Special Needs*.

HMI (1992) *Standards in Education 1991–92: The Annual Report of the Chief Inspector of Schools*

Her Majesty's Inspectorate

English

HMI (1986) *English from 5–16* (CMS).

HMI (1987) *Teaching Poetry in Secondary School* (CMS).

HMI (1991) *English Key Stages 1 and 3*.

HMI (1991) *English Key Stages 2–4* (N-S G).

Mathematics
HMI (1987) *Mathematics from 5–16* (CMS).
HMI (1989) *Mathematics from 5–16* (2nd Ed) (CMS).
HMI (1991) *Mathematics Key Stages 1 and 3.*

Science
HMI (1987) *Science from 5–16* (CMS).
HMI (1991) *Science Key Stages 1 and 3.*

Technology
HMI (1987) *Craft, Design and Technology from 5–16* (CMS).
HMI (1989) *Information Technology from 5–16* (CMS).
HMI (1991) *Information Technology and Special Needs in Schools.*
HMI (1991) *Teaching and Learning of Information Technology.*
HMI (1991) *Teaching and Learning of Design and Technology.*

History
HMI (1988) *History from 5–16* (CMS).
HMI (1991) *Training Teachers for the National Curriculum: History.*

Geography
HMI (1990) *Geography from 5–16* (CMS).

Music
HMI (1990) *Music from 5–16* (CMS).

Physical Education
HMI (1989) *Physical Education from 5–16* (CMS).
HMI (1990) *Physical Education from 5–16* (CMS).

Foreign Languages
HMI (1987) *Modern Foreign Languages from 5–16* (CMS).

Home Economics
HMI (1985) *Home Economics from 5–16* (CMS).
HMI (1990) *Home Economics from 5–16* (CMS).

Classics
HMI (1988) *Classics from 5–16* (CMS).

Drama
HMI (1989) *Drama from 5–16.*

Section 11 of the Local Government Act 1966: Background and Current (1990) Administrative Arrangements

G.K. Verma and P.D. Pumfrey

Section 11 of the Local Government Act was the first government inter-vention to provide assistance to multiracial areas. Originally such a grant was at the rate of 50 per cent of expenditure but this was later increased to 75 per cent. This grant, administered by the Home Office, has been used primarily by social services and education authorities although it was designed to cover all staff employed by local-authority departments.

The purpose of Section 11 as set out in the document is:

1 Subject to the provision of this section the Secretary of State may pay to local authorities who in his opinion are required to make special provision in the exercise of any of their functions in con-sequence of the presence within their areas of substantial numbers of immigrants from the Commonwealth whose language or customs differ from those of the community, grants of such amounts as he may with the consent of the Treasury determine on account of expenditure of such description (being expenditure in respect of the employment of staff) as he may so determine.

2 No grant shall be paid under this section in respect of expenditure incurred before 1st April 1967.

Although Section 11 grant has been interpreted as 'the only government finance earmarked directly and exclusively for combatting racial disadvant-age' (Home Affairs Committee, 1981, par., 48), many aspects of the grant's operation have been criticized. The main criticisms of Section 11 grant include its low take-up by some local authorities and the absence of any monitoring of Section 11 funded staff by the Home Office.

In response to various criticisms of Section 11 grant, the government issued revised administrative arrangements for the payment of this grant, which came into force on 1 January 1983. The changes in the arrangements were announced in the government's White Paper 'Racial Disadvantage' (Circ.

8476) and were set out in detail in the Home Office Circular 97/1982. The revised guidelines issued by the Home Office in 1982 were sound in principle, but were not taken in the same spirit by many LEAs. This was, in part, because of the 25 per cent of costs incurred. There was still a great deal of reluctance and inability to identify and account for Section 11 post-holders at local- and central-government levels.

In March 1986 the Home Office issued a further draft circular and proposed further adjustments for the administration of the grant. The suggested changes implied that Home Office's earlier circulars had been less effective than had been anticipated. The new Circular 72/1986 came into force on 1 October 1986. The latest review of Section 11 was conducted from October 1988. As a result Home Office issued Circular 78/1990.

Extracts from the Home Office Circular No.78/1990: Section 11 of the Local Government Act 1966

1 This Circular sets out the new arrangements for the administration of grant under Section 11 of the Local Government Act 1966. Separate guidance is being issued to Training and Enterprise Councils (TECs) to take account of their new responsibilities for the administration of arrangements (see para 14 below) in connection with the payment of grant to ethnic minority voluntary sector organisations presently outside the scope of Section 11. A copy of that guidance is also enclosed for information.

2 Under Section 11 of the Local Government Act 1966, the Secretary of State may pay grant in respect of the employment of staff to those local authorities who, in his opinion, have to make special provision in the exercise of any of their functions in consequence of the presence within their areas of substantial numbers of people from the Commonwealth whose language or customs differ from those of the rest of the community.

3 For the purposes of grant under Section 11 the qualifying group includes:

   i)   All those born in a country of the New Commonwealth however long they have been resident in the UK; and
   ii) their direct descendants.

There is no quantitative definition of what is meant by 'substantial numbers'. The essential requirement is to demonstrate a special need in the target group of sufficient size that it cannot be properly addressed without the additional help that may be obtained through Section 11 funding. Applications for grant should make clear the level of need.

Scrutiny Report

4 Following the publication in July 1989* of the report of an efficiency scrutiny of the current arrangements for the administration of grant, the Government confirmed its agreement with the conclusion that there was a continuing need for specific grant provision but that the present system of grant allocation needed substantial improvement in order to ensure that the available money was used to the best effect; that there should be established a clear framework of policy statements, approved by Ministers of the appropriate Government Departments, within which allocation of grant could take place. The Government has given full consideration to a number of other recommendations of the scrutiny, together with comments made in response to the consultation period which preceded the issue of this Circular. This Circular sets out the details of the new arrangements which supersede those in Home Office Circular 72/1986.

Principal Changes

5 i)   All provision must fall within the new criteria for grant as contained in the statement of policy accompanying this Circular.

ii) The grant is subject to an overall cash limit.

iii) Local authorities will in future be required to bid for provision within a fixed timetable (details at Annex A); bids to be project-based, the first bids — to cover the period commencing 1 April 1992 — to be submitted by 30 April 1991.

iv) All projects approved for funding will in future be time-limited; they will be annually reviewed and monitored against recognisable performance targets.

v)   Local authorities will be required to identify, within their bids, a proportion of provision for the voluntary sector.

vi) Payment of grant will be quarterly in arrears.

Section 11 Grant and the Govenment's Race Relations Policy

6 The Government's fundamental objective is to enable everyone, irrespective of ethnic origin, to participate fully and freely in the life of the nation while having the freedom to maintain their own cultural identity.

* Copies of the report are available through HMSO, ISBN No 0113409702.

The achievement of this objective involves central and local government; the private and voluntary sectors; and the ethnic minority communities themselves. The Government believes that at present there is a continuing need for specific grant to meet needs particular to ethnic minorities of Commonwealth origin that prevent full participation in the mainstream of national life. Barriers to opportunity arise in a number of areas, particularly through differences of language, in educational attainment, and through economic, social and cultural differences.

7   Genuine equality of opportunity is a Government priority. It is right that individuals from minority communities are given the assistance and encouragement necessary to enable them to particip- ate fully in the wider community. The Government believes that improved arrangements for Section 11 grant will help to achieve this objective. These aims and framework are set out more fully in the policy document which accompanies this Circu- lar and which forms the basis for the future use of Section 11 funding.

New Administrative Arrangements

8   The grant is subject to a cash limit reviewable annually. Future bids for funding will be invited on an annual basis to a fixed time- table geared to the financial year (Annex A). Existing provision approved under previous arrangements (i.e., posts approved following application up to 31 May 1990) will continue, subject to their being filled/not having been vacant for more than six months, to receive funding up to 31 March 1992. Bids under the new system may include bids both for existing Section 11 provision (submitted in project form) and for new provision, but *all* bids must be within the new criteria for grant. Bids may also be made for projects that are presently funded by central govern- ment and other similar agencies where that funding is due to run out, but must be submitted well before the final date of existing funding. Grant will *not* be approved for provision that is already receiving mainstream funding. Bids will need to include the following details:

i)   How the projects further the relevant Section 11 policy objectives and precisely what local needs they will address.

ii)   The specific objectives and quantifiable targets to be achieved by the proposed projects.

iii) The timescale over which objectives and targets will be measured.

iv) Proposals for monitoring the results.

v) The consultation procedures pursued with the involved communities and their responses to the proposals.

Purposes for which Grant may be Approved

11 The Government is anxious to ensure that grant is targeted at provision which will be effective in enabling members of ethnic minorities to participate fully in the economic, social and public life of the nation. The needs which a project is intended to meet must be either different in kind from, or the same as but proportionately greater than, those of the rest of the community. It is not enough that a project's client group are predominantly from an ethnic minority. Applicants must establish that there exists a need that requires special provision to redress. The policy document contains a statement of the functions in areas of local authority services which the Government considers may be appropriate for support through Section 11 funding. Those statements are not exclusive, but set out a policy framework for project bids. Projects may qualify for funding in areas to which policy statements do not specifically refer, nonetheless, if they comply with the general principles for the use of Section 11 grant laid down in the statements.

12 It is important that grant-aided provision should fall within a general strategy for meeting the needs of ethnic minorities.

The Voluntary Sector

13 The Government considers that the voluntary sector has an important contribution to make to the effective delivery of Section 11 provision. As part of this approach, the Government expects local authorities to include applications for projects placed in, and operating from, voluntary organisations. Such projects would remain under the overall control of the local authority who would continue to claim grant for them, but day to day responsibility for individual projects would rest with the organisation in which they were based. Examples of such projects can be found in the policy document.

14 To further the aim of greater voluntary sector participation, and in advance of legislation, a separate grant will be available to encourage projects from within the voluntary sector. The grant will be paid through the Training and Enterprise Councils (TECs) and will be available for voluntary sector projects

addressing ethnic minority need in training and enterprise under the same *policy* principles (see policy document) that apply to Section 11 grant but without some of the constraints of that grant. Where local authorities are proposing projects within the area of training and enterprise they must first consult with TECs or, where a TEC has not so far been established, Task Forces and City Action Teams where these exist. A copy of the guidance to TECs setting out their role in the administration of the grant, together with the scope of the grant, is enclosed.

Introduction of the New Arrangements

15 As indicated above, existing provision will cease when the new arrangements come into effect on 1 April 1992. To meet the requirement that all Section 11 expenditure conforms with the new policy, monitoring and targeting specifications, and in particular that ineligible expenditure is discontinued, existing projects and posts for which, in a local authority's view, there is a continuing need, will have to be bid for afresh under the new arrangements. Such applications will not be approved unless they meet the new criteria and monitoring requirements.

Enquiries

33 Enquiries about this Circular should be made to Ethnic Minority Grants (Section 11), I Division, Home Office, 50 Queen Anne's Gate, London SW1H 9AT.

Timetables

November 1991	— Final full quarterly payment in advance to local authorities.
May 1992	— Remaining quarterly payment for posts under previous system to local authorities.
July 1992	— Submission of first quarterly return for period Apr–Jun 1992 and projected costs for remaining 3 quarters of financial year 1992–93.
August 1992	— First quarterly payment under new arrangements (in arrears) for period Apr — Jun 1992.
30 September 1992	— Deadline for receipt of audited returns on previous financial year's grant expenditure.

Full Operation

January 1993	— Notification of approved provision for year commencing 1 April 1993.
30 September 1993	— See 30 September 1992 — detail to cover period 1 Apr 1992 — 31 Mar 1993.
July, October, January, April	— Submission of quarterly returns.
August, November, February, May	— Quarterly payments made to local authorities.

(The same annual timetable applies thereafter)

Introductory Timetable

October 1990 onwards	— Preparation and submission of project proposals under new arrangements for period 1 April 1992–31 March 1993.
	— Seminars/discussion by Home Office to explain new arrangements and assist in preparation of bids.
30 April 1991	— *Deadline for Receipt of Applications for April 1992 to March 1993.*
May 1991–October 1991	— Consideration of applications for April 1992–March 1993.
October/November 1991	— Applicants notified of decisions on project proposals for April 1992 — March 1993.
1 April 1992	— *Funding under new arrangements commences*

Annual operational Timetable

30 June (1992)	— Deadline for receipt of applications for year commencing 1 April (1993).
January (1993)	— Notification of grant available and project approvals for year commencing 1 April (1993).
1 April (1993)	— Continuation of existing approvals and new approvals take effect.
30 September (1993)	— Deadline for receipt of audited return of previous financial year's grant expenditure by recipient bodies.

Financial Timetable Introduction

30 September 1991	— Deadline for submission of final Fin Form C1 to Home Office.
October/November 1991	— Notification of grant available and project approvals for year commencing 1 Apr 1992.

Notes on Contributors

Robert Carroll is Head of the Centre for Physical Education at Manchester University. He works with teachers on curriculum matters and research methods and has published widely in the area of PE. Recently he has been engaged in research on ethnic groups, sport and PE.

Contact address — Centre for Physical Education, University of Manchester, Oxford Road, Manchester, M13 9PL.

Peter Figueroa is a senior lecturer in the School of Education, University of Southampton. He teaches Master's courses in: multicultural and antiracist education; curriculum policy; design and development; and philosophy and education. His interests include wider policy issues, evaluation, comparative education, sociology, and issues in social psychology.

Contact address — School of Education, University of Southampton, Southampton, S09 5NH.

Dawn Gill is the General Adviser for Humanities at the London Borough of Hackney Education Directorate. She has been involved in developing and implementing multicultural and antiracist policies for a considerable period.

Contact address — Hackney Education Directorate, 77 East Road, London, N1 6AH.

Horace Lashley is a lecturer in the Department of Community Studies at the University of Reading. Before joining the University of Reading he was Education Officer with the Commission for Racial Equality in London. He has written and researched into the area of multicultural and antiracist education.

Contact address — Department of Community Studies, University of Reading, Bulmershe Court, Earley, Reading, RG6 1HY.

Prabodh Merchant is an employment officer. He works for the Commission for Racial Equality (CRE) and has extensive knowledge of race-relations legislation and its effects. Currently he is working in the north west of England.

Contact address — Commission for Racial Equality, Maybrook House, 40 Blackfriars Street, Manchester, M3 2EG.

Anthony R. Neasham is Assistant Head of Modern and Community Languages in a 13–18 comprehensive school in West Yorkshire. Dr Neasham has also worked extensively with Professor Gajendra K. Verma on a number of research projects in the field of ethnicity and the curriculum.

Contact address — Hanson School, Swain House Road, Bradford, BD2 1JP.

Dudley Newell returned to England in 1969 from Canada where he went to University. He gained his first professional experience of the English education system by teaching part-time at a borstal. Currently he is an English and drama adviser in Manchester and has a wide experience of education in multicultural environments.

Contact address — Manchester City Council Education Department, Inspection and Advisory Service, the Greenheys Centre, Upper Lloyd Street, Moss Side, Manchester, M14 4HZ.

Glyn W. Price is involved in Initial Teacher Training (ITT) and the In-service Education of Teachers (INSET) with special responsibilities for technology (including design) at the University of Manchester School of Education. His work has been predominantly in areas characterized by cultural diversity. He has acted as a consultant both nationally and internationally in his specialist field.

Contact address — School of Education, University of Manchester (*v.s.*).

Peter D. Pumfrey is Professor of Education and Head of the Centre for Educational Guidance and Special Needs at the University of Manchester. His research and teaching interests include interethnic relationships, multicultural education, social psychology, and race-relations research. *Educational Attainments: Issues and Outcomes in Multicultural Education* (1988) and *Race Relations and Urban Education* were edited, and contributed to by him, in collaboration with Gajendra K. Verma.

Contact address — Centre for Educational Guidance and Special Needs, School of Education, University of Manchester (*v.s.*).

David Reid is Head of the Centre for Science and Technology, Director of Initial Teacher Education, and a senior lecturer in Education at the University of Manchester. He has had particular responsibility for training bilingual teachers from ethnic-minority communities.

Contact address — School of Education, University of Manchester (*v.s.*).

Jill Scarfe is an experienced teacher and lecturer in music education. Her particular concern has been the development of strategies to introduce world music in the curriculum. She has worked in the USA, India, Pakistan, and Trinidad. She has introduced steel-pan and Indian music as part of the curriculum in schools in the UK. She is now a freelance music-education lecturer and consultant.

Contact address — 39 Church Lane, Barrow on Trent, Derbyshire, DE7 1HB.

George Skinner is Senior Research Fellow in the Centre for Ethnic Studies in Education at the University of Manchester. He is a qualified and experienced teacher and has worked in the areas of equal opportunities and religious education on a number of major researches.

Contact address — Centre for Ethnic Studies in Education, School of Education, University of Manchester (*v.s.*).

Gajendra K. Verma is Professor of Education and Director of the Centre for Ethnic Studies in Education, School of Education, University of Manchester. He has been responsible for directing over twelve national and regional research projects concerned with education, social, and occupational adaptation of ethnic-minority groups. He was a member of the Swann Committee of Inquiry into the Education of Children from Ethnic-minority Groups.

Contact address — Centre for Ethnic Studies in Education, School of Education, University of Manchester (*v.s.*).

Julian S. Williams is Senior Lecturer in the University of Manchester School of Education and specializes in mathematics education. His research and publication interests include applied mathematics, the teaching of mathematical modelling and its applications in science and technology as well as multicultural dimensions of mathematics education.

Contact address — School of Education, University of Manchester, (*v.s.*).

Name Index

Subject Index